# The Body of Compassion

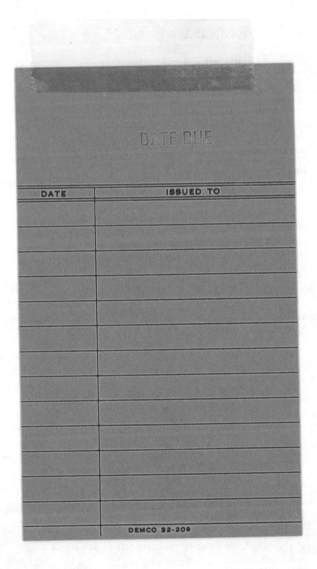

**RADICAL**
**TRADITIONS**

## Radical Traditions
## Theology in a Postcritical Key

Series Editors: Stanley M. Hauerwas, Duke University,
and Peter Ochs, University of Virginia

BOOKS IN THE SERIES

The Body of Compassion: Ethics, Medicine,
and the Church, *Joel James Shuman*

Church and Israel After Christendom:
The Politics of Election, *Scott Bader-Saye*

Reasoning After Revelation:
Dialogue in Postmodern Jewish Philosophy,
*Peter Ochs, Steven Kepnes, and Robert Gibbs*

Waiting for Godot in Sarajevo: Theological Reflections
on Nihilism, Tragedy, and Apocalypse, *David Toole*

Wilderness Wanderings:
Probing Twentieth-Century Theology and Philosophy,
*Stanley M. Hauerwas*

Revelation Restored: Divine Writ and
Critical Responses, *David Weiss Halivni*

FORTHCOMING

After the Spirit: The Story of the Holy Spirit
Eclipsed by Nature, Grace, and Law, *Eugene F. Rogers Jr.*

Ascending Numbers: Augustine's *De Musica*
and the Western Tradition, *Catherine Pickstock*

*Radical Traditions* cuts new lines of inquiry across a confused array of debates concerning the place of theology in modernity and, more generally, the status and role of scriptural faith in contemporary life. Charged with a rejuvenated confidence, spawned in part by the rediscovery of reason as inescapably tradition constituted, a new generation of theologians and religious scholars is returning to scriptural traditions with the hope of retrieving resources long ignored, depreciated, and in many cases ideologically suppressed by modern habits of thought. *Radical Traditions* assembles a promising matrix of strategies, disciplines, and lines of thought that invites Jewish, Christian, and Islamic theologians back to the word, recovering and articulating modes of scriptural reasoning as that which always underlies modernist reasoning and therefore has the capacity—and authority—to correct it.

Far from despairing over modernity's failings, postcritical theologies rediscover resources for renewal and self-correction within the disciplines of academic study themselves. Postcritical theologies open up the possibility of participating once again in the living relationship that binds together God, text, and community of interpretation. *Radical Traditions* thus advocates a "return to the text," which means a commitment to displaying the richness and wisdom of traditions that are at once text based, hermeneutical, and oriented to communal practice.

Books in this series offer the opportunity to speak openly with practitioners of other faiths or even with those who profess no (or limited) faith, both academics and nonacademics, about the ways religious traditions address pivotal issues of the day. Unfettered by foundationalist preoccupations, these books represent a call for new paradigms of reason—a thinking and rationality that is more responsive than originative. By embracing a postcritical posture, they are able to speak unapologetically out of scriptural traditions manifest in the practices of believing communities (Jewish, Christian, and others); articulate those practices through disciplines of philosophic, textual, and cultural criticism; and engage intellectual, social, and political practices that for too long have been insulated from theological evaluation. *Radical Traditions* is radical not only in its confidence in nonapologetic theological speech but also in how the practice of such speech challenges the current social and political arrangements of modernity.

# The Body of Compassion

## ETHICS, MEDICINE, AND THE CHURCH

### JOEL JAMES SHUMAN

Westview Press
A Member of the Perseus Books Group

*Radical Traditions*

Copyright © 1999 by Westview Press, A Member of the Perseus Books Group

Published in 1999 in the United States of America by Westview Press, 5500 Central Avenue, Boulder, Colorado 80301-2877, and in the United Kingdom by Westview Press, 12 Hid's Copse Road, Cumnor Hill, Oxford OX2 9JJ

Library of Congress Cataloging-in-Publication Data
Shuman, Joel James.
   The body of compassion : ethics, medicine, and the church / by
Joel James Shuman.
      p.   cm.—(Radical traditions)
   Includes bibliographical references and index.
   ISBN 0-8133-6704-2 (hc.)
   1. Medical ethics.   2. Christian ethics.   3. Health—Religious
aspects—Christianity.   I. Title.   II. Series.
R725.56.S54   1999
241'.642—dc21                                                            98-54406
                                                                              CIP

The paper used in this publication meets the requirements of the American National Standard for Permanence of Paper for Printed Library Materials Z39.48-1984.

10     9     8     7     6     5     4     3     2     1

# CONTENTS

Acknowledgments                                                     ix
List of Credits                                                     xiii
Introduction                                                        xv


1    Before Bioethics: The Moral Paradox
     of Modern Medicine                                             1

2    The "Birth" of Bioethics: Scientific Expertise and
     the Justification of the Modern Project                        47

3    After Bioethics: Toward a Christian Theology
     of the Body and Its Goods                                      79

4    Beyond Bioethics:
     Caring for Christ's Body                                       113

     Afterword: Awaiting the Redemption of Our Body—
     Life and Death in the Meantime                                 157


Notes                                                               161
Bibliography                                                        201
Index                                                               209

# ACKNOWLEDGMENTS

*A man by himself hasn't got a . . . chance.*
—Edward Abbey, *The Fool's Progress*

The culture of my baptism and the culture of my upbringing have at least this in common: Both have taught me that who I am and what I do are very much the results of the connections I have forged with others. This book, I hope, is both a product of and a tribute to some of those to whom I find myself connected.

Colleagues and friends at Duke and around the country have engaged me in useful and often entertaining conversation about the matters dealt with here and have commented on various parts of this book. Thanks are owed especially to Kate Joyce, Karen Westerfield-Tucker, Brett Webb-Mitchell, Hans Reinders, Scott Bader-Saye, Chris and Rachel Huebner, Kelly Johnson, David Cloutier, Therese Lysaught, Jim and Janine Fodor, Allyne Smith, Keith Meador, and Telford Work. Part of Chapter 2 was presented as a lecture to the students and faculty at Wheeling Jesuit University, and the substance of Chapter 3 was presented at the 1997 meeting of the Society for Health and Human Values. Both of these groups offered valuable input about the structure of my arguments.

I have been most fortunate to have an exceptional—and an exceptionally helpful—group of teachers who have offered me not simply knowledge but also friendship. Whether they like it or not, they are at least partially responsible for whom I've become. Richard Hays, who directed my final master's paper at Duke Divinity School on the Christ hymn from Philippians 2, has kept me interested in and excited about the Bible by making clear to me how the Scriptures can and must continue to play a central role in contemporary theological discourse. Geoffrey Wainwright helped me learn to think theologically and instilled in me a deep appreciation for the historical tradition of the church and a love for its liturgy. From Harmon Smith I learned to "speak the language of bioethics" and at the same time to appreciate and to critique that discipline from a theological perspective. Rom Coles has become not just my teacher but also my good and hopefully life-long friend. We have discovered that in spite of our considerable theological differences, we share many things in common. He has taught me as much as anyone about political philosophy and critical political economy, not to mention shown me a thing or two about bicycling and rock climbing. I hope only that one of us is able to move to the mountains and to play host frequently to the other before both of us go completely mad from the pressure of too much flatland sky.

I cannot say enough about the role Stanley Hauerwas has had in my life over the course of the last seven years. I came to Duke as a divinity student in 1991, intending to study with him and hoping to learn a little about Christian ethics in the process. In the meantime he has, through his considerable passion, changed my life by becoming not just my teacher but also perhaps my best friend. Although he has failed, thank God, to make me either a Texan or a Braves fan, he has helped make me a Methodist by introducing me to the people of his church, Aldersgate United Methodist, where my family and I have worshiped in recent years. Through their quiet example and under the leadership of Pastor Susan Allred, they have taught me as much as any text about what it means for Christians to be the body of Christ.

My editors at Westview have been most helpful. I owe them a tremendous debt of gratitude for nursing me through the publication of my first book. Laura Parsons and Michelle Trader have both been patient in taking me through the intricacies of the publication process. And my copy editor, David Toole, has been meticulous in his work on the manuscript. The book is much better because of his work and his exceptional literary sensibilities.

When I made the commitment to write this book, I did so with only a vague understanding of the impact that decision would have on my family. I remain in awe of them, for they have tolerated the considerable burden involved in my work better than I could have imagined or hoped for. My three children—Jessie, Amos, and Isaac—have accepted that burden with exceptional grace and a wonderful sense of humor that has kept me from taking myself too seriously. I thank them for letting me be a part of their lives, for it has been a pleasure to watch them grow up these past years. My wife, Chris, has been an amazing source of strength and support during this whole process. Her love, her friendship, her considerable sense of humor, and her gentle prodding have all in part made the writing of this book a possibility.

In addition to the many personal debts I owe others for helping with what is written here, I am grateful for permission to reprint copyrighted materials.

Finally, I wish to extend thanks to the people who have shaped me more than anyone, my parents and my grandparents. From them I have learned all of the most important things: My grandparents gave me a deep appreciation for the land on which I was raised and taught me to live close to it; they also taught me to work with my hands and to love that work. My parents, who were my first and best teachers, introduced me to books of all sorts, teaching me to love reading and learning and to be unrepentantly stubborn in pursuit of the truth. It is to them, with as much love and appreciation as I can muster, that I dedicate this book.

*Joel James Shuman*

# CREDITS

Wendell Berry. "Health Is Membership." In *Another Turn of the Crank*. Washington, D.C.: Counterpoint Press, 1995.

John Milbank. *Theology as Social Theory: Beyond Secular Reason*. Cambridge, Mass.: Blackwell, 1990.

Alasdair MacIntyre. *After Virtue*. 2d ed. Notre Dame, Ind.: University of Notre Dame Press, 1984.

Stuart Hampshire. "Fallacies in Moral Philosophy." In *Revisions: Changing Perspectives in Moral Philosophy*. Edited by Stanley Hauerwas and Alasdair MacIntyre. Notre Dame, Ind.: University of Notre Dame Press, 1983.

John Zizioulas. *Being as Communion: Studies in Personhood and the Church*. Copyright 1985 by Saint Vladimir's Seminary Press, 575 Scarsdale Rd., Crestwood, NY 10707.

John Zizioulas, "Communion and Otherness." In *Sobornost* 16, no. 1 (1994).

Flannery O'Connor. *The Habit of Being*. Edited by Sally Fitzgerald. New York: Farrar, Strauss and Giroux, 1979.

Flannery O'Connor. *Mystery and Manners: Occasional Prose*. Edited by Sally and Robert Fitzgerald. New York: Farrar, Strauss and Giroux, 1969.

Ray Anderson. *Theology, Death, and Dying*. Cambridge, Mass.: Blackwell, 1986.

Ruth Shalit. "When We Were Philosopher Kings." *The New Republic*, 28 April 1997, 24–28.

# INTRODUCTION

This is a book about Christian faith and its relationship to the maintenance and restoration of the health of the human body. Such a book would seem to fit well with certain trends in contemporary American culture; in recent years both the popular and technical media have been filled with articles suggesting that God—like raw vegetables, regular exercise, and properly used seat belts—is an essential component of a healthy life. Such articles typically begin by announcing the results of a recently concluded study done by researchers at a university medical center: The researchers found that people who regularly prayed or meditated or attended religious services lived longer or spent less time in the hospital, or had lower blood pressure or fewer incidents of impotence, than those who did not. In the popular media, the reporting of such results is sometimes followed by the testimony of someone who has been healed through prayer or meditation or who has seen his or her general health dramatically improved by regularly attending religious services. Finally, the author or the interviewer may solicit the opinion of an "expert," usually a neuroscientist or a psychiatrist, who explains, citing her own extensive research and that of her fellows (in language that is decidedly *non*-theological), precisely *why* religious activities are good for us.

Christian communities of various sorts seem generally to see such studies as good public relations, at the very least. After all, if people decide that the idea of God, whether God really exists or not, is good for their health, then maybe they'll start showing up in church on Sunday to see what else that idea can do for them. Such a consumerist mentality fits the strategic emphasis of the so-called "church growth movement," which says that if you want people to come to church, you have to provide "relevant" solutions to their most frequently expressed "felt needs," one of which is invariably good health. But this sort of facile, uncritical approach to the relationship between Christian faith and the health of the body is highly problematic because it fails to see that such perspectives *can*, unless care is taken, actually serve to undermine what Christianity has traditionally held to be true about the body and its goods.

Physical and emotional health are of course goods that Christians *should* desire; they are not, however, goods that should be pursued absolutely. What finally matters when Christians are sick or dying is not simply that they get well right away or die quickly, painlessly, in control, and without being a burden to others, but that they remain faithful to their most basic convictions about what it means to worship a crucified God. What *finally* matters when Christians find themselves in the presence of the sick and dying and charged with their care is that they take it upon themselves to *make space* in their lives for those persons as if they were making a space for Christ himself. Thus the central issue for Christians is not that illness is fundamentally bad or that God heals the sick (although both of these things are certainly true), but that God cares for and intervenes on behalf of the sick in a wide variety of ways. And because God cares for and intervenes on behalf of the sick, Christians must care and intervene as well, learning to do so in ways that are consistent with their most fundamental convictions about the particular God whose people they claim to be, the God who is of course the God of Israel and of Jesus and the Church. Only by so doing can they make the best—that is, the most *faithful*—use of the considerable resources at the disposal of contemporary biomedicine.

Consequently, those Christians who point uncritically to studies that seem to show some sort of positive causal link between certain "religious" practices and the goods of the human body may be missing an important point. They may be failing to see that one of the frequently held and central presumptions of such studies is that a particular account of God's character is in the end irrelevant, since everything, including God, can be explained finally without reference to God. Thus studies that show how prayer makes you healthy *can* be nothing but thinly veiled examples of a general trend in biomedicine toward a kind of hegemony, through which science and technology are used in the service of those modern bureaucratic institutions that would control our lives and destroy those usually older and decidedly "less efficient" ways of life that would resist such control.

There is a significant extent to which this book is simply an exercise in resisting such control, which is an explanation for the polemical tone in the first two chapters. What I have written there must not be construed as being categorically opposed either to science or to scientific medicine, but rather to the temptation of allowing those disciplines to *explain* everything about our body in their own languages; such explanations, I argue, tend to render certain aspects of Christian faithfulness irrelevant or even impossible. Medicine has always been—and remains—a significant and profoundly moral enterprise, one much richer and more textured than the story it tells about itself lets on. Yet that moral richness is becoming increasingly unintelligible because of a growing tendency among many of the practitioners of medicine to abandon this richness in favor of a purely technical expertise.

Thus one of the principle things that is at issue here is how we—and my "we" here is a broad one indeed, encompassing all those who are concerned with caring for the sick—might come to know everything we need to know about the body, about what the body *is* and what it is *for*, in order to care for it faithfully when it is sick. As I try to show in the first chapter, the sciences undergirding contemporary biomedicine can and do give us an incredible amount of extremely valuable information about what the body *is*, knowledge that may be effectively employed for the body's healing. However, because those sciences cannot—and in fact will not—say what the body is in any *teleological* sense, they can say nothing about what it is *for*. Consequently, a medicine whose practice is based solely in the natural sciences can talk about caring for the body only in terms of maintaining and restoring its usual physiological function or in terms of eliminating the efficient physiological causes of its suffering.

However, this view of the body serves to reduce it to an object of study and control, a reduction that (I argue) tends to alienate persons from their bodies, from the bodies of others, and from the meaningful performance of illness and dying—an alienation that ultimately serves the interests of neither the patient nor the caregiver but of the political economy in which the patient lives. Yet because (as I argue in Chapter 2) this sort of objectification and control is usually accepted as necessary for the effective maintenance and restoration of health, the practices making it possible are seldom called into question and are in fact underwritten by the now well-established professional discipline known as clinical bioethics. This discipline is all too frequently understood in reductionist terms as an attempt to determine the rights of individuals to adequate care based on existing practices, and to adjudicate competing claims to that care in situations of scarcity. Increasingly, clinical bioethics is rarely understood as a means of calling into question the modes of care themselves.

Over against these understandings, I propose, in Chapters 3 and 4, an alternative and explicitly Christian model of care for the sick, based upon a "theological ontology of the body." This Christian account does not supplant necessarily the contemporary biomedical account; it simply attempts to enrich it. Whereas the modern biomedical understanding of the body is drawn *exclusively* from the practices of the natural sciences, I suggest that there is also a *theological* understanding of the body based primarily in the Christian liturgical practices of baptism and Eucharist. This theological understanding holds that through baptism and Eucharist the body is reconstituted on its most basic level, such that it is bound to the bodies of other baptized persons and becomes part of the one body of Christ, a community whose goods and politics determine the way its members should be cared for when they are sick or dying. I do not attempt to explain precisely *how* this reconstitution takes place in terms of efficient causality, for to do so would discount the significance of the body for Christian existence by reproducing a subtle form of that same Cartesian dualism that privileges the immaterial mind (or soul) and disregards the body, giving it over to the whims of technological manipulation.

What such explicitly Christian care looks like in various situations can be specified only in concrete terms, as discrete examples of it are discovered and displayed. Hence the final chapter, where I try to name and display Christian virtues that might be especially relevant to the care of the sick, is fundamentally different in tone—and in approach—from the previous chapters. The reader will notice that my approach here is characterized more by narrative than by either analysis or polemics. This change in tone should not, however, be taken as a sign that I regard this chapter as less critically significant than the first two or as less constructively significant than the third.

The content of the final chapter is admittedly inadequate. It begs for a further development that can be achieved only as the practices of caring in and by the body of Christ begin to produce medical practices among patients and caregivers more clearly consistent with, and explicable in terms of, the Christian virtue of charity. The relative absence of such examples in contemporary culture is perhaps the main reason I turn at the end of the final chapter to the life and work of the late Flannery O'Connor, a devout Catholic who was sick for much of her adult life and whose correspondence, essays, and fiction provide especially good examples of what it might mean for Christians to be faithful patients and caregivers in the midst of the contemporary situation. Such faithfulness might well serve as an important first step in the recapturing of the strong moral tradition represented by the practice of medicine and other healing arts.

# The Body of Compassion

# 1

# BEFORE BIOETHICS

## The Moral Paradox of Modern Medicine

*A Decidedly—and Intentionally—*
*Unscientific Introduction*

In my grandfather's shed, there are hundreds of tools.
I know them by feel and by name.
Like parts of my body, they've patched this old place.
When I move them, they won't be the same.
—Kate Long, *Who'll Watch the Homeplace?*

On one level, this book is concerned with whether being Christian can and should make a real difference—a difference "all the way down," if you will—in the ways we live when we are sick and the ways we take care of the sick in our midst. But because it is almost certainly true, as Stanley Hauerwas has said, that "our particular stories ... provide us the training to understand how the Christian story may fit over our lives,"[1] this book is also in part a story about a part of my life and about the friendship I had with my grandfather; for as strange as it may sound, whenever I think about medicine—about hospitals or doctors or illness or dying—I think first about my grandfather.

He was one of my first real heroes, a tall man with strong, able hands, a man whose whole life seemed to be deeply inscribed on the contours of his body. Forever clad in khaki work clothes and an old cap pushed back on his balding head, he always had the appearance of being ready to work. He was a farmer and a woodsman and a master carpenter who taught me to hunt and fish and most importantly to work, to be with wild and domestic animals, and to make useful and sometimes beautiful things with my

*1*

hands; to this day I cannot pick up a hammer or a plane or smell freshly sawed lumber without thinking of him.

More than twenty years have passed since the summer of his death. That was the summer just before I turned seventeen, and I remember it in a way that I remember no other period of my growing up—as a collection of stark and frightening images that frequently force their way into my imaginings. It is my grandfather's significance in my own life, and the confusion his death caused me, that make this so. The year before he died he had gone to the local physician, one of only two in our rural county, feeling uncharacteristically tired. He was promptly sent to Charleston, the state capital, for a series of tests that revealed he had leukemia, which we in our relative ignorance understood simply as "cancer of the blood." I still remember my mother's weeping at our family dinner table the evening she received the call bringing us the news of this diagnosis. All of us children, though we knew very little about the nature of my grandfather's illness, understood from the intensity of her sadness that the news was especially bad.

My grandfather's new physicians in Charleston recommended that he have an operation, a procedure, they suggested, that might increase the span, and perhaps the quality, of his life, and he consented. They were, after all, doctors, whereas he was a farmer and a carpenter; they knew sickness and healing the way he knew how to judge the worthiness of a fine piece of red oak or cherry, or the likelihood that a big white-tailed buck would be bedded down in a blackberry thicket in the next hollow. This is how I imagine my grandfather reasoned about the treatment of his illness, whether or not it was so.

Hospital space was a precious commodity in West Virginia in that day, and my grandfather was told that he would have to wait—for weeks, perhaps—before he could make the two-hour drive to the city for his operation. In the meantime, he went about the usual business of his life as if nothing was wrong, working the same old farm his family had lived on for four generations. He built a new house for a close friend. He stretched and mended fence and tended the small herd of beef cattle pastured for the summer on the other side of the high knob where his house was located. And when the hay in the big ridge-top meadow across the road from the house ripened, he mowed it, returning the next day on his ancient Massey-Ferguson tractor to rake and bale the crop that would sustain the cattle through the winter.

From the time I was twelve years old I had worked in the hay fields. In spite of my childhood asthma, I looked forward to the time each year when I could go into the fields. I delighted in proving myself by lifting those heavy bales onto the truck as it passed slowly through the meadow. Haying was not simply a test of strength and a rite of passage into manhood, or at least adolescence, for me; it was also a means of financial success. Once I had proven myself capable of putting up hay, I could not just work in my grandfather's fields, but also hire out to other local farmers. Most importantly, though, working in the fields was another opportunity to be with my grandfather, who for years had been introducing me to the rhythms and riches of the woods and fields, and whom I had come by then to love more deeply than I could ever say.

The barn on my grandfather's farm was in those days situated at the very edge of the road, so close that it was possible to jump out the front door and land in the road with very little effort. I was standing in the door of that barn, unloading the hay truck with my uncle, when I saw my grandfather alive for the last time. He had received a call just a few minutes earlier, while we were in the meadow, informing him that a hospital bed had become available in Charleston and that his surgery could be scheduled for the next day if he could come right away. As he and my grandmother left the house and drove past the barn, he leaned out the passenger window of their car and waved good-bye to us, his face bearing a look of terrible sadness that haunts me to this day. My uncle and I waved casually, not daring to look for too long or to say anything to him or to one another, lest we begin crying in reaction to his and our obvious distress.

My grandfather died in the hospital two days later from complications following surgery. The next time I saw him, at his wake, he was lying in a polished casket, surrounded by hundreds of commercially grown flowers. He wore a light blue polyester-knit sport coat and a shirt and tie, and his cheeks had been rouged to a bright pink. I had never seen him looking even remotely like he looked then, and as I stood there in the funeral parlor, looking from a safe distance at what remained of him, I felt an awful, strange mixture of sadness and confusion. I knew that something had gone terribly wrong, but it was something I was unable to name.

My aunts were gathered in a cluster nearby, engaged in a typical funeral parlor conversation about how "good" my grandfather looked. The day before I had heard them talking with other family members in a similarly unconvincing tone about what a blessing it had been for him to have died in the hospital, rather than in the woods or the fields, where "someone might have been hurt." Having never before experienced the death of a close family member, I didn't know what to make of such conversation; it seemed to me only to aggravate what was an already absurd situation.

It was left to my mother, the oldest of my grandfather's children and a stubborn and unrepentant truth-teller, to inject a solitary word of passionate reality into what seemed to me a surreal madness. To my aunts' altogether innocent question, "Doesn't he look good?" she responded, quite abruptly, "No. I think he looks awful."

In retrospect, I cannot say whether the effect of my mother's response to so common and yet so ridiculous a question was immediate, or whether it came weeks, months, or even years later. I simply know that I have come over the years to regard her words as nothing short of revelatory; for in repeating to myself again and again the words she spoke to my aunts in that prophetic instant, I have developed at least some sense of why the events preceding and surrounding my grandfather's death were so terribly disconcerting. My grandfather, a man who had been born in the same house as his father, who had lived his entire life on the same few hundred acres of rocky, mountain land and attended the same little one room country church, who had seen his grandparents and parents and several of his siblings buried in the family cemetery on the hill overlooking that same house, and who had lived for years in close proximity to his children and grandchildren, had died alone in a hospital hours from home, denied an active role in the last days of his life and his death by a world that was almost completely foreign to him. That world had seduced him and had dared him to trust it and had then betrayed that trust. And yes, he did look awful.

I have no reason to question the competence or the professional judgment—much less the moral character—of the various physicians and nurses who cared for my grandfather during the last days of his life. Nor do I wish to suggest that his death would have been any less sad had it occurred at home. And I most certainly do not wish to be seen as some kind of reactionary, a medical Luddite who uncritically longs for a lost era that existed only in the minds of a few romantics, an era in which there were few doctors and fewer hospitals and in which everyone died happy and peacefully at home. I do want to suggest that there is something about the way my grandfather's illness was treated that shows what I take to be some typical problems inhering in the practice of medicine in contemporary American culture.

Specifically, I want to suggest that contemporary biomedicine faces a moral crisis that is a product of its fundamental inability to know and to care for its patients in any sense that takes seriously the ways those patients have learned to understand what it might mean to *be* bodies. This claim is the basis for the strong language I use above; I say that the world inhabited by my grandfather's physicians had seduced him to trust it and then betrayed that trust, not because those physicians were morally weak or unskilled in their areas of expertise, but because the trust he placed in them and in their world existed for the wrong reasons. That trust had no real basis in a commonly held, deliberatively arrived at vision of what it might have meant for my grandfather to live well for the remainder of his life; for though my grandfather's physicians knew as much as there was to know about his disease, they seem to have been totally oblivious—and in their minds, perhaps not unjustifiably—to the things that really made him the person he was—a simple man of remarkable character, with deep attachments to work and land and family, who had lived an exceptional life and who deserved a death consistent with that life.

I am suggesting that the ways in which we live when we are sick and the ways we care for the sick who live among us, as well as the ways in which we recover from sickness or not, are in some real and profound sense functions of how we have learned to identify ourselves as embodied persons. That identity, moreover, is not simply "there," not simply given, but is a function of the particular ways we learn to narrate our lives and to embody that narrative; of the joys and tragedies of our personal histories, our families, and our friendships; and of our particular convictions about what it means to live and die well. These, as a friend of mine might say, are the "matters that matter," and thus they are matters that ought to matter to those who care for us when we are sick.

Such matters are at their root theological. By this I mean their significance is shown finally to come from the ways we understand the world to be structured and to operate. Consequently, this book aims first to make explicit the theological foundations undergirding those social and natural sciences forming the epistemological and practical bases of modern biomedicine, and then to suggest that another, quite different theology, is a viable and even preferable alternative. Here I roughly follow John Milbank, whose work suggests that a kind of theological discourse lies at the root of all sorts of "secular" reasoning, including the social and natural sciences. Milbank remarks:

> On my reading, secular discourse does not just 'borrow' inherently inappropriate modes of expression from religion as the only discourse at hand (this is Hans Blumenberg's interpretation) but is actually *constituted* in its secularity by 'heresy' in relation to orthodox Christianity, or else a rejection of Christianity that is more 'neo-pagan' than simply anti-religious.[2]

There is thus a subversive element here, in that the medicine arising from the theology I narrate may at some points be different from and quite critical of some of the logics, languages, and practices of modern biomedicine. And because the Christian community has for the most part neither adequately accounted for its uncritical participation in modern medical practices nor offered any substantive alternatives to those practices, the constructive portions of this book are largely but an effort to *imagine* what it might mean for Christians to go about the business of helping one another live and die well in a world where the very concept of a good life—much less that of a good death—is quickly becoming nonsensical.[3]

Ultimately, then, this book is an attempt to establish a theologically truthful narration of the human body. In this sense what I do here differs substantially from most of contemporary bioethics. That discipline has tended to accept uncritically the biomedical view that the body is a largely passive object, one that is for the most part irrelevant to the autonomously rational decisionmaking process that is understood to be the sine qua non of modern morality. The best of the Christian tradition, on the other hand, has always believed that the body is irreducibly a part of human moral agency, at once created for eternal friendship with God and inevitably bound in this life for corruption and death. Because this distinctive contrast in understandings of the body lies at the foundation of this book, I begin with an account of the contemporary situation in biomedicine and of how things came to be the way they now are.

### The Irony of Modern Medicine

> The assertion of value-free cure and care is obviously malignant nonsense.
>
> —Ivan Illich, *Medical Nemesis*

The irony of the contemporary situation is profound: At the very time medicine has become more successful than ever as an enemy of disease and a prolonger of human life, it has become increasingly incapable of contributing meaningfully to our living and dying well. Whether Ivan Illich is right to claim that the "medical establishment has become a major threat to health" remains a matter of significant dispute; what is much less disputable is that as medicine has become increasingly modern—that is, as it has become increasingly scientific, bureaucratic, and professionally autonomous—it has experienced what James Browder calls an increasing "inability to respond with a human face to the suffering which confronts it," a profound discrepancy between its increasingly abundant means and its growing poverty of ends.[4] These problems are due largely to the character of modern culture itself, and to the fact that modern biomedicine, as much as any human endeavor, exists as both a creator and a product of the thinking and practices of modernity.

Medicine in the modern era has increasingly been burdened with social and moral functions traditionally ascribed to religion and religious institutions.[5] The contemporary political philosopher Michael Walzer, for example, proposes that any modern state daring to call itself just must make adequate medical care widely available to all persons, regardless of their ability to pay for it, in much the same way that medieval Christianity made its means of grace universally available to the masses of people. Walzer makes this recommendation not because he personally believes medicine is more important than religion but because of the growing perceived importance of medicine—especially in the popular understanding—and the accompanying "shift in [important public] institutions from the church to the clinic and the hospital." His argument is thus based on the observation that "we have lost confidence in the cure of souls, and we have come increasingly to believe, even be obsessed with, the cure of bodies."[6] Insofar as the liberal state is supposed to reflect the concerns of its citizenry, Walzer reasons, its policies should display an ever-increasing concern with the equitable provision of bodily cures.[7]

Medicine has become more socially important than religion precisely to the extent that medicine has permitted itself to become associated with a particular kind of scientific reasoning—a kind of reasoning typically placed over against those types of enquiry, religious and otherwise, that are dismissed in contemporary culture as matters of freely chosen private beliefs, at best, or as primitive superstitions, at worst. When medicine falls short of the increasingly unrealistic expectations placed upon it by contemporary culture, that culture's significant and ever-increasing faith in science as a savior is typically not considered as a possible cause of the disappointment.[8] Rather, the scientific day of salvation is held up as a not-yet-arrived-at goal. Ivan Illich puts it this way:

> The proponents of higher scientific standards in medical research and social organization argue that pathogenic medicine is due to the overwhelming numbers of bad doctors let loose on society. Fewer decision-makers, more carefully screened, better trained, more tightly supervised by their peers, and more effec-

tively in command over what is done for whom and how, would assure that the powerful resources available to medical scientists would be applied for the benefit of the people.[9]

From a *moral* perspective, however, these proponents of a "more scientific medicine" miss the point; for in spite of the fact, as Illich remarks, that "medicine tells us as much about the meaningful performance of healing, suffering and dying as chemical analysis tells us about the aesthetic value of pottery,"[10] biomedicine continues to pursue its ends relentlessly, without adequate attention to the phenomenon of human suffering. This lack of attention to suffering is largely the result of the assumption that suffering itself is ultimately curable and hence finally irrelevant to the project of modern medicine. "The [contemporary biomedical] imperative," says Gerald McKenny, "is to eliminate suffering and to expand the realm of human choice—in short, to relieve the human condition of subjection to the whims of fortune and the bonds of necessity."[11]

Yet, as Eric Cassell has so eloquently stated in his essay, *The Nature of Suffering*, this imperative is a misguided one. "Suffering," he explains, "must inevitably involve the person—bodies do not suffer, persons suffer."[12] And because contemporary biomedicine's understanding of the body is largely impersonal, suffering as a discrete phenomenon is frequently overlooked to the extent "that even in the best settings and with the best physicians it is not uncommon for suffering to occur not only during the course of a disease but as a result of its treatment."[13]

Illich notes that practitioners of medicine at one time understood themselves as "an association of artisans who use tradition, experience, learning and intuition"; however, in modernity they have

> come to play a role reserved to ministers of religion, using scientific principles as its theology and technologists as its acolytes. As an enterprise, medicine is now concerned less with the empirical art of healing the curable and much more with the rational approach to the salvation of mankind from attack by illness, from the shackles of impairment, and even from the necessity of death.[14]

Thus a conflict has come to exist between the expectation that medicine should be globally efficacious and its ability to meet that expectation; this conflict has left clinical medicine on the horns of a profound moral dilemma. Physician A. E. Clarke-Kennedy realized this more than a half century ago when he addressed a history of science seminar at Cambridge University: "The greater the growing power of medicine, the more often will medicine be confronted by moral issues, and with increasing frequency will problems, now decided mainly on an ethical basis, come to be settled entirely on grounds of medical expediency and judgment."[15]

Clarke-Kennedy's prediction was not a celebratory proclamation of the triumph of science over superstition but a warning about the moral future of medicine. The scientific turn taken by modern medicine, for all its remarkable achievements, has been accompanied by a profound moral poverty that is not unique to medicine but is, rather, symptomatic of nearly all discourse in modernity.[16] Alasdair MacIntyre has referred to such discourse as "that state of confusion which we sometimes dignify with the name of moral pluralism."[17] The present era may increasingly be characterized, MacIntyre notes, by an almost absurd discursive fragmentation, wherein there seems to exist "no rational way of securing moral agreement."[18] The development of this inability to agree morally has a long and complex history that culminates philosophically not simply in disagreement about the content of morality but in the abandonment of any expectation that substantive moral agreement can be attained. For now, it will suffice simply to say with MacIntyre that the "distinctively modern standpoint" is one "that envisages moral debate in terms of a confrontation between incompatible and incommensurable moral premises and moral commitment as the expression of a criterionless choice between such premises, a type of choice for which no rational justification can be given."[19]

Rational justification cannot be offered for moral positions taken by persons in our contemporary culture because one of the fundamental tenets of modern thought is that the proper ends of human life, if such things in fact exist, are not demonstrable. And if the ends of life are not scientifically demonstrable, if one cannot say in scientific terms what a good person is, then social relations between persons need to be ordered in such a way that each person is maximally free to pursue what he or she freely chooses as his or her own end or ends.

Thus one of the central tenets of modern sociopolitical thought is that freedom and autonomy are the sole bases for a just society, a tenet that is displayed nicely in the work of John Rawls, who has argued that "no general moral conception can provide a publicly recognized basis for a conception of justice."[20] Rawls says further that in the absence of such a general moral conception individuals are empowered to "conceive of themselves and one another as having the moral power to have a conception of the good."[21] Because each person has this power autonomously, for that person the "good is determined by what is *for him* the most rational long-term plan of life given reasonably favorable circumstances. A man is happy when he is more or less successfully in the way of carrying out this plan. To put it briefly, the good is the satisfaction of rational desire."[22]

   In this sociopolitical context, the ways people understand what it means to be healthy or ill are steadily transformed, such that health often comes to be understood as a (particularly important) commodity. As an inhabitant of a modern society, I am essentially an individual in search of that "something" that will satisfy my supposedly rational desire. And while health, strictly speaking, may or may not be in and of itself that "something," I will probably come to understand that I must have health in order to continue the search, to pursue my own freely chosen, rational, long-term plan of life. Medicine is thus transformed into a kind of industry that is in the business of selling an especially desirable product, namely health.[23] And because that product is marketed in such a way as to be considered scarce, its distribution must be regulated by a complex bureaucratic apparatus.[24] This bureaucratic control contributes to the morally paradoxical nature of modern medicine and to the characteristic inability of its practitioners to know and care adequately for their patients. Because the bureaucracy *surrounding* medicine and the methodology *of* medical practice so tightly controls the patient's access to the caregiver, and increasingly the *nature* of their interaction, the patient finds herself in a situation in which many of her particular concerns—specifically those that can properly be called *moral*—are likely to be ignored because they are deemed insignificant.[25] The paradox in contemporary medicine—namely, that caregivers can know all *about* the patient's body without really having to know the patient *as* a body—is both accounted for and masked by the story medicine tells about itself.

### The Story Medicine Tells About Itself: A Critical Retelling

   There is probably no more fascinating story than the rise of scientific medicine. Its beginnings were in mystery and superstition; its progress encumbered with ignorance and quackery. Above these it has risen to become the most beneficent science in the modern world.
          —Howard W. Haggard, *Mystery, Magic, and Medicine*

   There is no one definitive history of medicine, no universally accepted narrative account of how biomedicine has come to understand, describe, and treat the human body in the particular ways it does. Historians of medicine have for some time argued that writing the history of medicine is a profoundly complex endeavor and that the historiography of medicine has, most often implicitly, been the setting for a multitude of ideological and sociopolitical conflicts.[26] In spite of these claims about its complexity, however, it is possible to identify a fairly definitive standard account of the history of medicine, which I call here "the story medicine tells about itself." Partly because of medicine's immediacy to everyday modern life, and partly because "the historiography of medicine lacks such striking landmarks as Boris Hessen's famous 1931 paper on the social and economic roots of Newton's *Principia* or Thomas Kuhn's *Structure of Scientific Revolutions* (revolutionary texts in the historiography of science), the history of medicine is still often understood and articulated in terms that are if not triumphalist, at least positivist."[27]

The story medicine tells about itself reveals a great deal about how modern biomedicine understands and orders itself and about the ways in which that self-understanding is inscribed on popular thought and practice. Medical sociologist Deborah Lupton notes: "The linguistic and visual representations of medicine, illness, disease and the body in elite and popular culture and medico-scientific texts are influential in the construction of both lay and medical knowledges and experiences of these phenomena."[28] Lupton's point is an important one that is well worth emphasizing. The fact that more than one social history of medicine has persuasively deconstructed the standard account of that history does not mean that medicine does not at some level continue to understand itself—and, perhaps more importantly, to be understood popularly—in broadly positivist terms. When I speak of "the story medicine tells about itself," I am speaking of an informal and even popular summary synthesis of these classical, more or less positivist histories of medicine. This story is about the steady, historically driven movement from various sorts of superstition about the causes of illness to true knowledge of the human body via scientific investigation and experimentation.

James P. Browder has argued persuasively that Comtean positivism has been a significant force in the development of modern biomedicine, in terms both of its methodology and its self-understanding. Browder suggests (following Du Plessis) that Comte's thinking was characterized above all by an "optimistic progressivism"[29] that understood the way humans attained knowledge of things in their world, as well as the way they organized their societies in order to maximize the application of that knowledge, as evolving through three distinct and exclusive stages. The names Comte gave to these stages reveal a great deal about what he meant when he said *progress:* The first and most primitive stage he called the "theological"; the second, "metaphysical"; and the third and ultimate, "scientific." In the last stage scientific enquiry is regarded as the only acceptable and legitimate means of attaining real knowledge.

What the scientific knowledge attained in the third stage reveals, say the positivists, is that *all* phenomena are "subject to invariable natural *laws*."[30] Characteristic of this stage, Browder explains, is the rejection of "all a priori knowledge," as well as an absolute denial of "the possibility of knowledge about religious or metaphysical questions."[31] Positivism thus envisions humanity as aspiring, Browder argues, to a kind of asceticism in which a sound scientific knowledge of "the imperturbable laws of natural science" would afford humanity a serenity arising from the capacity of science not simply to understand but also to *control* the physical world.[32] When that anticipated understanding and control were made part of the social fabric, the ensuing social order would be predictably utopian.

The classical histories of medicine are striking in the degree to which they conform to Browder's description of positivism, both in terms of their optimistic progressivism and their ever-increasing portrayal of instrumental scientific reasoning as the single acceptable means of knowing and narrating the truth about the human body. Henry Sigerist's classical work, *The Great Doctors*, subtitled *A Biographic History of Medicine*, is an ideal exemplification of this point. At the conclusion of his book, Sigerist boldly places the development of scientific medicine at the very center of human history by identifying history with progress, and progress with science. "History," he says, "continues its unceasing march. Acting and creating, each of us in his place, we form part of its progress." Physicians, he notes, have taken part in this progress—and ostensibly may continue to do so— by being "above all students of natural science . . . those who, with the scalpel, the microscope and the test tube did [and do] their utmost to wrest her secrets from nature in order to *win control over nature, in order to burst the fetters that hamper us, so that man can become free to fulfill his mission.*"[33] The implication is obvious; science offers control over contingency, and control of contingency offers freedom from the vicissitudes of nature. And, as Iago Galdston remarks (speaking of modern medicine's self-understanding), although "medicine is not as exact a science as is chemistry or physics, it is *au fond* an exact science, becoming increasingly so as more and more of its besetting uncertainties are cleared up. In this view, medical history is the story of the emergence and evolution of medicine from ignorance, superstition and empiricism up to its present state as a scientific discipline."[34]

At the center of modern medicine's self-narration and its narration of the human body, then, is a dependence upon instrumental scientific reasoning that is so comprehensive as to be frankly ideological.[35] Indeed, as the more or less classical account of one historian suggests, it is medicine so conceived that is in large measure responsible for *all* of modernity's scientific orientation; for medicine, by making science immediately and obviously relevant to the everyday experience of human life, "has resulted in science making a greater contribution to [the entirety of ] thought than would otherwise have been the case."[36] The well-known historian of medicine Erwin Ackerknecht echoes this sentiment. Ackerknecht suggests that modern medicine has its most immediate origins in the scientific discoveries of the eighteenth and nineteenth centuries, discoveries that

> led to the development of a new type of clinical medicine in the second half of the nineteenth century. This new clinical medicine is the medicine of the present day. One of its early protagonists, Claude Bernard, pronounced that the laboratory was the 'sanctuary' of medicine. Thus the new period can properly be called that of laboratory medicine, as opposed to the library medicine of the Middle Ages, the bedside medicine of Hippocrates, Boerhaave, and Sydenham, and the hospital medicine of Laennec and Graves.[37]

Ackerknecht's description of contemporary medicine as increasingly scientific medicine is quite accurate, and the triumphalism detectable just beneath the surface of his writing is not altogether unjustified. One can hardly deny, for example, that the first "modern" anatomy based on extensive human dissection, Vesalius's *De Humani Corporus Fabrica*, represented a vast improvement over the long-accepted but inadequately researched work of Galen.[38] And the good done by antibiotic drugs is indeed "unimaginable to anyone who has not witnessed the miseries of the preantibiotic era."[39] What Ackerknecht and other classical historians typically fail to account for, however, is that medicine's positivist turn has come at a cost. When an instrumental scientific understanding of the body is seen as uniquely adequate and is praised without restraint, the account of medical practice that results from that understanding is likely to be a morally impoverished one.

Sherwin Nuland, a physician and historian of medicine, comes close to this position at times in his book, *Doctors: The Biography of Medicine*. His ideological attachment to science as the sole basis for knowing about the body is suggested by his claim that "minds capable of solving the mysteries of DNA will, . . . in some distant future, elucidate what are now seen as the miraculous mysteries of human nature." Nuland lauds the rational science begun in the Renaissance and brought to fruition in the Enlightenment as the turning point of contemporary medicine, not to mention of human history itself. "These men," he says, with reference to the thinkers of the Enlightenment, "inherited a dark world and illuminated it. . . . The scientific thinkers among them sought the truth that only experience and experiment could teach them, through the evidence of their senses. The ultimate test of truth was that it could be demonstrated and confirmed by anyone who had the desire to learn—it had to be convincing to the most skeptical."[40]

## Medical Knowledge and Social Context

In the world depicted by functionally positivist thinkers like Nuland, science becomes not simply *a* way of knowing about the human body, but *the* way, to the exclusion of all others, including those derived from theological discourse. One of the methodological problems with such an exclusively objectivist account of knowing, however, is that it fails to acknowledge that there is virtually no new knowledge attained purely independently of knowledge that already exists. All means of attaining knowledge, and hence all descriptions of the human body—the medical-scientific among them—are dependent upon some tradition of inquiry. They all, in other words, come *from somewhere,* and only in that sense should they be offered to the exclusion of others.[41] For example, Ivan Illich's suggestion that "disease is a socially created reality"[42] is not a denial of the real existence of disease so much as it is an assertion that the knowledge of the body requisite to describing a phenomenon as a disease is attained through a particular, socially established and maintained educational process.[43]

However, as MacIntyre notes, to say that all knowledge is tradition-dependent does not mean that "what is said from within one tradition cannot be heard or overhead by those in another."[44] There is no reason *in principle* that a description of the body derived by using the methods of the physical or natural sciences cannot be rendered compatible with one or more truthful and useful descriptions derived from other methods, and that taken together these multiple descriptions cannot provide a richly textured account of the body and its goods that contributes to human flourishing in ways that an exclusivist alternative precludes. When the science that is the basis for such a description is conceived in positivist terms, however, means of knowing and descriptions deriving from discourses like theology are by definition excluded or reduced to the status of mere opinion.[45]

## The Biomedical Account of the Human Body

Peter Freund and Meredith McGuire posit the existence of a modern "biomedical model" for understanding and describing the human body. This model, they explain, is constituted by a series of five tightly interwoven methodological assumptions about how true knowledge of the human body may be acquired and put to use in the service of medicine.[46] Each of these assumptions has its roots in the earliest strands of modern thinking, and each is at once tremendously useful and fundamentally problematic when applied to clinical medical practice. An examination of these assumptions enables us to understand some of the origins of the unhappy moral poverty faced by modern scientific medicine.

One of the most basic and perhaps the most widely held assumptions of modern biomedicine is that humans exist in a dualism of mind and body. "The medical model," Freund and McGuire say, "assumes a clear dichotomy between the mind and the body."[47] This dualism has its philosophical origins in the work of René Descartes, who is often referred to as the father of modern philosophy.[48] Descartes suggested, proceeding from a methodology of universal doubt, that the mind, the *res cogitans*, was an immaterial thing interior to and completely distinct from the body, the *res extensa*.[49] His now famous axiom *cogito ergo sum* arises from "the intuition that while everything else can, in principle, be doubted, it is impossible for any person to doubt that he or she exists as a thinking thing."[50] Descartes thus saw the mind as the essence of the human individual and as the locus of human agency; absolutely free, the mind was conceived as the center of "an agent whose behavior is governed by no other law than that which the agent himself creates."[51] This assertion is striking, in part because of how remarkably close Immanuel Kant, who is often seen as the paradigmatic modern moral and political thinker, comes to it some 140 years later in the *Foundations of the Metaphysics of Morals*: "By this principle all maxims are rejected which are not consistent with the universal lawgiving of will. The will is thus not only subject to the law but subject in such a way that it must be regarded also as self-legislative and only for this reason as being subject to the law (of which it can regard itself as the author)."[52] The modern tendency to privilege individual autonomy as a moral principle sine qua non is at least partly connected to a dualist assertion that the body is passive and inert and thus obedient to the self-legislating will.

Modern medical practice has at least tacitly accepted this dualism and has consequently come to treat the mind as either radically separate from or as simply an epiphenomenon of the body; Cartesian dualism and reductionist materialism are in this sense but two sides of the same coin. MacIntyre remarks that this treatment is not simply a function of medical theory but also of "the way in which our culture, in thinking about human beings, oscillates between two unsatisfactory metaphysical alternatives: an inadequate materialism and an equally inadequate dualism. Sometimes we behave like the heirs of Descartes, at others like those of La Mettrie."[53] In either case, the body is understood more as a passive machine than as an aspect of personal agency and identity.

Thus we can see that the highly prevalent metaphor of the body as a machine has its origins in Cartesian thinking, as well. In opposition to the mind's absolute freedom, Descartes saw the body as totally constrained by physical laws—that is, as mechanical. As such, he understood the body to be quite incidental to such activity as could properly be called human.[54] Whereas he understood that the mind was immaterial, and thus free and active, he saw the body as wholly material, and thus governed by physical law. Moreover Descartes saw the body as essentially passive, acting only in response to stimuli, either from the mind or from some source external to the body.

As MacIntyre says, when the body is understood as material and passive, it can readily be seen as "an object for or an exemplification of the results of scientific research."[55] In this view, the body can be reduced to and understood on the level of its constitutive parts; and sickness thus can be defined in terms of what Dubos referred to as the "doctrine of specific etiology," which is the "belief that each disease is caused by a specific, potentially identifiable agent."[56] The doctrine of specific etiology is closely related to the machine metaphor; sickness is understood primarily as a sign of disease, which is the failure, due to contamination or structural defect, of one or another of the parts of the machine.

### *Progress or Pathology?*

The smartest and most educated people are the scientists, for they have already found solutions to all our problems and will soon find solutions to all the problems resulting from their solutions to all the problems we used to have.
  —Wendell Berry, *Sex, Economy, Freedom, and Community*

Men may not pursue their moral ideals indefinitely within a conceptual framework that denies reality to them.
  —Michael Polanyi, *Scientific Outlook: Its Sickness and Cure*

Certain of the unhappy practical and moral consequences of the biomedical model—specifically those deriving from dualist and reductionist accounts of the body as a kind of machine—are fairly easy to show. In what follows, I describe those consequences in terms of alienation: the alienation of the patient's body from her experience of illness; the alienation of the patient's body from its environment and especially from other bodies occupying space within that environment; and finally, the alienation of the person from any sense that ethics might be as much about the formation of the body as the autonomy of the mind.

Insofar as the medical practitioner is trained into a method that understands or assumes the person to be constituted by a dualism of a free and active immaterial mind and a mechanical and passive material body, she understands illness to have little to do with the patient as a moral agent. Rather, illness has to do with the patient's body, which is understood first of all as a scientifically quantifiable object, one composed by "blood pressure and cholesterol level . . . damaged muscles or emphysematous lungs." The subjective experiences of suffering and illness thus become increasingly irrelevant to the practitioner of a medicine more and more concerned with objective quantification. When the practice of medicine assumes a dualism of mind and body, then, "the logical framework for a new purpose of medicine had been laid. Instead of suffering man, sickness was placed in the center of the medical system and could be subjected to (a) operational verification by measurement, (b) clinical study and experiment, and (c) evaluation according to engineering norms."[57]

Because this objective narration of the body is reductionist, it tends to make certain aspects of the patient invisible or at least irrelevant to the concerns of the practitioner.[58] Modern biomedicine understands the patient's body as at once the objective locus of her illness and as something other, in a strict sense, than the patient herself; thus the patient finds that she is alienated from her own body and from her personal experience of illness. What matters primarily is not that the patient has a complaint but that her body may be analyzed. This prioritization is effected not simply by modern medicine's understanding of itself as an applied science, but also by the way its institutional practices and the practices of its professional education enforce that basis. I remember quite well that in my own training as a physical therapist, I was constantly reminded to "objectify and quantify" my patients' difficulties. Moreover, I was trained always to mistrust, in at least some sense, their subjective complaints. It was a mistake, I was told, on more than one occasion, to attend too readily to a patient's "pain behavior," since such behaviors were invariably an attempt to manipulate me and gain my sympathy in order that the patient might attain some secondary benefit. Rather, I was to ignore such behaviors and rely instead on my own scientifically based knowledge and my own skills of objective examination. I am not suggesting that patients never attempt to manipulate their caregivers by exaggerating their symptoms, nor that well-developed objective examination skills are not an essential part of good medicine. The problem arises, in my mind, when the objective examination is, *as a matter of course,* placed "over against" the patient's subjective history.

This sort of training is by no means unique to me and my classmates. Arthur Kleinman explains that the very way a physician is trained to conduct a medical history and to record the details of a patient's illness in the chart "is in fact a profound, ritual act of transformation through which illness is made over into disease, person becomes patient, and professional values are transferred from the practitioner to the 'case.'" The very act of the physician's providing a written account of her transaction with the patient, Kleinman says, "turns the sick person as *subject* into an *object* first of professional inquiry and eventually of manipulation."[59]

The particular case Kleinman uses to illustrate this process of objectification is an especially good example of how the concerns of the patient disappear as her body is transformed into an object. The patient is "Mrs. Flowers," a middle-aged, single mother of five children and the sole caretaker of her disabled elderly mother. Mrs. Flowers's medical diagnosis is hypertension. The matriarch and sole provider in a household fraught with social and economic difficulties, she has come to her physician's office complaining of headaches and especially of "pressure." From the transcript Kleinman provides of her visit, it is fairly evident that when she refers to "pressure" she is talking not about her hypertension so much as the incredible emotional pressure she feels as the head of her household and the person responsible for her elderly mother, who is almost totally disabled and whose condition is steadily becoming worse.

The transcript shows that Mrs. Flowers's physician is not particularly interested in her concerns, however. During the course of their time together, he continually tries to redirect their conversation toward the objective aspects of her illness. When Mrs. Flowers insists on telling him about her significant family and personal problems, he responds, dismissively, "Any other problems? I mean *bodily* problems?" To the physician's suggestion that he perform a physical examination in order to "see how you're doing," her response is, "I ain't doin' well. Even I can tell you that. There's too much pressure and it's makin' *my pressure* bad." To this the physician responds, taking control and discounting Mrs. Flowers assessment: "Well, *we'll soon see* how things are going."[60]

Mrs. Flowers, Kleinman observes, has been unwittingly transformed. Insofar as she is permitted to speak, it is of her disease and not of her experience of illness or of the multitude of social, cultural, and economic forces that, along with her disease, constitute that particular experience.[61] The patient's "I" is transformed into medicine's "this," an object that may be subjected to intense scientific scrutiny and treated as a complex machine that has broken down.

None of this means that scientific investigation of the patient's body is morally wrong, much less medically unimportant. Such investigation, remarks Arthur Frank, "is an essential part of the story of illness, but it is never more than half of the story." In recounting his own experience of being treated for testicular cancer Frank recalls one of his physicians remarking that the results of a diagnostic ultrasound would "have to be 'investigated.'" He remembers his reaction: "Hearing this phrase, I was both relieved and offended. The relief was that someone was assuming part of the burden of what was happening to me. But I was also offended by his language, which made my body into medicine's field of investigation."[62]

Frank's concerns are not without merit, for it is not just the patient's body that is affected by illness but the life that is lived in and through and by that body.[63] As he so clearly explains, "The body I experience cannot be reduced to the body someone else measures."[64] But to "colonize" the patient's body—to use Frank's language—as an object of scientific investigation and manipulation is precisely to presume that her body can be so reduced, that those things that make the patient a person are located somewhere other than her body; it is, as Bryan Turner suggests, to ignore the fact that "the social actor is not a Cartesian subject divided into body and mind but one embodied actor whose practicality and knowledgeability involve precisely this embodiment."[65] Everything we know and do, whether sick or well, we know and do through—and in some very real way because of—our bodies. "Indeed," as philosopher of science Michael Polanyi explains, "the structure of perception throws light on all the rest. Because our body is involved in the perception of objects, it participates thereby in our knowing of all things outside."[66] The Cartesian pretense to "have no body" is exactly that—a pretense.[67]

Scientific medicine's dualist/reductionist account of the body contributes to the patient's alienation not only from her own body but also from the surrounding environment, including the bodies—and thus the embodied lives—of other persons. To say that the human body may be understood simply by subjecting it as a discrete object to scientific investigation and analysis is to ignore the multitude of ways in which the boundaries of the human body are continually open to what Freund and McGuire (among several others) call the "social body."[68] An exclusively objective, scientific view of the body is, as Wendell Berry observes, "fanatically individualistic." To see the body as nothing more than a "defective or potentially defective machine" is to see it as "singular, solitary, and displaced, without love, solace, or pleasure," a view that implies that an individual body can become and remain perfectly healthy in a less-than-healthy environment, such as a "disintegrated family or community or in a destroyed or poisoned ecosystem."[69]

Freund and McGuire develop a point complementary to Berry's, suggesting that the very ways in which someone understands what it means to be healthy or sick are inextricably connected to that person's social context:

> The fates of individual bodies are thus linked to the workings of the social body. A person's life chances are not some deterministic fate nor a purely accidental, random result. Rather, a person's chances for illness and successful recovery are very much the result of specifiable social arrangements, which are in turn products of human volition and indeed deliberate policy choices made by identifiable groups and individuals. In large part, illness, death, health and well-being are socially produced.[70]

But modern medicine tends, at least methodologically, to be largely unconcerned with the place any given body occupies in the world or with the ways in which that body's world affects its health. Practitioners who tacitly assume the correctness of the machine metaphor are conditioned by that acceptance not simply to consider the body in isolation from other bodies but even to think on occasion of the various parts of a given body in isolation from one another. This approach, remarks Wendell Berry, makes medical care more the imitator of disease than of health. "If, for example, intense and persistent pain causes you to pay attention only to your stomach, then you must leave home, community, and family and go to a sometimes distant clinic or hospital, where you will be cared for by a specialist who will pay attention only to your stomach."[71] It is here, he explains, that the occasionally helpful machine metaphor runs up against its very pronounced limits; for "like any metaphor, it is accurate only in some respects."[72] But to the extent that the machine metaphor is treated as completely accurate, it makes invisible all of the important ways the human body is not like a machine. Berry continues:

Like all living creatures and unlike a machine, the body is not formally self-contained; its boundaries and outlines are not so exactly fixed. The body is not, properly speaking, a body. Divided from its sources of air, food, drink, clothing, shelter, and companionship, a body is, properly speaking, a cadaver, whereas a machine by itself, shut down or out of fuel, is still a machine. Merely as an organism (leaving aside issues of mind and spirit) the body lives and moves and has its being, minute by minute, by an interinvolvement with other bodies and other creatures, living and unliving, that is too complex to diagram or describe.[73]

### *Knowledge as Control: Subduing the* Factum

The mechanistic tendency to examine and manipulate certain parts of the body separately from the whole—along with the tendency to see and treat the body in isolation from other bodies and from the rest of its environment—has developed historically just to the extent that modern medicine broadly has adapted itself to certain of the canons of scientific positivism. Concerning the metaphor of body as machine, Berry remarks that "a metaphor must be controlled by a sort of humorous intelligence, always mindful of the exact limits within which the comparison is meaningful."[74] And it is precisely this practical "humorous intelligence" that is made impossible by medicine understood as a science conceived in strictly positivist terms. Illich explains:

> By turning from art to science, the body of physicians has lost the traits of a guild of craftsmen applying rules established to guide the masters of a practical art for the benefit of actual sick persons. It has become an orthodox apparatus of bureaucratic administrators who apply scientific principles and methods to whole categories of medical cases. In other words, the clinic has turned into a laboratory. By claiming predictable outcomes without considering the human performance of the healing person and his integration in his own social group, the modern physician has assumed the traditional posture of the quack.[75]

Illich's pejorative language notwithstanding, his point must be taken seriously; for although it is certainly true that many physicians at least partly share his concerns about the transformation of medical practice from art or craft to technique, it remains the case that there is a strong current of thought both inside and outside the medical community that understands the practice of medicine to be more or less science per se. When medical practice is posited as a "pure" science, certain presumptions about what it means for the healer to know about the body of her patient are being made.

It is not simply, as one classical history of medicine notes, that "as science progressed, the canons of evidence became more rigorous and the explanations . . . more exact."[76] Rather, as history moved into the modern era the canons of *what counted* as genuine knowledge actually began to change.

Two interrelated aspects of this change are especially significant for the particular point I am trying to make here. The first of these is modernity's rejection of an explicitly teleological account of the created world—in which the structural and functional interrelationship and interdependence of all things, the human body among them, is given *a priori*—in favor of a growing tendency to examine and to explain phenomena and their causes completely and in absolute isolation from one another. The second is the emergence of an increasingly instrumental account of reason, one that is manifested methodologically in an objectivism wherein the object is isolated from its observer and from other objects as a step necessary to achieve control of it.[77]

Robert James Hankinson explains that the "empirical" medicine of the premodern era was characterized by a relatively loose account of causality and by the Aristotelian conviction that "first principles, the *archai* or axioms of a science, cannot be proved or demonstrated, and hence cannot be given an explanation."[78] He notes that for physicians of that time this was not just a matter of metaphysical conviction but also of practical expediency; it was simply thought that it was "of no practical use to try to aetiologize absolutely everything," since "for ordinary, everyday medical purposes explanation must stop somewhere."[79] Hence for these practitioners "all the epistemological work . . . is done at the level of the phenomena, the appearances, and the concatenations upon which their therapeutics are based are all perfectly evident sequences of repeated, observable events."[80]

## Science and the Abandonment of Ecology

These events, moreover, were understood to stand in a particular kind of relationship to one another. Galdston explains:

> In Greek medicine—and Greek medicine in effect prevailed in Europe for close to two thousand years—Man was seen not merely as dependent upon Nature but as an inseparable part of manifest Nature. In classical Greek culture, the concept of *physis*, of Nature, was central and dominant, and in medicine it afforded the physician a rationale for health and sickness, and a rationale, too, for his therapeutic efforts. Health was the resultant of living in accordance with Nature's requisites; disease the result of failure to do so. The good physi-

cian was one schooled and skilled in diagnosing what was the trouble and whence it came, and in helping Nature by means of the prescribed regimen to reestablish the patient's health.[81]

Galdston calls this sense of the fundamental interdependence of all things—a notion that permeated ancient and medieval thought and served as the basis of medical practice during those periods—the "ecological concept." He sees it crystallized in the admonition of the Ionian philosopher Anaximander, who said: "Things must pay one another the penalty and compensation for their injustices according to the ordinance of time."[82] The Greeks, and the ancient and medieval Jews, Christians, and Muslims after them, understood that the interrelationship and interdependence of things was to be taken seriously, and violated only at a cost. Galdston continues:

> The Greeks understood the meaning of ecology and they understood its dynamics. So, too, did the medieval thinkers. They viewed man as the lesser image of the greater universe, the microcosm of the macrocosm. But with the advent of modern science, this insight into the interrelationship of man with the rest of the world, both living and inanimate, was obscured. Science dazzled man's vision, and the tragedy of Prometheus was compounded a "thousand thousandfold."[83]

An ecological view of the world, and those practices of healing based upon that view—called variously by historians of medicine: Greek, Hippocratic, Galenic, or Scholastic—dominated medicine through the Middle Ages and began to erode only with the advent of nominalist thinking in the fourteenth century and the subsequent emergence of modern scientific thought during the Renaissance. With nominalism came a fundamental reinterpretation of the place of woman and man in the created order. As John Milbank says, the Christian notion of human *dominium* over the creation was no longer understood as "the rational mastery of the passions and . . . the basis for one's legitimate control and possession of external objects," but instead came to be "redefined as power, property, active right, and absolute sovereignty."[84]

With human *dominium* redefined purely as a matter of the exercise of human will and the absolute right of humans to control the *factum*—that is, the existent, created, material realm—comes the emergence of the secular sphere.[85] The secular realm is the domain of the essentially private, isolated individual, whose nearly unrestricted exercise of power may be legitimized not only sociopolitically, but also theologically:

*Dominium*, as power, could only become the human essence, because it was seen as reflecting the divine essence, a radical divine simplicity without real or formal differentiation, in which, most commonly, a proposing 'will' is taken to stand for the substantial identity of will, essence and understanding. . . . The later middle ages retrieved in a new and more drastic guise the antique connection between monotheism and monarchic unity. . . . In the thought of the nominalists, following Duns Scotus, the Trinity loses its significance as a prime location for discussing will and understanding in God and the relationship of God to the world. No longer is the world participatorily enfolded within the divine expressive *logos*, but instead a bare divine unity starkly confronts the other distinct unities which he has ordained.[86]

Power thus came to be understood as the essential, defining human attribute, and Machiavellian *virtù*—the skillful, heroic, and frequently violent exercise of manly individual will—as its highest expression not simply philosophically but sociopolitically, as well.[87] As Paolo Rossi demonstrates, this understanding found its practical scientific expression first of all in the practices of the alchemists and magicians of the early Renaissance, and then, more significantly, in the work of the earliest modern philosophers and scientists, in particular Sir Francis Bacon.[88] Rossi notes that from the alchemists and magicians Bacon took "the idea of science as the servant of nature assisting its operations and, by stealth and cunning, forcing it to yield to man's domination; as well as the idea of *knowledge as power*."[89] Bacon's *Novum Organum* provides the clearest expression of this ideal. It is here that his thinking is most clearly descended from the nominalists. Galdston explains:

*Novum Organum* most clearly expounds the spirit of the new and dawning age of modern science. Therein he propounded his theory of science as the means to discovery and invention. But his was not an idle curiosity, nor a vain pursuit. Bacon was a very practical man and thinker. A science that was not practically useful was, in Bacon's eyes, worth nothing. By means of science, Bacon argued, it would be possible to establish the "dominion of man," the *regnum hominis*, over all things, so that the wants of Man's life might be satisfied, his pleasure multiplied, and his power increased. The dominion of Man over things, Bacon urged, is the highest and indeed the sole end of science.[90]

Bacon held that this new science, or more properly, this new philosophy of science, demanded a complete break with traditional thought. Thus as Rossi points out, Bacon believed "that a new era in the history of mankind was at hand," and that this new era brought with it a new way of thinking about humanity and its relationship to the world.[91] The thinking of those who had gone before was faulty, Bacon thought, not simply because they had committed theoretical errors but because, as Rossi notes, their *ethics* were clearly inadequate.[92] In criticizing the ethics of those who had gone before him, Bacon was referring the term in the broad, generally Aristotelian sense of human acts conducted consistently with a usual and customary way of life directed toward the pursuit of certain ends agreed upon by a specific, concrete community. On this point, as Max Horkheimer and T. W. Adorno note, Bacon established the paradigm for Enlightenment thinking:

> The program of the Enlightenment was the disenchantment of the world; the dissolution of myths and the substitution of knowledge for fancy. Bacon, the "father of experimental philosophy," had defined its motives. He looked down on the masters of tradition, the "great reputed authors" who first "believe that others know that which they know not; and after themselves know that which they know not."[93]

Rossi notes that Bacon proposed instead of the old ethics "an entirely new attitude to nature involving new principles and a different kind of argument, and different aims: in fact a new concept of truth, a new ethic, and a new logic."[94] What had to be different about the new philosophy, Bacon believed, was that it needed to be directed toward the newly understood end of humanity, the willful human control of the world.[95]

In the course of striving to attain sovereign control *over* creation, man and woman came to be understood as the controlling masters of creation and at the same time as part of a given order of creation only insofar as they were subject to control by other, more knowledgeable women and men. Thus in a sense the ecological concept became increasingly irrelevant and, for Bacon and his followers, as Galdston remarks, "alien and repugnant . . . romantic and reactionary."[96] Gone was the sense of women and men being inherently dependent upon the rest of creation, much less upon one another. In its place had been erected the notion of the solitary willful individual with the capacity to understand and ultimately to master everything, including the human body. The problematic implications of this shift for the biomedical view of the human body are summarized aptly by Wendell Berry:

> Where the art and science of healing are concerned, the machine metaphor works to enforce a division that falsifies the process of healing because it falsifies the nature of the creature needing to be healed. If the body is a machine,

then its diseases can be healed without reference to anything outside the body itself. This applies, with obvious differences, to the mind; people are assumed to be individually sane or insane. And so we return to the utter anomaly of the creature that is healthy within itself.[97]

## Science and the Abandonment of Teleology

One of the central tenets of Bacon's thought was that the *ethics* of the pre-modern philosophers were inadequate because of their adherence to an ecological concept of the world and their related failure to place humanity above and in sovereign, unrestricted control of the rest of creation. With the rise of the modern scientific world view and its strictly instrumental account of the *factum* came the abandonment of the idea that the proper ends of human life might be somehow given as part of the order of creation; with this abandonment came the fundamental alienation of what was regarded as real human knowing from substantive moral discourse.[98] No longer could the fundamental moral question (which once had at least tacitly preceded all others) be, as Aristotle posed it, "What is the proper function of man?" or, in Wendell Berry's more modern idiom, "What are people for?"[99]

Put another way, we can say that in modernity, science and morality are placed on fundamentally opposite trajectories. Insofar as the modern world is one in which true knowledge is thought to be attainable only scientifically, moral precepts are relinquished to the secondary status of "values," which in the end come to be thought of simply as subjective preferences.[100] This is the case to a significant extent because of the increasingly reductionistic and mechanistic tendencies that arrived with the birth of modern science. MacIntyre puts it this way:

> The explanation of action is increasingly held to be a matter of laying bare the physiological and physical mechanisms which underlie action; and, when Kant recognizes that there is a deep incompatibility between any account of action which recognizes the role of moral imperatives in governing action and any such mechanical type of explanation, he is compelled to the conclusion that actions obeying and embodying moral imperatives must be from the standpoint of science inexplicable and unintelligible. After Kant the question of the relationship between such notions as those of intention, purpose, reason for action and the like on the one hand and concepts which specify the notion of mechanical explanation on the other becomes part of the permanent repertoire of philosophy.[101]

In this latter world, governed by mechanical explanation, one can no longer speak intelligibly about what it might mean for someone to be a good person. Gone from discourse is any notion of women and men as what MacIntyre refers to as "functional concepts," in which "'man' stands to 'good man' as 'watch' stands to 'good watch.'"[102] Yet, this was a fundamental part of moral discourse prior to modernity, when "the concept of *man* [was] understood as having an essential nature and an essential purpose or function."[103] MacIntyre continues:

> Within that teleological scheme there is a fundamental contrast between man-as-he-happens-to-be and man-as-he-could-be-if-he-realized-his-essential-nature. Ethics is the science which is to enable men to understand how they make the transition from the former state to the latter. Ethics therefore in this view presupposes some account of potentiality and act, some account of the essence of man as a rational animal and above all some account of the human *telos*.[104]

Science, however, says nothing from a functional point of view about the human *telos*, nothing about the human essence, and nothing about potentiality and act in this Aristotelian sense. The knowledge science claims to offer—and this includes knowledge of the embodied human—is an ostensibly detached, objective knowledge freed from the prejudicial superstitions of opinion or of "mere belief." This is taken in modernity to be the sort of knowledge that really matters. But, as Michael Polanyi has shown convincingly, "there are a great number of things our knowledge of which dissolves if we look at them in a thoroughly detached manner."[105] He suggests that there is a "tacit" knowing that "forms an indispensable part of all knowledge," and that the significance of this tacit knowledge renders the "ideal of exact science . . . fundamentally misleading and possibly a source of devastating fallacies."[106]

Polanyi's point is that scientific explanation, important as it is, is an inadequate way to account for all of human existence because "we can know more than we can tell."[107] That tendency in science to explain completely objects and phenomena in terms of increasingly smaller units of organization is problematic, inasmuch as

> nothing is relevant to biology, even at the lowest level of life, unless it bears on the achievements of living beings: achievements such as their perfection of form, their morphogenesis, or the proper functioning of their organs; and the very conception of such achievements implies a distinction between success and failure—a distinction unknown to physics and chemistry.[108]

We cannot, in other words, speak completely and intelligibly about organisms—and this certainly includes human beings—without reference to their function. Such references to function, moreover, must be taken as seriously as scientific references to structure and organization, if not more so; for in speaking about human function *qua* human function—about whether a human life or a human death is good or bad—we are making a kind of *ontological* claim and not merely offering an opinion or even a "value judgment." As Polanyi says, "the kind of comprehensive entities exemplified by skillful human performances are real things; as real as cobblestones and, in view of their far greater independence and power, much *more* real than cobblestones."[109]

A strictly mechanistic view of the world, however, denies that moral judgments about human function have to do with human ontology. This denial is not simply a product of modernity's abandonment of philosophical scholasticism, but also of the closely related rejection of the social, political, and economic structures of the premodern world. As MacIntyre notes, according to this premodern tradition "to be a man is to fill a set of roles, each of which has its own point and purpose: member of a family, citizen, soldier, philosopher, servant of God. It is only when man is thought of as an individual prior to and apart from all roles that 'man' ceases to be a functional concept."[110]

We have thus come full circle, returning to the claim I made briefly above about how the moral poverty faced by modern biomedicine is closely related to the general state of moral discourse in modernity. There is a subtle, albeit inextricable, relationship between modern science's abandonment of an ontological, teleological account of humans—and of their relationship to one another and to the rest of the world—and the rise of modern political liberalism. When the notion of a functional account of human being is no longer taken seriously—when it is held that there is no essential connection between what I am known to be and what I do—then the only logical "scientific" alternative for social organization is that which allows each individual the freedom to *choose* to enter into or depart from relationships that carry with them the burden of behavioral expectations.[111]

## *Biomedicine and Biopower: Controlling the Body*

> Today, when any human thought can be discredited by branding it as unscientific, the power previously exercised by theology has passed over to science.
>
> —Michael Polanyi, Scientific Outlook: Its Sickness and Cure

In the modern world, science is regarded as the only acceptable means of attaining real knowledge. In that world, ethics becomes a matter of subjectively-held "values" that are thought to be nothing but "mere belief"; and freedom, which is understood in modernity as autonomy or self-legislation, becomes the guiding principle of moral discourse. Gone is the notion that a person's identity is constituted by particular, socially sustained ways of life; instead, as McKenny says, "the self is now thought of as criterionless, because the kind of *telos* in terms of which it once judged and acted is no longer thought to be credible."[112]

Ironically, however, individual autonomy in modernity has not been allowed to go unrestrained. Even the most libertarian political philosophers admit to the necessary existence of at least a minimal state, ostensibly in order to adjudicate conflicting individual rights claims.[113] The vast majority of contemporary political thinkers, moreover, go beyond this and posit the need for a more significant, yet still extremely liberal, state in which individual rights include certain entitlements that may by nature place certain restraints on the freedom of others.[114] The advocates of these positions are confronted by what is perhaps the primary issue in modern political philosophy: the justification of the sociopolitical regulation of individual autonomy. This justification is typically accomplished by the employment of a peculiar "politics of modernity," which, according to MacIntyre, juxtaposes "an individualism which makes its claims in terms of rights and forms of bureaucratic organization which make their claims in terms of utility."[115] And these politics find their legitimation, finally, in a variation on the modern account of scientific knowledge.

This sort of strategy of justification is especially prevalent in modern biomedicine. Freund and McGuire, in enumerating the last of the tenets of their biomedical model, explain:

> Partly as a product of the machine metaphor and the quest for mastery, the Western medical model also conceptualizes *the body as the proper object of regimen and control*, again emphasizing the responsibility of the individual to exercise control in order to maintain or restore health. Modernizing trends toward rationalization have further encouraged the notion of the standardization of body disciplines, such as diets, exercise programs, etiquette, routines of hygiene, and even sexual activity.[116]

To show the interrelationship of the body, medicine, and power, it is necessary that I account first, in more detail than I have previously done, for the relationship in modernity between knowledge and power. Michel Foucault shows, consistent with what I have said above, that the most significant characteristic of knowing in modernity is the role given to the subject, the ostensibly detached observer. Whereas in the premodern era man and woman were understood to be participants, albeit of a very special sort, in the great chain of being that was given and ruled by God, in modernity there opens up a very particular kind of interrogative space between the object and its observer. Into this space enters the questioning—and answering—subject, man. And this subject, this human, suddenly finds herself in the radically new position of being both a subject *and* an object. This position is radically new because from the time the nominalists, and then Bacon, developed the notion of the human as the sovereign of the created realm, the human had not located herself thoroughly as an objective and epistemologically embedded part *of* that realm.[117] In the modern era, however, this omission of the human from the realm of scientific objectification begins to break down. Romand Coles explains:

> Foucault contends that the man emerging in modernity discovers that he is indicated by the positive forms of life, labor, and language in which he finds himself. . . . Yet as man is indicated at the *center* of life, labor, and language, he simultaneously finds that his existence is accessible only in these very forms, and that they are older than he is and determine him. Man can only be known as he works, speaks, and lives. . . . Everything indicates man, and everything man can reveal about himself indicates an "irreducible anteriority," gestures towards his ineliminable finitude.[118]

What Coles is saying is that according to Foucault, the very developments that privilege the modern subject in such a profound way, the same developments that make her knowing the only possible solution to the otherwise insoluble problem of human life, are the very same factors that make her "an object of nature, a face doomed to be erased in the course of history."[119] Thus Foucault says that the subject that is deemed capable of transcendence is also the corporeal subject who by virtue of her corporeality must soon cease to exist:

> At the foundation of all the empirical positivities, and of everything that can indicate itself as a concrete limitation of man's existence, we discover a finitude— which is in a sense the same: it is marked by the spatiality of the body, the yawning of desire, and the time of language; and yet it is radically other; in this sense, the limitation is expressed not as a determination imposed upon man from the outside . . . , but as a fundamental finitude which rests on nothing but its own existence as fact, and opens up the positivity of all concrete limitation.[120]

Foucault claims that this paradox indicates the practical end of metaphysics. The very modernity that enables and elicits the possibility of a sovereign, transcendent subject is the same modernity that challenges that possibility by showing that the very life, labor, and language that define the knowing human in modernity also demonstrate human finitude; that they "express the end of metaphysics: the philosophy of life [i.e., biological science] denounces metaphysics as a veil of illusion, that of labor denounces it as an alienated form of thought and an ideology, that of language as a cultural episode."[121] In the subsequent emergence of what Foucault calls the "analytic of finitude," the human subject emerges fully as what he refers to as an "empirico-transcendental doublet," a subject caught between being defined and even determined by her own mortal corporeality and yet possessing a unique capacity: the capacity to see and to *understand* that her own being has been constituted by a tremendous variety of contingencies.[122] Yet, at the very instant of this understanding, the same finitude that constrains the subject is challenged constantly by another possibility, by the possibility that "there *must* also exist a truth that is of the order of discourse—a truth that makes it possible to employ, when dealing with the nature or history of knowledge, a language that will be true."[123]

The modern subject is thus caught in a strange tension, at once Cartesian and anti-Cartesian, between what Foucault refers to as the "cogito" and the "unthought." Certainly the modern human is, as Descartes argued, the thinking subject; however, the very content of her thought concerning the world consists primarily in the specter of her death. The subject cannot then be one of pure *cogito*. Neither, however, can she "inhabit the objective inertia of something that, by rights, does not and never can lead to self-consciousness."[124] Modern thought, suggests Foucault, consists in a "double movement," whereby the "'I think' does *not*, in this case, lead to the 'I am.'"[125] Thought always has its origins and owes its existence to the particular conditions brought about by the thinker's biological life or by her labor or her language, and the subject from which this thought proceeds is left always to wonder whether her existence is bound *only* to the analytic facts of her physiology, her work, and her speech. The *cogito*, we discover, leads not so much to a Cartesian affirmation of being, but rather to a persistent questioning of being.

What must I be, I who think and am my thought, in order to be what I do not think, in order for my thought to be what I am not? . . . What is man's being, and how can it be that that being which could so easily be characterized by the fact that 'it has thoughts' and is possibly alone in having them, has an ineradicable and fundamental relation to the unthought? A form of reflection is estab-

lished far removed from both Cartesian and Kantian analysis, a form that involves, for the first time, man's being in that dimension where thought ad-
dresses the unthought and articulates itself upon it.[126]

Foucault argues that it is here, in the onset of this particular kind of questioning, that ethics as traditionally understood becomes an impossibility for
the modern subject; for the epistemological parameters established by
modernity offer her only one imperative, and that is to *know*, not simply
everything that may or should be known, but even that which is almost certainly unknowable, as well.[127] Horkheimer and Adorno characterize this
way of thinking as fundamentally self-destructive: "Ruthlessly, in despite of
itself, the Enlightenment has extinguished any trace of its own self-consciousness. The only kind of thinking that is sufficiently hard to shatter
myths is ultimately self-destructive . . . There is to be no mystery—which
means, too, no wish to reveal mystery."[128]

Coles notes that the Enlightenment's "constant obsession with and inter-
rogation of the unthought does not culminate in the dissolution of opacity,
however."[129] The object of thought, whether it be another person or another thing, always maintains an element of strangeness and is never
brought fully within the conceptual boundaries maintained by the thinker.

Modern thinking is thus destined always to be "plagued by an unthought residue," a characteristic that gives it a relentless attachment to
power; for although the object of thought never fully conforms to the efforts of the subject to conceptualize it, the subject nevertheless ceaselessly
moves cognitively in that direction, "towards that region where man's
Other must become the same as himself."[130] Because it has been given that
the *telos* of modern thought is mastery of the object, the modern subject
cares nothing for the differences displayed in and by the body of the other,
but strives constantly to force the other to fit into her own conceptual presumptions. The Cartesian/Baconian impulse becomes especially frenetic as
human knowing in modernity becomes "in its very being . . . a type of
power."[131]

None of this should be construed as a denial that the ways in which humans ordered their worlds prior to modernity were free from the effects of
power. Rather, it is simply to say that the most basic characteristic of modern thought is the thinking subject's exertion of power on its object, while
insisting that *all* that is actually occurring is the pursuit of value-neutral,
factual information, of purely objective truth. In the emergence of Foucault's analytic of finitude, the human subject was challenged, in the dis-

covery of that finitude, with the impossibility of her sovereign control of the world. Yet she failed, in a very real sense, to take that impossibility seriously.[132] In this failure, power concurrently became a factor in the creation and extension of bodies of knowledge and in their social embodiment.

Modern societies are characterized by these sorts of multiplications of knowledge and power partly because they are reflections of modern notions of human subjectivity. A return to the work of MacIntyre is helpful here. On the one hand, MacIntyre says, modernity has posited a human subject with a certain transcendent character whereby "each of us is taught to see himself or herself as an autonomous moral agent." On the other hand, however, "each of us also becomes engaged by modes of practice, aesthetic or bureaucratic, which involve us in manipulative relationships with others."[133] Thus, as I have already used MacIntyre to say, we live in a "culture of bureaucratic individualism" characterized by "overt political debates . . . between an individualism which makes its claims in terms of rights and forms of bureaucratic organization which make their claims in terms of utility."[134]

These societies are fraught with incoherence, however; for, as MacIntyre suggests, the debates characterizing these societies are rooted in a "mock rationality."[135] The fallacious character of this rationality indicates that those employing it are dependent upon their desire to manipulate or control others; this concealment is most often accompanied by the claim that the other is irrational or simply not in possession of an adequate reservoir of knowledge about the topic of the debate. The rationalities employed by all sorts of modern bureaucracies in their assertions of managerial and therapeutic expertise are especially dense loci of this phenomenon. Yet, such expertise is rooted in a claimed capacity and right to manipulate or control human behavior on the basis of certain scientific bodies of knowledge that are for the most part either nonexistent or not adequate to justify the kinds of claims being made.[136]

MacIntyre's account of bureaucratic power makes explicit the social and political manifestations of Foucault's denial that ethics is possible in modernity. It is Foucault who claims that the exertion of this peculiarly modern type of power "has been a fundamental instrument in the constitution of industrial capitalism and the type of society that is its accompaniment."[137] He, in a way that corresponds to the account given by MacIntyre, speaks of modern societies as expressing the analytic of finitude and hence of having a fundamentally binary character:

Modern society, then, from the nineteenth century up to our own day, has been characterized on the one hand, by a legislation, a discourse, an organization based on the public right, whose principle of articulation is the social body and the delegative status of each citizen; and, on the other hand, by a closely linked grid of disciplinary coercions whose purpose is in fact to assure the cohesion of this same social body. . . . The powers of modern society are exercised through, on the basis of, and by virtue of, this very heterogeneity between a public right of sovereignty and a polymorphous disciplinary mechanism. . . . They engender, for the reasons of which we spoke earlier, apparatuses of knowledge *(savoir)* and a multiplicity of new domains of understanding. They are extraordinarily inventive participants in the order of these knowledge-producing apparatuses.[138]

We can say, then, that there is an interrelationship between knowledge and power in modern societies that is both complex and inextricable.[139] The managerial bureaucrat alluded to by Foucault and described explicitly by MacIntyre is the archetypal example of the subject created by modern thought and knowledge, one who discovers herself as the executor of a will to power in all of her interactions with the other and who nonetheless in some way assents to that power's being masked by the questionable claim to be one who knows things—usually scientifically—as they really are. This exertion of power concealed as knowledge is not, however, *simply* the consequence of an individual decision to act in such a way. As Foucault remarks: "Power relations are [at the same time] *both* intentional *and* non-subjective. If in fact they are intelligible, this is not because they are the effect of another instance that 'explains' them, but rather because they are imbued, through and through, with calculation: there is no power that is not exercised without a series of aims and objectives."[140]

What Foucault and MacIntyre both suggest is that claims of managerial and therapeutic expertise are to some significant extent self-interested or institutionally-interested calculi that present themselves as being based on bodies of knowledge that are for the most part regarded as esoteric. Following this, we can say that power functioning under the guise of expertise is among the most accurate ways of naming social relationships in modernity. This is not to say that any institution that justifies its exertions of control on the basis of its expertise is *simply* masking a will to power; Foucault explains that modern societal relations cannot be characterized simply as the overt repression of knowledge. Rather, he argues, one of the principle functions of these relations is to *produce* knowledge.[141] It is not, in other words, people's ignorance, but their production and possession of certain kinds of knowledge that permits them to be subjected to bureaucratized forms of control.

Put another way, we may say that in modern societies there exists a three-way interrelationship between power and what Foucault calls "two points of reference, two limits: on the one hand, to the rules of right that provide a formal delimitation of power; on the other, to the effects of truth that this power produces and transmits, and which in their turn reproduce this power."[142] This production and reproduction of power is dependent upon the "production, accumulation, circulation, and functioning of a discourse," he notes. It thus becomes important for each person in modern societies to develop a familiarity with the discursive resources that serve in those societies to produce and exercise power; for Foucault suggests that it is precisely this familiarity that enables one to limit the application of power to one's self, one's body.[143]

Paradoxically, however, it is this very familiarity that initiates a person into the discourses of the society in which she lives and makes her a participant in its economy of power. Foucault explains:

> There can be no possible exercise of power without a certain economy of discourses of truth which operates through and on the basis of this association. We are subjected to the production of truth through power and we cannot exercise power except through the production of truth. . . . We are forced to produce the truth of power that our society demands, of which it has need, in order to function: we *must* speak the truth; we are constrained or condemned to confess or to discover the truth. Power never ceases its interrogation, its inquisition, its registration of truth: it institutionalizes, professionalizes and rewards its pursuit. . . . In the end, we are judged, condemned, classified, determined in our undertakings, destined to a certain mode of living or dying, as a function of the true discourses which are the bearers of the specific effects of power.[144]

Let me summarize what I have said to this point before I try to show how modern biomedicine can be seen in part as the kind of modern knowledge Foucault describes and as a kind of social power masked as expertise. First, I have suggested that there is a particular method of knowing and ordering the world that is peculiar to modernity. This mode of knowledge and order has two especially significant traits: It depends on a particular kind of ostensibly free and autonomous subject who possesses the cognitive capacity to discover the "real" order of things. This order is, because of its depth, largely hidden from the understanding of the common person and must be sought by a highly rigorous, typically specialized, and esoteric investigation.

Second, I have suggested that the knowledge produced and possessed by such persons, knowledge that is frequently employed in the service of hidden coercive power, has both an exoteric and an esoteric component. The esoteric component of such knowledge is first of all and ultimately the property of a typically institutionalized community of designated authorities called experts. The exoteric component, on the other hand, exists in that the success of such knowledge as a means of exerting power is dependent upon its broad public acceptance as a "discourse of truth." The practical application of esoteric knowledge by bureaucratic and therapeutic experts represents the creation and promulgation of this sort of discourse, whereas the application of somewhat smaller or less specified bodies of exoteric knowledge corresponds to the generalized popular acceptance of those discourses and, paradoxically, to both the limitation of power exerted on the individual *and* to the perpetuation of the discourse in the society's economy of power.

The basis of all these characteristics of modern knowledge is that modern conception of human subjectivity that is traceable from the nominalist theologians of the fourteenth century to the philosophers of the Renaissance and to the political and scientific positivists of the nineteenth century and beyond. In that genealogy we see concentrated the paradoxical character of modern bureaucratic individualism. Romand Coles notes that "at the same time people are abstracted as commodified labor, made exchangeable in highly routinized labor processes, and become formally equal members of political systems," they are also taught to understand themselves as discrete, autonomous individuals.[145] When people understand themselves in this way, moreover, they are endowed with a particular facility for comparing and contrasting themselves to others. The existence of this ability to compare the self to another makes the concepts "normal" and "abnormal" especially significant, in that a significant part of the onus for determinations of normality is placed upon the individual.

What it means for someone or something to be normal is thus an essential part of life in modern society. *Normalization* represents the most fundamental way the esoteric knowledges of various experts are promulgated as widely accepted discourses of truth that function openly within a society. The individual is trained by these discourses to take ownership of the knowledges underlying them, to make them her own, and to employ them for her own purposes and ends, purposes and ends that she has ostensibly freely chosen for herself. The individual in modernity thus becomes adept at plumbing the depths of her own being in order to understand herself in a way that ultimately works to strengthen the hold that bureaucratically administered power has on her. This "self-reflection," explains Coles, "tends to normalize as it observes, both by impregnating the self with self-definitions constituted by hegemonic discourses and practices and by engendering certain 'desirable' characteristics while reducing those that are 'undesirable' or 'other.'"[146] Indeed, as Deborah Lupton says, the very bodies of individuals "become inscribed by dominant discourses in the public sphere."[147]

The regime through which the individual acquires this capacity for self-examination is part of the "over-all strategy" by which social power is exercised. Foucault notes that it is inappropriate to think of the conditioning of the self as being discontinuous with the exercise of bureaucratic power upon that self; rather, he says, there exists an "double-conditioning" effect by which persons are trained to make the esoteric knowledge of experts their own.[148] This conditioning finds its moment of application as the person internalizes and comes to own the institutionalized knowledges of experts. Jeremy Bentham's panopticon is the metaphor Foucault uses to demonstrate how this internalization is carried out.

A significant aspect of power that must be masked if it is to be applied successfully in the long term is power's capacity for surveillance. Power must, in other words, have certain means by which it can consistently determine over time the relative compliance of those to whom it is being applied. Bentham's panopticon represents a "technology of power designed to solve the problems of surveillance."[149] Foucault explains that the panopticon is literally an "architectural figure" (e.g., a military barracks, a prison, a hospital, or more overtly, various systems of electronic surveillance equipment) through which several persons are subjected to the constant or *potentially* constant gaze of one supervisor.[150] Panopticism achieves its solution first of all based upon its polyvalence; it is an extraordinarily widely applicable concept. It represents a monitoring that is at once constant and exhaustive while itself remaining always invisible; the watched person is never certainly, but always potentially, being subjected to examination.[151]

Panopticism's most effective exercise is expressed non-architecturally through the notion of internalization. In internalization, the surveillance exercised by power becomes a self-surveillance at the moment the power in question gains credibility as an accepted discourse of truth. Power then explicates the order of things under the guise of scientifically-determined truth. So received, power is tacitly made part of the broad exoteric knowledge constituting the daily lives of persons living in a society. As each individual makes this knowledge her own, she assumes that it constitutes standards of normativity. Through the application of such self-surveillance, the "ordering of human multiplicities" is assured.[152] Certain ways of thinking and acting are designated as normal, not simply because they are so named by institutional authority but also because they have come to be acknowledged by the masses of people as self-evidently so.

Corresponding to the concepts of "normalization" and "normal" are those of "differentiation" and "abnormality." The subject who is immersed in the discourses of a society is endowed by those discourses with the capacity to make judgments about what counts as normal or not. Foucault refers to such judgments as "dividing practices." He notes that these practices are the means by which a "subject is either divided inside himself or divided from others. This process objectivizes him."[153] The differentiation of the self and its characteristics from other selves and their characteristics occurs in several spheres; what is central to my concerns here is that each of these occurrences is potentially a function of the exercise of power.

It is important not to overdetermine the subjectivity behind these notions of internalization and self-surveillance, as if they were the fault of some individual or another. To do this would be to disregard the subtlety with which they function. An individual need not possess an especially large amount of knowledge to function integrally in a society; she needs merely to accept the normativity of that society's practices in order to embody their rationality and make them her own. The examination, which Foucault says is a combination of "the techniques of an observing hierarchy and those of a normalizing judgment" becomes an important concept in this process.[154] In the examination, the expert and the institutions she represents have a means of exercising power precisely to the extent their expertise is accepted by the examinee. This acceptance of examining expertise, which is best described as a form of trust, is a significant means by which discourses of truth are internalized.

The part played by all of this in the practices of modern biomedicine are best displayed narratively. It is difficult to ignore the fact that the full emergence of what Foucault calls the modern *episteme* and the mechanisms of power associated with it roughly parallels the emergence of industrial capitalism. Peter McMylor, in his useful work on MacIntyre, notes that capitalism is "the fundamental reality of western, 'modern' societies." The central question facing these societies, he claims, is how, given their presumption of and emphasis on the existence of a human subject who is no longer governed by particular communal forms of life, they are able to marshal the "mechanisms of control and power" requisite to their successful existence.[155] He indicates that it is those "apparently neutral, managerial and bureaucratic forms of power" that have typically fulfilled this role; the rise of management-based complexes of power and knowledge explicated above, in other words, is to a significant extent inextricably linked to the emergence of a capitalist political economy.[156] In capitalist societies, notes McMylor, "social coordination must take the form of either 'legitimate' coercion in the name of rational necessity or the manipulation of other apparently 'independent' wills, in accordance with social 'need' or 'utility,' as expertly as possible, by those with knowledge, competence, and above all else, power."[157]

The complex relations of power characteristic of modernity are thus largely relations having to do with production and consumption.[158] The division of labor, so intrinsic to the emergence of eighteenth-century capitalism, demanded the implementation of an extraordinary economy of power in and through which some form of surveillance could be extended to each participant in the production and consumption of goods and services.[159] This surveillance, Foucault explains, had to be of a particular sort; "it had to have methods of power capable of optimizing forces, aptitudes, and life in general without at the same time making them more difficult to govern."[160] Surveillance had, in other words, to present itself to producer/consumers as something that would be for their ultimate benefit.

The concepts "normal" and "normalization" are especially relevant to these modes of the distribution of surveillance. Because capitalist political economies demand of power that it gives the appearance of being at the service of the individual, autonomous will of each producer-consumer, it is necessary, as Foucault notes, that power be exercised primarily through non-juridical means:

> Law cannot help but be armed, and its arm, *par excellence*, is death; to those who transgress it, it replies, at least as a last resort, with that absolute menace. The law always refers to the sword. But a power whose task is to take charge of life needs *continuous* regulatory and corrective mechanisms. It is no longer a matter of bringing death into play in the field of sovereignty, but of distributing the living in the domain of value and utility.[161]

By virtue of its being brought into the sphere of everyday life, power attains a newfound subtlety. The loci of its exercise shifts from the juridical and punitive realms to those areas charged with the establishment of standards of normativity through managerial expertise, including, perhaps paradigmatically, modern medicine.[162] The modern person is thus trained to see herself first of all as a producer/consumer; the capacity to produce and consume becomes one of the significant standards by which she is judged as normal or not.[163]

It is tempting, but unacceptably simplistic, to link directly the exertion of power by managerial bureaucracies in capitalist political economies to certain of the practices of modern biomedicine. Yet, a subtler form of such a connection does indeed exist. Foucault argues that the most widely accepted discourses of truth in late modernity are those promulgated by experts in the biological and physical sciences. The scientific expert, he explains, "has at his disposal . . . powers which can either benefit or irrevocably destroy life. He is . . . the strategist of life and death."[164] To the same extent that medicine can be shown to represent the widely beneficent pole of such expertise, it can also be shown to exist as the servant of disciplinary mechanisms of power in modern political economies.[165]

The connection between medicine and power seems to be of two different, albeit closely related, types. First, the standards of human normativity implied by modernity—that is, by capitalist modes of production and consumption—coincide with those suggested by the expert knowledges and practices of modern medicine. Insofar as capitalism and modern medicine both treat persons as discrete and autonomous individuals, health becomes associated at least implicitly with the ability of the individual to function independently of other individuals, to produce and consume and accumulate wealth in her own self-interest.

None of this is to say that modern medicine is not properly devoted, in the words of Edwin Dubose, to "the values of restoring and maintaining health and relieving suffering."[166] Rather, it is to suggest that the particular health modern medicine devotes itself to maintaining and restoring is nonetheless not morally neutral. Although the special scientific expertise of the caregiver does indeed usually serve these ends, the success of the medical enterprise is also dependent upon the patient's acceptance of just enough about the politics of the entire medical enterprise to trust that the caregiver's expertise does indeed provide the truest account of the patient's body. Thus, as Wendell Berry notes, we develop an extreme dependence upon medical expertise to tell us whether or not our bodies are normal.[167] Dubose puts it this way:

Medical knowledge is the key to power and authority within the field of medicine and the field within society. It is in the self-interest of the profession to foster the attitude that this power is beyond the ability of lay people to understand. The emphasis on the physician's personal judgment maintains the importance of each physician's personal knowledge and personal experience as a component of the doctor's authority and professional persona. The prerogative for decisionmaking thereby remains in the doctor's hands. The assumption of a clinical perspective serves to separate the physician from the patient and reinforces the value of the physician's expertise. The emphasis on a clinical perspective determines the way knowledge, techniques, skills are selected, mastered, and applied in the world of working.[168]

A second way of relating modern medicine to capital-driven exertions of power is to see the vast array of institutions and practices that compose health care as in their own right a complex instantiation of the capitalist political economy.[169] Health, from this perspective, is not simply an accepted means of adjudicating human normativity but also a valuable commodity to be produced and sold. This perspective is completely compatible with my earlier suggestion that those discourses by which we learn to name our bodies as normal or not derive from and serve the political economies in which we are willing or unwilling participants; for when health is seen both as a necessary condition for successful participation in the political economy *and* as a product that is bought and sold in that economy, a reciprocal relationship is established, one that assures the perpetuation of both the political economy and the medical industry that at once serves and benefits from that economy. Hence, as Berry notes:

> We are now pretty clearly involved in a crisis of health, one of the wonders of which is its immense profitability both to those who cause it and to those who propose to cure it. That the illness may prove incurable, except by catastrophe, is suggested by our economic dependence on it. Think, for example, of how readily our solutions become problems and our cures pollutants. To cure one disease, we need another.[170]

The effects attributable to these complex relationships are many and varied. Any condition affecting one's ability to participate in the political economy tends to be seen as in some way constituting an unacceptable difference, and hence a pathology. The rise of various types of institutional care for the aged or for those with mental retardation could be understood in this way, for example, and seen as corresponding both to the notion that these persons are not normal because they are unable to participate fully in the economy *and* to the notion that their abnormality requires a special institutional type of care that enables others to participate fully in that economy.

The generally diminished capacity of the elderly or those with retardation to participate in modes of production and consumption, a capacity corresponding to age- and disability-related differences, could be seen as a justification for segregating them from the wider population; these differences would be understood as constituting an abnormality when seen through the lens of capitalist power. The need for segregation, moreover, justifies the creation of specialized models of institutional care in a society that devalues communal interdependence. Ostensibly, these newly created models would be to the benefit of the aged and would present themselves as such through the creation and promulgation of scientific discourses that claim to represent the truth.

Political economy would benefit potentially from the acceptance of these models in at least two ways. First, the general perception that professional care is necessary would remove the responsibility of caring for the aged or those with retardation from families or other smaller, more localized nonprofessional communities. Under the rubric of better care, the entire network of those who would have served as caregivers in more traditional communities would thus be freed to more fully participate in the economy of production and consumption. Second, the lives of the elderly themselves will have become commodified; an entire industry, with its requisite expert managers and disciplined workers will have been developed, and the considerable wealth of the elderly, otherwise relatively inactive, will have been circulated in the economy.

The moral issue here is what such models of care make invisible and thus, in a sense, impossible to imagine. When the elderly, for example, are segregated from the wider community, the community is deprived of, among other things, their collective wisdom. Gradually (this point is developed in depth in the final chapter) the community forgets what it means to care well for the sick and the dying and to be sick and to die well.

If the argument I make here about certain ways of understanding scientific knowledge, modern biomedicine, and political and economic power is correct, then the issue becomes one of asking what possible and more desirable alternatives to the status quo might exist and how those alternatives might be developed. I intend to develop these very points in some detail in Chapters 3 and 4; however, I would first like to deal with them in a more general manner here. Foucault, for one, affirms the possibility of alternatives to the status quo. He notes that the nearly ubiquitous exertion of power always carries with it another possibility. "For . . . at the heart of power relations and as a permanent condition of their existence there is an insubordination and a certain obstinacy on the part of the principles of freedom." This suggests that "there is no relationship of power without the means of escape or possible flight. Every power relationship implies, at least *in potentia*, a strategy of struggle, in which two forces are not superimposed, do not lose their specific nature, or do not finally become confused."[171] In medicine, this is displayed as a subtle paradoxical antimony between physician and patient, as Dubose explains:

> The professional and social commitment to knowledge by physicians . . . also fosters an uneasiness, a suspicion, on the part of the public in its contact with the medical province. The basic orientation in medicine towards biomedical science nourishes an inverse psychological and social relationship between doctor and patient. The greater the drive toward knowledge, the more power and authority the profession exhibits. In spite of additional knowledge, medical technology, and miracle cures, the public feels less satisfied and more uncertain in relation to physicians.[172]

Such dissatisfaction and uncertainty create the possibility of a counternarrative and of accompanying counterpractices. The very possibility that there is another way of doing things, one that might call into question the existing one, demands an examination of the possibility that the expert knowledges constituting medicine's discourses of truth do not completely account for the way things actually are. The "strategy of struggle" embodied by such an examination creates a space for those "subjugated knowledges" denied and dismissed by expertise.[173] The histories of these knowledges, which Foucault calls genealogies,

> entertain the claims to attention of local, discontinuous, disqualified, illegitimate knowledges against the claims of a unitary body of theory which would filter, hierarchize, and order them in the name of some true knowledge and some arbitrary idea of what constitutes a science and its objects. Genealogies are therefore not positivistic returns to a more careful or exact form of science. They are precisely anti-sciences.[174]

Genealogies are thus potentially emancipatory, in that they found the possibility of hope for an alternative.[175] Although they do not suggest anarchy, neither do they purport to be free from the effects of power. "It's not a matter," Foucault, reminds us, "of emancipating truth from every system of power (which would be a chimera, for truth is already a power) but of detaching the power of truth from the forms of hegemony, social, economic and cultural, within which it operates at the present time."[176]

When expert knowledges are detached from their hegemonic status as truth, possibilities for the discovery and embodiment of lost ways or new ways of thinking and living may emerge. When persons are no longer defined strictly by the power-laden discourses of modernity, they are free to discover and embody other narratives that more fully account for who they are and how they should live. They come to understand that a way of thinking that refers to itself and is referred to by others as "expert" need not be uncritically privileged, and that their own stories, stories that in their own right tell them who they are and how they should live and die, are well worth hearing.

## Conclusion

Modern biomedicine has to a significant extent been a discipline shaped by the thinking and practices of the Enlightenment, that way of thinking and living that, according to Kant, would release women and men from their "self-incurred tutelage" and free them to know and especially to master their world.[177] The "story medicine tells about itself" reflects this shaping by portraying the development of medical practice, in broadly positivist terms, as a journey from superstition to true knowledge, from helplessness in the face of sickness and death to the hope of final victory over those terrible enemies.

This narration of medicine's history is so compelling because it is largely true. Biomedical science and technology have made and continue to make amazing strides toward the elimination of many horrible illnesses, illnesses once regarded as incurable. Yet the same program of thought that made possible these developments in medical practice has also worked hegemonically within modern societies to make certain traditional ways of understanding human life and its goods untenable. Horkheimer and Adorno accurately characterize this way of thinking, saying that for Enlightenment thought, "that which does not reduce to numbers, and ultimately to the one, becomes illusion; modern positivism writes it off as literature."[178] Any way of life that suggests that the final end of humankind is not found in the quantification and finally in the mastery of the world is rejected a priori.

To the considerable extent that it has been shaped by this aspect of the Enlightenment program, medicine has been one of the institutional forces in modern capitalist societies that has worked in this way. As such, it has operated to help alienate modern persons from their bodies, from one another, and hence from meaningful, community-based ways of living and dying, all the while masking its coercive alienating tendencies under the guise of the final truth about human life and death.

# THE "BIRTH" OF BIOETHICS

## Scientific Expertise and the
## Justification of the Modern Project

### *The Death and Rebirth of Ethics in Modernity*

The scientific ideals of objectivity and specialization have now crept into the humanities and made themselves at home. This has happened . . . because the humanities have come to be infected with a suspicion of their own uselessness or worthlessness in the face of the provability or workability or profitability of the applied sciences. The conviction is now widespread, for instance, that a "work of art" has no purpose but to be itself. . . . A poem, in short, is a relic as soon as it is composed; it can be taught, but it cannot teach.
    —Wendell Berry, *What Are People For?*

My father was very sure about certain matters pertaining to the universe. To him, all good things—trout as well as eternal salvation—come by grace and grace comes by art and art does not come easy.
    —Norman Maclean, *A River Runs Through It*

Professional bioethicists did not—and could not—offer any assistance to my grandfather during the last days of his life. So far as I know, bioethicists did not participate in his medical care at all. In that day bioethics was still a relatively insignificant discipline, and most hospitals probably hadn't yet seen any need to employ a bioethicist. And insofar as ethicists were and are typically involved in patient care only in "tough cases" dealing with "hard decisions," there is no reason to think that, had an ethicist been available, she would have been asked to consult on my grandfather's case; the care he received was, from a medical perspective, fairly unproblematic.

If my grandfather was able to talk about any of this today, I doubt that he would be have much to say about the absence of an ethicist from his medical care team. He probably would not have been able even to offer much of a definition of the word "ethics." As a technical term, it had no place in his farmer-carpenter-woodsman's lexicon. In spite of this, he was undoubtedly one of the most "ethical" men—and here I use that term in a very particular way—I have ever known; for he was a man happily captured by tradition, a storyteller and creature of strong habits whose body had been trained from childhood in the ways of his father and grandfather. He was ethical because traditions, stories, and habits, it turns out, are the most basic stuff of ethics.

For Aristotle and his ancient and medieval followers, ethics was nothing less than the act of living well, an art that impinged upon the conduct of every aspect of common human life. As such, ethics dealt primarily not with knowledge but with action.[1] A moral person was not simply one who was well informed about how to be good but one who had acquired certain habits of body and mind in conformity with the customary standards of a community of friends.[2] The members of such a community shared above all a way of life rooted in a provisional agreement about the ends—and especially about the End—of human life.[3] This is why at the close of his most significant theoretical work on ethics, Aristotle explains that even the most complete knowledge of ethical theory is only one very small step on the way to being good. He explains that "if discourses on ethics were sufficient in themselves to make men virtuous, 'large fees and many' (as Theognis says) 'would they win,' quite rightly."[4] Such discourses, however, are clearly not adequate to the task of developing good character; something more is needed: "In order to be good a man must have been properly educated and trained, and must subsequently continue to follow virtuous habits of life, and to do nothing base whether voluntarily or involuntarily, then this will be secured if men's lives are regulated by a certain intelligence, and by a right [political] system, invested with adequate sanctions."[5]

Hence Aristotle often compares becoming a moral person to being apprenticed to learn a craft from a master artisan, who conveys to the apprentice not simply a body of propositional knowledge about the art, but also a sense of the history of the art and of the habits requisite to the art's perfection. He would suggest that just as one does not become a master artisan alone or simply by reading a book about some art or craft, neither can one become moral alone or simply by reading a book about ethics. One must have a teacher who is also a friend, one who sees in the apprentice the potential embodiment of the art and who is willing to spend with the apprentice the time necessary to make that potential actual.[6]

This is the account of ethics made impossible by the relentless quest for knowledge and mastery and the antagonistic politics of modernity; for in modernity, as I showed in Chapter 1, individual autonomy is understood to be the defining human moral trait.[7] Consequently, there is no broadly accepted notion of the human good that may offer normative standards for enquiry and practice. The only imperative is to maintain the freedom to investigate, know, and master everything, regardless of the cost; and only in the name of knowledge—especially objective, supposedly scientific knowledge—may the freedom of another person or group of persons be restrained. Knowledge of this sort has thus shown itself to be a powerful force in controlling human behavior. As Bacon maintained and Foucault showed much later in a rather different way, modern scientific knowledge was and is a kind of power. Thus on a popular level it is the case, as Neil Postman notes, that in modernity "almost no fact, whether actual or imagined, . . . will surprise us for very long, since we have no comprehensive and consistent picture of the world that would make the fact appear as an unacceptable contradiction."[8] So long as a claim is ostensibly scientific, it is generally regarded as acceptable.

It should thus come as no surprise that the same thought and politics that renders traditional notions of ethics so problematic also gives rise to a distinctly modern, quasi-scientific discipline bearing the same name; for in modernity, "ethics," conceived as a set of dispositions and formative practices, is reduced to being a matter of strictly private, subjective preference. Public ethics—those minimal moral judgments that should ostensibly be shared by all members of a society—on the other hand are conceived in increasingly procedural terms and become more and more the purview of the courts and of legal experts.[9]

According to Stuart Hampshire, this way of understanding ethics originated with Immanuel Kant, who introduced to moral philosophy a method based upon what he believed was the *"unbridgeable* separation between moral judgments and factual judgments."[10] Kant's distinction, says Hampshire, has generally been accepted by the overwhelming majority of post-Kantian philosophers who regard "the logical independence of moral and empirical beliefs as defining the main problem of ethics."[11]

One of the principal differences between ethics in modernity and ethics in earlier eras, then, is the perspective from which moral problems are addressed. Whereas "Aristotle is almost entirely concerned to analyse the problems of the moral *agent*," notes Hampshire, "most contemporary moral philosophers seem to be primarily concerned to analyse the problems of the moral *judge* or critic":

> Aristotle describes and analyses the processes of thought, or types of argument, which lead up to the *choice* of one course of action, or way of life, in preference to another, while most contemporary philosophers describe the arguments (or lack of arguments) which lead up to the acceptance or rejection of a moral *judgment about actions*. . . . Aristotle's principal question is—What sort of arguments do we use in practical deliberation about policies and courses of action and in choosing one kind of life in preference to another? What are the characteristic differences between moral and theoretical problems? The question posed by most contemporary moral philosophers seems to be—What do we mean by, and how (if at all) do we establish the truth of, sentences used to express moral judgments about our own or other people's actions?[12]

Ethics in modernity is thus no longer understood as being analogous to art or craft but to the *criticism* of art, a distinction that turns out to matter a great deal. The concern of the expert in ethics is not so much to be a good person or to help others become good persons as it is to pass judgments of praise or blame on the actions or potential actions of others. Such judgments are made, moreover, by those in possession of an increasingly esoteric body of knowledge. But, as Hampshire explains:

> No one will be inclined to dispute that the processes of thought which are characteristic of the artist or craftsman in conceiving and executing his designs are essentially different from the processes of the critic who passes judgment on the artist's work; it is notorious that the processes involved in, and the gifts and training required for, the actual making of a work of art are different from those which are required for the competent appraisal of the work; the artist's problem is not the critic's problem.[13]

But if ethics as a discipline is to have any practical meaning for us, it must be concerned first of all with teaching us how to live our lives well on a day-to-day basis and not with formulating criteria for making expert decisions on our behalf when we are trapped in difficult circumstances. The "typical moral problem is not," explains Hampshire, "a spectator's problem or a problem of classifying or describing conduct, but a problem of practical choice or decision."[14] Yet this is quite the opposite of the direction in which the discipline of ethics has moved in recent years, as ethics has become increasingly concerned with displaying a kind of scientific certainty that validates the authority of a group of experts.

This tendency in the disciplines of applied ethics and moral philosophy is closely related to the steadily increasing authority the notion of scientific objectivity has attained in modernity. The notion of ethics as an applied science perhaps has its origins in the philosophy of Jeremy Bentham, who argued for the elimination of evaluative language from moral discourse in favor of an objective "science of morals in which all moral problems would be experimentally decidable as technical problems."[15] And although the kind of strict utilitarianism advocated by Bentham and his followers has to an extent fallen from favor among ethicists, the goal of a kind of scientific objectivity in ethical decisionmaking has not.

Wendell Berry laments the moral impoverishment arising from modern culture's increasing tendency toward dependence upon scientific objectivity, noting that the problem with objectivity as a sole criterion of decisionmaking is that it disallows all references to affection. Yet, he insists, "to be well used, creatures and places must be used sympathetically, just as they must be known sympathetically to be well known."[16] Berry goes on to make a point similar to Hampshire's distinction between performance and criticism. The point in question appears as an epigraph at the beginning of this section, but it is worth quoting again and at more length:

> The scientific ideals of objectivity and specialization have now crept into the humanities and made themselves at home. This has happened, I think, because the humanities have come to be infected with a suspicion of their own uselessness or worthlessness in the face of the provability or workability or profitability of the applied sciences. The conviction is now widespread, for instance, that a "work of art" has no purpose but to be itself. Or if it is allowed that a poem, for instance, has a meaning, then it is a meaning peculiar to its author, its time, or its convention. A poem, in short, is a relic as soon as it is composed; it can be taught, but it cannot teach. The issue of its truth and pertinence is not raised because literary study is conducted with about the same anxiety for "control" as is scientific study. The context of a poem is its text, or the context of its history and criticism as a text. I have not, of course, read all the books or sat in all the classrooms, but my impression is that not much importance is attached to the truth of poems.[17]

Berry's observations are especially salient with regard to the way medical ethics has developed in recent modernity, where there has emerged a new sort of expert, the applied or clinical medical ethicist.

## Medical Ethics as Bureaucratic and Scientific Expertise

With purity and holiness I will pass my life and practice my art.
—from the *Oath of Hippocrates*

Moralism in our common life is dangerous precisely because it dominates distributive systems outside the private and the religious spheres.
—Dan Beauchamp, *The Health of the Republic*

In one significant sense, there is nothing modern about medical ethics. A significant portion of the well-known and highly influential *Corpus Hippocratum* from the third century B.C. concerns itself with the moral comportment of the physician.[18] Medical practice in the nineteenth century was characterized by a renewed interest in ethics, as exemplified by the British physician Thomas Percival's 1803 *Code of Ethics*. Beginning in the middle of the nineteenth century and following Percival's lead, physicians made strong efforts to assure high moral standards among themselves through the founding of professional associations with their own codes of ethics.[19]

In quite another way, however, medical ethics is very much a product of the late twentieth century and its characteristic technical, sociopolitical, and economic developments. In 1992, a conference held at the University of Washington celebrated the thirtieth anniversary of what organizers referred to as the "birth" of bioethics. Albert Jonsen explains:

The occasion of this conference was the thirtieth anniversary of the publication of an article in *Life* magazine, "They Decide Who Lives, Who Dies" (9 November 1962). That article told the story of a committee in Seattle whose duty it was to select patients for entry into the chronic hemodialysis program recently opened in that city. Chronic dialysis had just been made possible by Dr. Belding Scribner's invention of the arteriovenous shunt and cannula in 1961. It quickly became apparent that many more patients needed dialysis than could be accommodated. The solution was to ask a small group, composed mostly of nonphysicians, to review the dossiers of all medically suitable candidates and sort out those who would receive the lifesaving technology.[20]

Jonsen was one of the keynote speakers at the Washington conference, and he claimed that since the publication of the *Life* article, "bioethics has matured into a minor form of moral philosophy practiced within medicine."[21] The impetus for this "new ethics of medicine," he explained, came about in the dialysis case because "authorities of the past, namely physicians, seemed inadequate."[22] This inadequacy Jonsen attributes not to the inadequate moral character of contemporary physicians but to changes in the "very nature of biomedical science" that necessitated a new approach to medical decisionmaking in morally difficult cases.[23]

Thus Jonsen argues that it is the rapid evolution of biomedical technology that led to the changes that have allowed bioethics to flourish as a full-blown profession. No longer a concerned lay or clergy person, the medical ethicist has become an acknowledged health care expert among others, and though it may be true that the contemporary ethicist occasionally challenges the unbridled acceptance of technological advance with, in Jonsen's words, a "critical, analytic, and even prophetic voice," it is more often the case that the ethicist's role is one of blessing and sanctioning existing or cutting-edge medical practices based upon her expertise.[24]

The clinical ethicist is understood to have legitimate medical authority rooted in the exclusive possession of expert knowledge, knowledge analogous to that possessed by medical specialists like neurosurgeons or nephrologists. Ruth Shalit says of these individuals:

> The clinical ethicists . . . regard themselves as authorities in the medical as well as the pastoral sphere: in their view, an ethicist's advice on moral matters carries the same weight of a surgical consultant in his specialty. "If you're a cardiologist, and a foot problem arises, you may call in a consultant in that particular specialty to help identify the problem," explains Thomas May, an ethicist at the Memorial Medical Center in Springfield, Illinois. Similarly, moral quandaries beyond the grasp of doctors "will seem obvious to a philosopher," he says, "because, you see, we deal with these concepts every day."[25]

The expert bioethicist justifies her authority not simply on the basis of familiarity with the moral implications of difficult cases but also on the basis of the possession of esoteric knowledge about how to solve those cases. Oblivious to the Aristotelian admonition that mathematical certainty in moral matters may be unattainable, clinical ethicists "weigh empirical data, parse risk-benefit ratios and wield 'ethics case analysis grids' with algorithmic certainty."[26] Perhaps even more significantly, clinical ethicists lay an exclusive claim to the bases by which their decisions are made, as Shalit demonstrates:

> Those who have entered the guild are quick to warn moral rookies against the dangers of lay ethical analysis. "It simply is not within the purview of most patients and family members to understand the complex nature of the moral judgments facing them," sighs Nancy Dubler, a lawyer-ethicist for the Montefiore Medical Center and author of *Ethics on Call*, a book about her fledgling profession. "One would have to be able to abstract from what is, at this point, a rather large literature."[27]

In Chapter 1 I suggested that modernity—and this includes modern biomedicine—could not be properly understood philosophically or politically apart from the development of capitalist markets. Not surprisingly, the market forces of capitalist political economy are a significant influence in the emergence of bioethical expertise. As medicine has become more technical and more oriented toward highly individualized, pathocentric notions of health, it has increasingly come to be understood as a commodity subject to market scarcity. It is a simple tenet of the market that valuable commodities are valuable in part because they are scarce, meaning that not everything technically possible can be done to every patient, particularly when the goal of one or more of the parties involved is profit.[28]

The emergence of explicitly for-profit medicine has brought this point into sharp relief. If hospitals or payers (i.e., insurance companies and HMOs) are to yield a profit for their investors, they must at some point limit their distribution of goods and services. Such limitations must to a significant extent be accepted by patients, however, for reasons other than purely financial ones. Enter the medical ethicist. Shalit notes:

> increasingly, medical-ethics consultants are being retained by HMOs to assist them in decisions about grievance cases, risk management and "noncompliant patients." Robert Wagener of the Center for Medical Ethics and Mediation in San Diego says that for-profit HMOs striving to do the right thing compose an ever-increasing share of his clientele. "The movement away from traditional fee-for-service care . . . has raised . . . complex issues," writes Wagener in a 1997 journal article. "These issues give new meaning to the struggle between the ethical principles of autonomy, beneficence, distributive justice, and fidelity." Wagener, whose conversation is an exuberant melange of John Stuart Mill and *Getting to Yes*, could not be more enthusiastic about the changes afoot. "There is a much higher consciousness about the ethics of managing scarce fiscal resources," he says. "Now, notice that I never say, 'saving dollars.' I say, 'managing resources.'"[29]

Shalit makes the point that although explicitly for-profit medicine certainly does make medical practice more complex morally, it is worth asking whether an ethicist employed by the payer is the best person to adjudicate such complexities.[30] If the kinds of expert, scientific knowledge the clinical ethicists claim to possess does not in fact exist—and I am clearly convinced that it does not, at least not in the sense the ethicists say it does—then the potential for conflicts of interest, not to mention frank unintelligibility, is enormous.[31] "Ethics" becomes simply another way of masking coercive power under the guise of knowledge.

Perhaps this is best illustrated by considering an issue around which clinical ethicists vie with physicians for the power to make difficult decisions, namely whether caregivers should seek to extend a patient's life through the utilization of so-called "extraordinary measures."[32] Doctors Daniel Waisel and Robert Truog, in a 1995 article in the *Annals of Internal Medicine*, discussed medical and moral concerns surrounding the recent advent of the "unilateral do-not-resuscitate order." A unilateral do-not-resuscitate order (DNR) is an order written by the attending physician instructing hospital staff not to perform cardiopulmonary resuscitation on a patient in the event of cardiac or respiratory arrest. The order is unilateral because it is issued independently of the patient's consent; the issue is controversial because traditionally "CPR held a unique position. Unlike all other therapies, one had to get consent to withhold CPR, not to administer it."[33] The authors stress that these orders have their basis in medical, rather than moral, judgments. "Unilateral do-not-resuscitate policies," they explain, "presume that cardiopulmonary resuscitation is a *medical* therapy and that physicians have no obligation to undertake a medical therapy that does not offer achievable and appropriate goals."[34]

The explanation the authors offer for the emergence of unilateral DNR policies is an exceptional example of the presence in medicine of the fundamental modern antagonism between individual freedom and expert control. They say:

Physicians may be frustrated by the glare of autonomy compelling them to provide, in the physician's mind, inappropriate treatment. Because the patient's autonomy may not allow the physician to give what he considers the best possible care, physicians may feel hindered in fulfilling their fiduciary relationship. This requirement to give unsuccessful and inappropriate care can be demoralizing to the caregiver. Tomlinson and Brody have argued that the current primacy of the patient's wishes does not provide true autonomy. By instituting a therapy in a futile situation, one falsely offers hope to the family and patient that undermines the patient's ability for rational judgment and autonomy.

. . . Finally, the pressure to control costs is greater now than it has been in the past, and providers may be looking for ways to ration care; expensive and marginally effective care may be a place to start.[35]

Whether the unilateral DNR policy is good medicine or not is an interesting and important question, but to put the matter in exactly this way misses what I believe is the main point; for this very way of *describing* patient-caregiver interaction—that is, by opposing professional expertise to individual patient autonomy—belongs to the politics of modernity discussed in Chapter 1 and is from a moral perspective profoundly problematic. What is even more interesting, in my estimation, is the way in which clinical ethicists are being placed in positions similar to experts in order to uphold the decisions of physicians.

Consider the cases of patients James Bland and Brianne Rideout, discussed by Shalit in her article. Bland was a comatose hospital patient, very near death, who was ventilated by a respirator. Prior to his becoming comatose, he had explained that above all else he feared suffocating, and that he wanted to be allowed to die while being ventilated. His insurance company, however, wanted him to be transferred to hospice care, a move that would require him to be taken off the respirator. A physician-ethicist employed by the insurance company advised that the move was appropriate, ostensibly on moral as well as medical grounds. Predictably, Bland died a short time after being taken off the respirator, in spite of his concerns.

Rideout, on the other hand, was a three-year-old patient who became comatose and had to be ventilated while being treated for a brain tumor. Her parents were informed by her physician that the hospital's ethics committee had decided it would be appropriate to shut off Brianne's ventilator; when the parents protested, an ethicist was appointed to consult with them and informed them that the decision to terminate their daughter's treatment was appropriate and therefore final. "At the appointed hour, the Rideouts rushed to their daughter's room, where they were 'restrained by hospital security guards and police officers as they thrashed and wailed,' according to a newspaper account. As predicted, the child died when the plug was pulled."[36]

The most significant thing about these various cases, from the perspective of the argument I am developing here, is not that the decisions made by physicians and ethicists were bad ones (this may or may not be the case), or that they had tragic consequences. Rather, what is problematic is that contemporary clinical ethics conceives these situations according to the politics of modernity—that is, as a bipolar opposition of wills.

Harmon Smith and Larry Churchill offer a substantial critique of the modern incarnation of the notion of Aesculapian authority, which calls upon the patient to take up the "sick role" by which "a person becomes a patient when he or she becomes ill, is excused from normal responsibilities, places him/herself in the hands of a competent physician, and cooperates with the regimen recommended by the physician."[37] At the same time, however, they warn against an absolutized notion of patient rights that renders the physician's judgment irrelevant.[38] "The answer to Aesculapian authority," they explain, "is not populism."[39] They argue that if medical ethics is to escape the antagonism of the politics of modernity, that escape must begin with a renewed understanding of the notion of *consent*. Whereas the politics of modernity causes us to understand consent as the abandonment of patient agency, Smith and Churchill (following Edmund Pellegrino) suggest that true consent occurs when patient and caregiver think *together* about the proper course of action and come to a reasoned agreement.[40]

Yet the opposition of patient autonomy to caregiver (and institutional) authority is the fundamental assumption of most contemporary medical ethics. In what follows, I will consider three well-known and highly regarded works in medical ethics and the philosophy of medical practice, each of which is to a greater or lesser extent rendered problematic and occasionally even unintelligible by its ultimate acceptance of the politics of modernity. I begin with a fairly detailed and critical examination of the work that seems to embrace the politics of modernity most uncritically: *The Principles of Biomedical Ethics*, by Tom Beauchamp and James Childress. This book is very sophisticated, in the sense that it engages in a variety of kinds of ethical analyses in order to show how moral dilemmas in modern medicine might be approached and resolved. It is also an excellent illustration of the problems associated with ethical discourse in modernity, inasmuch as the authors seem to presume throughout the book that there is nothing wrong with contemporary medical practice that rigorous ethical analysis cannot fix.

I then bring that book into conversation with a more sophisticated dialectical analysis of clinical practice that challenges many of the assumptions of modern thought: *A Philosophical Basis for Medical Practice*, by Edmund Pellegrino and David Thomasma. Pellegrino and Thomasma are much more willing to engage the politics of modernity than are Beauchamp and Childress; they recognize that there are deep problems with medical practice in modernity and seek to resolve those problems by asking fundamental questions about why physicians and other caregivers do what they do. Their work falls short of its goal, however, because their dialectic leads them to the conclusion that medicine itself, as a discrete discipline, possesses moral resources adequate to effect its own repair.

I then proceed to engage a third work:, *The Foundations of Bioethics*, by Tristram Engelhardt. This is a radically skeptical attempt to do a kind of minimalist medical ethics within the modern situation. Engelhardt is fully aware of the fragmented nature of moral discourse in modernity and has no hope that a substantive, content-full medical ethics can be developed given the constraints of modernity. Yet, he is willing to assume some of the tenets of modernity, especially the distinction between the public and private spheres and the possibility of a pure procedural ethics in the former realm. It is in this acceptance that Engelhardt's work finally fails.

All three of these works are ultimately unsatisfying because they finally accept too many of the tenets of modernity. What is needed, as Engelhardt readily admits and in fact strongly advocates, is an ethics of medical practice that can speak intelligibly in the midst of—but without having to embrace—the politics of modernity. At the conclusion of this chapter, I will indicate what I believe are the necessary conditions for the development of such an ethics, which is the project of the second half of this book.

## The Principles of Biomedical Ethics:
### *Principles Are All You Need*

> Hegel thought all "content and specification" in a living code of ethics had been replaced by abstractness in Kant's account. Ethical theory that features principles has been similarly accused.
> —Beauchamp and Childress

Perhaps the best-known and most highly regarded contemporary attempt at a comprehensive introduction to medical ethics is *Principles of Biomedical Ethics* by Tom Beauchamp and James Childress, first published in 1979 and most recently revised in 1994. *Principles* is a book classically representative of modernity, in that it has as its aim "to show how ethical theory can illuminate problems in health care and can help overcome some limitations of past formulations of ethical responsibility."[41] Beauchamp and Childress thus share (and in some sense may be understood as the codifiers of) the fairly common presumption among contemporary medical ethicists that a modern, technocentric medicine demands a correspondingly modern medical ethics; they are proponents of the fairly typical position that, as Gerald McKenny says, a "new, philosophically grounded bioethics is . . . necessary."[42] Beauchamp and Childress defend this claim by explaining:

> Medical ethics enjoyed a remarkable degree of continuity from the last days of Hippocrates until its long-standing traditions began to be supplanted, or at least supplemented, around the middle of the twentieth century. Scientific, technological, and social developments during that time produced rapid changes in the biological sciences and in health care. These developments challenged many prevalent conceptions of the moral obligations of health professionals and society in meeting the needs of the sick and injured.[43]

The authors follow Henry Sidgwick and William Frankena in assuming the existence of a fairly substantial common human morality that although "not faultless or complete in its recommendations . . . forms the right starting place for ethical theory."[44] Such a morality, they explain, does not necessarily have, nor does it require, shared metaphysical commitments or widespread agreement on the human good. It exists rather as a function of "the morality shared in common by the members of a society—that is, unphilosophical common sense and tradition."[45] There is thus a close, albeit not necessarily direct, relationship between morality and public policy.[46]

As the title suggests, the theoretical foundations of this work are a cluster of principles that may be applied, usually in tension with one another, to particular dilemmas in clinical ethics. These principles—autonomy, nonmaleficence, beneficence, and justice—are not, the authors insist, self-evident absolutes but general rules for human action arising dialectically over time from "considered judgments in the common morality and medical tradition"; principles, in other words, both come from and are applied to particular cases.[47] They are thus "both prima facie binding and subject to revision":

> So understood, a prima facie principle is a normative guideline stating conditions of the permissibility, obligatoriness, rightness, or wrongness of actions that fall within the scope of the principle. The latitude to balance principles in cases of conflict leaves room for compromise, mediation, and negotiation. The account is thereby rescued from the charge that principles cannot be compromised and so become tyrannical. In stubborn cases of conflict there may be no single right action, because two or more morally acceptable actions are unavoidably in conflict and yet have equal weight in the circumstances. Here we can give good but not decisive reasons for more than one action.[48]

Although Beauchamp and Childress rightly deny that theirs is a "monistic" approach to ethics, one in which a "supreme, absolute principle supports all other action guides in the system," their general adherence to the canons of political liberalism requires them to allow one of their enumerated principles—respect for the autonomous choices of other persons—undeniable centrality.[49] Following the philosophical work of Kant and Mill, the authors summarize their principle of autonomy as follows: "*Autonomous actions should not be subjected to controlling constraints by others.*"[50] They insist that this should not be interpreted as a call for an uncritical patient populism, however; where the medical caregiver is concerned, respect for the patient's autonomy means primarily that there is an "obligation of respectful treatment in disclosing information and fostering autonomous decisionmaking."[51]

Therefore "*express* and informed consent" forms one of the bases for Beauchamp and Childress's account of patient autonomy.[52] The physician may rightly execute only those procedures explicitly consented to by the well-informed patient. Proper consent requires two conditions from the patient: First, she must be *free* to decide; second, she must be *capable* of deciding.[53] On their interpretation of these two conditions—which it seems to me turns out to be more than a little equivocal—hangs the authors' account of autonomy and hence of the other principles.

In order for a patient properly to give or refuse express consent for a particular procedure, she must by judged competent to make such decisions. "Competence judgments serve a gatekeeping role in health care by distinguishing persons whose decisions should be solicited or accepted from persons whose decisions need not or should not be solicited or accepted."[54] The *power to adjudicate* competence thus has a significant role here; the person vested with that power provides an important hedge against caregivers merely serving the potentially anarchic—and wrongheaded—desires of their patients. A knowledgeable and sensitive caregiver might make a huge difference in the way a patient is treated.

Competence, argue Beauchamp and Childress, is a fluid concept. Whether a person is competent or not depends not simply on the person but also on the task in question. In spite of this qualification, they note that "the gatekeeping function of competence requires sorting persons into one of two classes: competent or incompetent." Competence is thus referred to as a "threshold" concept: "Above the threshold, persons are equally competent; below the threshold they are equally incompetent. Gatekeepers test to determine who is above and who is below this threshold."[55]

The fundamental criterion for judging competence "in biomedical contexts" is the ability of the patient to understand her situation and the freedom to decide whether to accept or reject the proposed course of action. Specifically, a person is to be judged competent to give (or to withhold) consent if she is first of all "able to understand a therapy or research procedure, to deliberate regarding major risks and benefits, and to make a decision in light of this deliberation."[56] Competence thus depends on a person's ability to offer *rational* reasons for choosing one option over another.[57] Those reasons, moreover, must be the person's own; they must be given without influence from other persons or groups of persons.[58]

Two closely related questions must be put to Beauchamp and Childress at this point. First, when a person is judged incompetent, in whose interest is that judgment made? Whose notion of the good, in other words, is at work in the adjudication? Second, what criteria are to be employed in making such judgments? The authors acknowledge the significance of these questions and attempt to provide satisfying answers. They note:

> In practice challenges to a patient's competence rarely emerge unless a disagreement exists about values. As long as a patient concurs with the physician's recommendations, his or her competence to understand, to decide, and to consent to treatment is rarely examined. But conflict between the patient' wishes and the physician's judgment about that patient's best interests typically provokes an inquiry into the patient's competence.[59]

The prospect of "an inquiry into the patient's competence" may of course be a matter of some concern, given the questions about patient interest I have put to the authors in the preceding paragraph. Beauchamp and Childress seem to be aware of this and appear to side with the patient in cases of conflict by putting the less arguable criterion of capacity for decision, rather than the question of what is best for the patient, at the center of the debate. At the same time, however, they remind us that respect for autonomy is only one of their principles, and that it must be balanced with others that more fully "take account of risks, benefits, and best interests."[60] Just as the principle of respect for autonomy protects patients against the undue exercise of Aesculapian authority, the interwoven principles of nonmaleficence and beneficence protect medical practice from being totally subject to undesirable patient autonomy.

Nonmaleficence and beneficence may be seen as belonging to a cluster of moral obligations that begins with the obligation to refrain from acting in such a way as to willfully harm another person (nonmaleficence) and ends with the obligation to act in such a way as to promote that person's well being (beneficence).[61] Beauchamp and Childress, however, maintain that non-maleficence and beneficence are distinguishable principles that involve different concepts, namely harm and best interest, and that the differences between these concepts matter in distinguishing "between killing and letting die, intending and foreseeing harmful outcomes, withholding and withdrawing life-sustaining treatments, and extraordinary and ordinary treatments."[62]

The authors readily acknowledge that a certain ambiguity attends the determination of what constitutes harming or helping another person: "What counts as a harm to one person may not be a harm at all to another person because of their competing visions of what constitutes a setback of interests."[63] In spite of this admission, however, they indicate that in a medical context a patient's ostensibly objective physical interests—including "pain, disability, and death"—should be considered first of all.[64] Thus there are certain fairly universal prima facie moral rules arising from the principle of nonmaleficence:

1. Do not kill.
2. Do not cause pain or suffering in others.
3. Do not incapacitate others.
4. Do not cause offense to others.
5. Do not deprive others of the goods of life.[65]

In the same way, the authors list what they take as corresponding universal prima facie rules of "obligatory beneficence" that are active in a medical context:

1. Protect and defend the rights of others.
2. Prevent harm from occurring to others.
3. Remove conditions that will cause harm to others.
4. Help persons with disabilities.
5. Rescue persons in danger.[66]

It stands to reason that there will likely be less disagreement about what sorts of actions constitute violations of nonmaleficence than those constituting violations of obligatory beneficence. What is apparent in both cases, however, is that Beauchamp and Childress are constrained by their acceptance of the highly individualized and antagonistic politics of modernity to explain both nonmaleficence and beneficence with reference to their central principle of respect for autonomy. Their treatment of one issue in particular makes this clear.

In the course of considering what sorts of actions constitute nonmaleficence, the authors discuss the distinction in medical practice between killing and letting die and between the traditionally held moral and legal sanctions against physician-assisted suicide. They maintain that "merciful physician interventions in the form of voluntary active euthanasia are not inherently wrong or incompatible with the role of a health professional" and that "prohibitions in biomedical ethics against certain forms of assisted suicide should be eased, making physicians more comfortable in helping certain patients achieve what for them is a comfortable and timely death."[67]

They begin their argument by stating what they believe is a maxim of the common morality: "It is not always wrong . . . to cause someone's death."[68] What determines whether a particular instance of killing is maleficent or beneficent is not the act itself but the circumstances surrounding the act. Killing is thus prima facie, but not absolutely, wrong. Causing the death of another person is not morally wrong because the act itself is evil or because of the effects that death has on society or the friends and relatives of the deceased, but "because of a harm or loss to the person killed, not because of the losses that others encounter." It is wrong because it inflicts "the loss of the capacity to plan and choose a future, together with a deprivation of expectable goods."[69] It is a violation of that person's autonomy.

Whether a particular act interferes with the right of the autonomous individual to plan and choose her future is thus the basis of adjudicating that act's morality. When the act in question is causing the death of another person, the question that must be asked is whether the person *wants* to die and whether her desire to die is *reasonable*. If death is her choice, and if she is competent to make that choice, then she may rightfully request the assistance of a physician in reaching that goal. The physician may kill the patient in an absolutely nonmaleficent way. Autonomy rules.

This does not mean, however, that the physician is morally obligated to terminate the life of every patient who wants to die, nonmaleficence notwithstanding. The principle of beneficence—or more properly the *limits* of that principle—may be invoked by the physician at this point. Although she is obligated to act beneficently toward her patient, the physician is not bound by the patient's definition of what constitutes beneficent action; for the physician, like the patient, is an autonomous moral agent with her own plans for the future. The general rules of beneficence do not require her to act in such a way as to interfere with her *own* life plan.[70] If her life plan does not include terminating the life of a patient, she has no obligation under the principle of beneficence to do so. Once again, autonomy—in this case that of the caregiver—proves to be the dominant principle.

At this point a brief recapitulation is in order. Beauchamp and Childress argue that there exists a common morality from which four broad principles may be taken. These principles will sometimes conflict with one another and must be balanced against one another. However, the authors fail to give any real material specification to their principles of nonmaleficence and beneficence; these are reduced to matters of autonomous personal choice. What is for me medically beneficent is what I want, and as an autonomous agent I have the right to seek that from a caregiver or caregiving institution. My caregiver, however, is under no obligation to provide me with the services I want if those services are not consistent with *her* understanding of what constitutes nonmaleficent/beneficent treatment; she is also an autonomous agent whose autonomy must be respected.

This way of practicing health care would seem to work well so long as the life plans of patient and caregiver correspond to or compliment one another; in such cases, health care tends to be pretty much like any other good or service exchanged in a free and open market.[71] When there is a conflict, however, between a patient's desire and a provider's unwillingness or inability to satisfy that desire for whatever reason, the conflicting autonomies of the two parties must be resolved.[72] This resolution is the function of the principle of justice.

Justice, broadly understood, is making sure that persons receive what is due them: "A situation of justice is present whenever persons are due benefits or burdens because of their particular properties or circumstances, such as being productive or having been harmed by another person's acts."[73] When Beauchamp and Childress discuss justice, they are typically referring to *distributive* justice. The principle of distributive justice is applicable "under conditions of scarcity and competition," conditions ostensibly applicable to contemporary medical practice, involving as it does the considerable employment of expensive and not-yet-universally available technology.[74] Distributive justice determines how much someone should receive of what they want or need or what someone else wants them to have.

This is not to say that all desires are immediate concerns of the principle of justice. Some desires are obviously more important than others; for Beauchamp and Childress distributive justice is concerned with *fundamental needs:* "To say that a person has a fundamental need for something is to say that the person will be harmed or detrimentally affected in a fundamental way if that need is not fulfilled."[75] The authors suggest a series of acceptable material principles of justice, noting that the applicability of any one given material principle depends upon the context and the nature of the need or desire in question:

1. To each person an equal share
2. To each person according to need
3. To each person according to effort
4. To each person according to contribution
5. To each person according to merit
6. To each person according to free-market exchanges[76]

Beauchamp and Childress argue that a certain level, or what they call a "decent minimum," of medical care is a fundamental need of every person and that the provision of a certain amount of medical care is thus a problem of distributive justice.[77] The free market, they argue, fails to justly distribute the minimum of health care, and a just society will seek to distribute care at some level by some other material criteria. Their arguments for developing criteria of just distribution consist in comparing and contrasting various libertarian and non-libertarian theories of justice and arriving finally at the relatively egalitarian conclusion that all persons have an "enforceable right" to a decent minimum level of care.[78] More significant for the argument I have been developing here, however, is their discussion of exactly what constitutes such care, "of how to specify the entitlements and limits" mandated by such a right.[79]

These two issues are of course closely related. In the liberal state Beauchamp and Childress envision, assuring the right to minimal care is a problem of distributive justice precisely to the extent that such care is understood as scarce. "Because," as they say, "health needs and desires are virtually limitless, every health care system faces some form of scarcity, and not everyone who needs a particular form of health care can gain access to it."[80] It is clearly one thing to say that everyone who has acute appendicitis has an enforceable right to an emergency appendectomy (not that contemporary Americans can even agree upon that) and quite another to say that an infertile couple has a right to in vitro fertilization, even though both acute appendicitis and the inability to conceive and give birth to children could readily be understood as interfering with a person's autonomously conceived life plan.

To their credit, Beauchamp and Childress go a long way toward systematically framing these issues by suggesting that certain questions must be answered in determining how health care is to be distributed:

1. What kinds of health care services will exist in a society?
2. Who will receive them and on what basis?
3. Who will deliver them?
4. How will the burdens of financing them be distributed?
5. How will the power and control of those services be distributed?[81]

In spite of their repeated insistence upon its existence, the common morality seems to do very little work for Beauchamp and Childress in providing answers to these questions. There continues in modernity to be a relative absence of agreement about what is required for the pursuit of a good life and about what we owe one another to enable that pursuit. Hence the authors' argument that the problem of distributive justice in health care is "far too complex to be addressed by ethical theory":

> An acceptable system of entitlements to a decent minimum of health care must remove the gaps in health insurance discussed above, without at the same time deeply disturbing levels of employment, employment opportunities, and incentives to employers. Health policy should also not frustrate vital social goals, such as government allocation to other entitlement programs and the system of free-market competition in the development of health care technologies. No reason exists to believe that any single plan is the only one that can be just and justified. Complex social, political, economic, and cultural beliefs therefore will all play a legitimate role in shaping how a community that recognizes a rule of fair opportunity implements an entitlement to health care.[82]

Here the authors' position becomes a good deal clearer. Certainly it is correct to suspect the ability of Americans to arrive at an agreement about what constitutes a just distribution of medical care. To say that the situation is complex is an understatement. But to claim that the "social, political, economic, and cultural beliefs" that are part of arriving at such an agreement are something distinct from the moral considerations is to accept modernity's attenuated account of ethics and become dependent on what is essentially a crude prudential utilitarianism.[83]

Certainly the authors are right when they claim in conclusion that "great ethical theories converge to the conclusion that the most important ingredient in a person's moral life is a developed character that provides the inner motivation and strength to do what is right and good."[84] They are naive, however, if they believe that the theories in question converge in the same way concerning the *content* of the right and the good. So long as they are unwilling or unable to specify what is in fact right and good or to discuss the possible sources from which such shared judgments might arise, their principles are of little help; for in the absence of such specification, ethical theory is but a thin veil for the antagonistic juxtaposition of wills to power that is the essence of modern life.

### *Pellegrino and Thomasma's* A Philosophical Basis of Medical Practice: *Does Medicine Know Where It's Going?*

> Medicine really cannot be successful until it knows exactly what it is trying to achieve, whether this achievement is possible, and whether it reflects a desirable goal of contemporary human culture.
> —Pellegrino and Thomasma

The beginnings of Edmund Pellegrino and David Thomasma's *A Philosophical Basis of Medical Practice*, published in 1981, are promising, in that they display a willingness to call into question the way medical practice is presently conceived and conducted. Modern medicine, the authors claim, "does not have the tools within its methodology to critique its goals and values."[85] Although medicine rightfully has a good deal to do with science, it is not purely a science; the human body is not *just* an object for scientific study:

> As clinical science, medicine must study the human entity, in which purpose, values, consciousness, reflection, and self-determination complicate the laws of chemistry and physics even more than do the special micro-environments of living things in general. Medicine, even as a science, must encompass the special complexities of *man as subject* interacting with *man as object* of science.[86]

Because it deals with purposeful human activity, medical practice, in order to be morally intelligible, must be able to speak teleologically, to say why it does what it does on more than a technical level.[87]

Pellegrino and Thomasma avoid undue philosophical abstraction by beginning in the middle. They explain that both medical practice and philosophy properly center themselves around a conversational meeting between two persons, and that in the case of medicine, this meeting is a "dialectic of human beings, a dialogue about sickness and health."[88] Hence reflection on medical practice begins with a consideration of medicine's *Lebenswelt*, or life-world, which is the clinical interaction between patient and caregiver, both of whom are active participants in the process:[89]

Two personal intentions at least are needed to form a clinical interaction, both with a curative intent, one to seek help and the other to extend it. The link between intentions is the special character of the event . . . The clinical interaction establishes medicine as a *tekne iatrike*, a technique of healing. *Tekne* here means a knowledge of how to act according to what is the case and why it is the case.[90]

As a meeting between two persons, the clinical interaction is a meeting of two human bodies, neither of which can be reduced to a merely passive object of study or manipulation.[91] The irreducibility of the clinical interaction requires the caregiver to know her patient as an embodied person and not simply as inhabiting an objectifiable body whose ontology is given by scientific study.[92] Although it is certainly true that the patient who seeks help from a caregiver displays in and through her body a state that is for her not normal, what *is* normal "cannot be reduced to a single form of physiological knowledge because it rests in part on man's action in his environment."[93]

Pellegrino and Thomasma do not suggest that anything goes or that medicine must not remain significantly dependent upon science. They introduce an important distinction here between the notions of a "lived self" (that set of characteristics often referred to as "personality"), the "lived body" ("that experience of being a body that cannot be objectified"), and a "living body" (which "refers to the *ontologically prior* realm of individual survival as a physical organism, ingesting, interpreting, and modifying its environment in the struggle and defense of its own existence").[94] There is thus a scientifically established, objectifiable ontology of the body that is in some sense distinct from the human experience of living through that body. There is a "bionomic order" that leads the living body to desire biological health as a "perduring value."[95] Together, the quest of the lived/living body for biological health suggests the possibility of "an ethics based on the value of health and an ontology of living bodies. Since medicine cannot fully explain itself by understanding the body in fully mechanical terms, neither can human life be so explained. Furthermore, the ancient conjunctions of value and medicine are shown to have their roots in the common and unique functions of living bodies."[96]

Pellegrino and Thomasma thus center their philosophy around the "clinical event," the discrete interaction in the clinical setting between the patient, who seeks to be healed, and the caregiver, who seeks to heal.[97] Although the interaction centers around the ontological priority of the patient's illness (or perceived illness), the goal of the caregiver must be to treat the patient, and not the illness only. Differences between patients must be accounted for in such a way that the action taken is "the *right* one for this patient," meaning it must be "as congruent as possible with his or her particular clinical context, values, and sense of what is 'worthwhile' or 'good.'"[98] Thus the practice of medicine is an inherently moral activity, insofar as the actions taken on behalf of the patient are performed for the sake of what she considers good.

When the physician meets her patient in the clinical setting, she must decide how to act in the best interests of that particular patient. Her judgment, if it is to be "complete and authentic," must take into consideration not simply the patient's disease state but also her particular presence as a person. Although a consideration of the patient's particularity makes the clinical event a highly contingent occurrence, the process is "reducible to three *generic* questions: *What can be wrong? What can be done? What should be done for this patient?*"[99]

Although the first and second questions—the "diagnostic" and the "therapeutic"—are rightly based primarily in applied scientific reasoning, the third question is decidedly moral.[100] In asking herself how a particular patient should be treated, the physician may discover that what she believes is scientifically the best course of action is not what the patient believes is best. There may be conflict, and the way that conflict is resolved determines whether or not the clinical event has been conducted morally.[101]

In spite of their repeated affirmations of each patient's irreducible moral particularity, the authors' focus here is on the role of the caregiver. There is a "dialectical" component to the reasoning involved, they admit, but:

> Once the ethical and logical possibility and "strength" of argument for one action over another are assessed by dialectic, then the reasoning becomes "rhetorical"—in the classic sense of artful persuasion, of relating a dialectically established decision to prudent action, generating belief of another kind from scientific or logical cogency, belief that this particular action should be taken in preference to all others.[102]

Certainly there is nothing wrong with rhetoric per se having a role in the meeting of physician and patient. Rhetoric is an essential element of many human enterprises, including the moral enterprise. The politics of modernity, however, makes the use of rhetoric in the clinical setting problematic. Rhetoric is persuading another to act in a particular way, for a certain end that is taken to be good. But in modernity, there is no presumption of agreement about the good, or even about the possibility of such agreement; each person is left to decide for herself what is good. Rhetoric is thus especially susceptible to the distortions of power I discussed in Chapter 1. Pellegrino and Thomasma admit as much when they claim that a "central problem in technological societies is the judicious containment of the expert."[103] The difficulty with the solution they offer to this problem is their apparent assumption that expertise exists as an esoteric body of knowledge and that it must be contained by things like a "patient's 'Bill of Rights'" rather than called into question or incorporated into a wider account of a tradition of enquiry and judgment.[104]

The authors seem to recognize that there is a problem here, that either a simple balancing of principles or the juxtaposition of rights to paternal authority is an inadequate solution to the modern situation. In a discussion of contemporary changes in the role of the physician in modern society, they note:

> There is least danger in limiting physician discretionary latitude in his relationships with society as a whole, a little more in his relationship with the hospital, and most in his dealing with the individual patient. As we have shown, the essence of medicine is its concentration on particularities—on the uniqueness of each patient encounter. The move to patient participation and respect for the patient's value system is healthy. A more adult relationship will result based on mutual respect for the truly inviolate realm of personal moral choices. More and better disclosure of technical details should enhance rather than hamper the physician's decisional prerogatives. Nonetheless, the exercise of clinical judgment is too easily stifled. It is a precious commodity of the experienced clinician—too often alluded to, too rarely present, yet indispensable when the accepted regimen must be modified, abandoned, or replaced.[105]

These concerns are justified precisely to the extent that they are endemic to the modern situation. There is a familiar presumption here, albeit a subtle and for the most part unspoken one, that the role of medical ethics is primarily to resolve judiciously conflicts between patient autonomy and physician authority; such conflicts are ostensibly the consequence of life in a world of moral pluralism. The best medical outcome, in other words, is not necessarily the best ethical outcome of the clinical event; a "correct" decision from a medical-scientific standpoint might not be a "good" one from an ethical standpoint.[106]

But is this a solvable problem, given the way Pellegrino and Thomasma have described it? They believe it is, and that the answer lies in the appropriation by medicine of the language of *values*.[107] They explain that medicine, like many human endeavors, is a value-laden activity; as a "movement toward an end, its actions on behalf of patients, as well as its desire to understand disease processes, would both be forms of valuing."[108] The end of medicine is health, which may be seen as "an intrinsic value of organisms which is not only a condition of the positive *medical* event but also of the positive *ethical* event. . . . Because health is basically a way of coping with the environment, the principle that *it is good to be healthy* functions as a moral absolute."[109]

If in fact health "is a value that takes precedence over others," then the authority to articulate a definition of health is central to the ethical practice of medicine; for if a patient values something other than health, that something may be seen as relatively insignificant or as a mere subjective preference by comparison.[110] And this, it seems, is exactly the course Pellegrino and Thomasma follow. In spite of their claim that they "are not referring to any particular interpretation of health," they indicate that since the living body is ontologically prior to the lived body or the lived self, then "the norm for medical ethics is also grounded in that body."[111] Thus, "the common good as it affects medicine should not clash with the common structures of living bodies."[112]

The difficulty here is a subtle one and lies primarily in the authors' use of the language of values. That language, at least in modernity, implies that what is good for an individual is whatever she freely *chooses* to hold as good, what she subjectively *values*. The good of medicine, on the other hand, is the health of the patient, a good based not in subjective choice but in the ontology of the patient's living body, an ontology prescribed at least for the most part by the facts of medical science. If there exists a conflict between the patient's (or the physician's) chosen good and the good of the patient's living body, then the good of the living body, because it is ontologically prior, takes precedence over the patient's chosen good and the physician is apparently obligated to pursue it. What Pellegrino and Thomasma need to make their project a success is an account of the body's good that is neither autonomously chosen nor simply determined by science. But their tacit acceptance of the modern situation, in which there is agreement neither about the human good nor the goods of the body nor the relationship between the two, makes it impossible for them to provide such an account. Consequently, they end up simply reproducing the problematic modern distinction between facts and values, a distinction that, as Horkheimer and Adorno say, causes "that which does not reduce to numbers, and ultimately to the one," to become "illusion; modern positivism writes it off as literature."[113]

## *Engelhardt's* Foundations of Bioethics:
## *Medical Ethics in the Ruins*

To be free is to be free to choose very wrongly.
—H. Tristram Engelhardt

H. Tristram Engelhardt is fully convinced that the politics of modernity makes concrete discourse in bioethics difficult, if not impossible.[114] His *Foundations of Bioethics*, published in 1986 and again in a second edition ten years later, is in part a rejection of the views of those "cosmopolitan ecumenists"[115] who believe that "real men and women share enough in common so that a concrete and authoritative moral consensus can be discovered in societal undertakings that will allow them to justify a particular bioethics and to direct health care policy with moral authority."[116] In the modern world, with its radical diversity of moral perspectives, such undertakings are futile and self-deceiving. Nonetheless Engelhardt does not stop there; he believes that a kind of bioethics can be done in modernity. It is simply that what can be done is far less substantial than is commonly thought. *The Foundations*, he says, "justifies a moral framework by which individuals who belong to diverse moral communities, who do not share a content-full moral vision, can still regard themselves bound by a common moral fabric and can appeal to a common bioethics. It offers a moral perspective that can reach across the diversity of moral visions and provide a moral lingua franca."[117]

Engelhardt's work is thus a version, albeit a very skeptical one, of the by-now familiar liberal claim to moral neutrality.[118] He insists that his refusal to advocate a particular moral position is not equivalent to an endorsement of moral anarchy; it is simply the case that in the absence of common thinking about the moral authority of "God or reason, authority can only be derived from the concurrence of individuals."[119] Such a concurrence is morally neutral because it "is not antagonistic to the moralities of concrete moral communities whose peaceable commitments may be far from libertarian."[120] Whether this is in fact true is more than a little questionable, as a closer examination of Engelhardt's argument will show.

Engelhardt seems convinced that apart from some form of liberal democracy the modern world, which stands teetering on the edge of disaster, will be plunged into widespread anarchy and social chaos. The deconstruction of modernity initiated by Nietzsche and made manifest by the Holocaust has brought the contemporary world to the "brink of nihilism," creating the need to "save a shred of the modern philosophical project."[121]

The aspect of the modern project Engelhardt is most concerned to save (one that turns out to be quite a bit more than a shred) is the right of the individual to choose what is for him or her a good life. The principles of tolerance and permission are central to such an ethics, which can be distilled into one statement illustrating the two dimensions of the moral life: "The patient had a right to do that, but it is wrong."[122] The locus of the first dimension ("The patient had a right") is the content-less public realm, represented by the state, which has only the responsibility to protect the right of the individual to do with her body as she wishes. The locus of the second dimension ("it is wrong") is the private realm, represented by those communities with particular concrete moral commitments. Those communities have the right in Engelhardt's world to speak against behavior they find morally objectionable but not to interfere with others who pursue those behaviors. They have the right and in fact the responsibility to speak out against things they believe are wrong, but they must be tolerant and "eschew contemporary versions of the *writ de haeretico comburendo*."[123]

The question that must be asked here is whether these two realms can in fact coexist peacefully, or whether the secular public realm will, in spite of its pretensions to moral neutrality, tend always to undermine the private realm of concrete moral commitment. The latter in my estimation turns out to be the case; content makes its way into Engelhardt's public ethics through the portal of his account of the person, and this content threatens to destroy those communities with strong moral commitments for whose welfare he is so obviously concerned.

Engelhardt's secular bioethics is built on the foundation of the assumption that in the morally fragmented modern world, (content-less) morality in the public realm exists on the basis of one thing only, and that is permission. "Secular moral authority is derived from a bare will to morality. Competence to give permission is the ability to so will."[124] Without competence, one has no place and no voice in the public arena; without competence, one is not a person:

> Persons, not humans, are special—at least if all one has is general secular morality. Morally competent humans have a central moral standing not possessed by human fetuses or even young children. It is important to understand the nature of these inequalities in some detail, for physicians and medical scientists intervene in numerous ways in the lives of adult humans, children, infants, fetuses, and laboratory mice.[125]

A person is a human who can "envisage *the notion of the peaceable. (moral) community*."[126] Persons are those humans who are self-reflective and above all responsible for their behavior. "It is because members of *Homo sapiens* are usually self-conscious, rational, and possess a moral sense that being a human is so significant—or at least in general secular moral terms."[127] Persons are those who are capable of choosing; it is they who make morality possible.[128] Persons have rights and may own property, including perhaps their own bodies.[129]

This definition of persons turns out to be quite modern, and even scientific. The capacity to choose requires a certain level of higher brain-center function.[130] Hence a person must have a certain level of rational capacity.[131] Humans with severe mental deficiencies, whether because of age, injury, or birth defects, are not persons, nor are human fetuses, human infants, or young human children.[132] Such human non-persons are dependent for their lives upon humans who *are* persons. In the absence of these advocates, non-persons are ostensibly without rights and are subject to the vagaries of life in a world on the brink of nihilism.[133]

But this way of understanding what it means to be a person or to treat someone as a person is very particular. It arises from a particular set of historical circumstances, in a particular place at a particular time, and the morality associated with it is, in spite of Engelhardt's assertions to the contrary, equally particular; that is, it is *content-full*.[134] And if this very central aspect of the secular morality advocated by Engelhardt is indeed content-full, then there is considerable question as to whether it can allow other, more explicitly content-full moralities to exist alongside it in the way Engelhardt envisions. This is not to say that a secular public morality will respond to other ways of life by violently crushing them. The coercive power exercised by public institutions, as I suggested in Chapter 1, is considerably more subtle than that, which is one reason we typically find it so unthreatening.[135]

Such powers are more subtly corrosive to particular moral commitments than Engelhardt believes. He claims that in the world of public morality, the greatest of the virtues are "tolerance, liberality and prudence." He is precisely correct to refer to these qualities as virtues, for they are transformative moral habits and are embodied at the expense of other moral habits, including those associated with particular, content-full moralities.[136] It is no wonder that Engelhardt finds that "in actually delivering health care . . . the lived morality of many is quite distinct from the moral commitment announced, or once announced, by that particular religious or ideological group."[137] Such a discovery is nothing more than a display of the validity of Alasdair MacIntyre's expression of concern for such persons in the closing pages of *After Virtue*:

Even ... in such communities the need to enter into public debate enforces participation in the cultural *melange* in the search for a common stock of concepts and norms which all may employ and to which all may appeal. Consequently the allegiance of such marginal communities to the tradition is constantly in danger of being eroded, and this in search of what, if my argument is correct, is a chimera.[138]

Although Engelhardt seems to be unaware of the ways in which the modern account of autonomous personhood is itself reflective of a concrete and even hegemonic moral commitment, he is completely aware of the inadequacy of a content-less ethics. His insistence that "one should want more" than "secular reason can disclose"[139] is correct, although the attainment of that "more" is not quite the simple matter of free choice that he takes it to be.[140]

## Something More: The Book Engelhardt Didn't Write

Somewhere is better than anywhere.
—Flannery O'Connor

Engelhardt's admonition to his readers that they should "want more" is to be taken as seriously as anything he writes. Perhaps the most important passage in the vast *Foundations* is found in the preface to the second edition:

Canonical moral content will not be found outside of a particular moral narrative, a view from somewhere ... Although I acknowledge that there is no secular moral authority that can be justified in general secular terms to forbid the sale of heroin, the availability of direct abortion, the marketing of for-profit euthanization services, or the provision of commercial surrogacy, I firmly hold none of these endeavors to be good.[141]

Engelhardt's position that "none of these endeavors" is good goes directly to the central issue of all moral discourse, the question of what things are good—and what thing is Good—for women and men. And this is as true for medical ethics as it is for ethics in general. Ezekiel Emanuel suggests that it is "only by appeal to our shared political conception, to our conception of what constitutes justice and the good life, that we can know" whether to say that a given medical practice is moral.[142] The very phrase "essential health care" is laden with implicit moral judgments and presumes some agreement about what is good; it reflects, says Emanuel, "considered moral judgments about the worth of different opportunities secured and foregone, which, in turn, depend upon the person's conception of the good life."[143]

But whence come such shared conceptions of the good life? The moral fragmentation of modernity makes it perfectly clear that such conceptions are neither universal and self-evident nor scientifically discovered or determined. Pellegrino and Thomasma are certainly correct in their claim that "all human disciplines do not possess a methodology capable of formulating the proper ends of a good human life."[144] Their claim that medicine per se is not such a discipline is, however, incorrect. As Smith and Churchill indicate, in the absence of "some sense of mutual interdependence and personal collaboration between doctors and patients," there is no assurance that the ends pursued in the clinic will be morally appropriate.[145]

Smith and Churchill's insistence that caregivers allow for "patients' interpretive grids for their own illnesses," so as to give "due regard and even legitimation" to those perspectives, is proper, but, as they admit, it seems possible only insofar as physician and patient are willing and able to hold certain things in common.[146] Giving due regard to the concerns, desires, and commitments of the patient presumes "a commonality *between* physician and patient."[147] It requires that they share something besides the facts of the patient's illness and the physician's expertise. Without such a commonality, "no rule or principle or process or procedure will be of any use; and these can only be hollow forms, void of a center."[148]

These are compelling claims. Yet they may be subject to the same accusations of formalism that Smith and Churchill level against others. Smith and Churchill refer to an "essential humanity" held in common by patient and caregiver, an awareness of a shared "human countenance." There is, they say, a primordial "sense of community, an intuition of finitude, an awareness of fragility and vulnerability between human beings" upon which the practice of medicine may be based.[149] Yet it is not at all clear that "moral strangers"—to borrow a term from Engelhardt—have such intuitions in common or, if they do have them, that such intuitions are materially similar. Christians, Jews, and secularists, for example, are likely to have different understandings of what it is to be human or to be part of a community, or even of whether being human means being inherently fragile and vulnerable. These differences are morally significant and are the reason Engelhardt does not believe that a content-full secular ethic is possible.

The moral practice of medicine derives neither from the application of a set of abstractly reasoned principles nor from the technically competent practice of medicine itself, nor even from a common intuition of human finitude and fragility. It derives rather from the politics of particular communities whose members share the same stories, the same practices, and the same (at least) provisional accounts of what constitutes a good life. In order to develop a sufficiently thick account of medical practice, such communities must show how the good practice of medicine contributes to and is subordinate to other established practices and goods. Specifically, these communities must show how the practice of medicine can and does contribute to their peculiar accounts of what constitutes a good life and a good death.

It is important to add that an account like this must first of all be the account of one particular community and not a generic display of how communities in general might conceptualize the practice of medicine. To claim material usefulness for the latter would be to engage in a nuanced version of the liberal search for a common morality, as is the habit of the so-called liberal communitarians, and to suggest that there is indeed a view from nowhere, a neutral place from which to adjudicate competing moral schemata.[150] No such place exists.[151]

It is to the account of a particular community that I turn in the next two chapters, where I attempt to develop an explicitly theological account of how the Christian community should practice medicine, both as caregivers and as patients. I want, in other words, to offer an account of what it might mean for Christians to be sick and to die and to care for the sick and the dying among them in ways that are shaped by the claims they make about the ends and the End of human life.

# 3

# AFTER BIOETHICS

## Toward a Christian Theology of the Body and Its Goods

At the beginning I said that this book was to be about whether being a Christian made a difference in the ways we behaved when sick or when caring for the sick living among us. Being a Christian made a difference for my grandfather, I think, but probably not the kind of difference it should have made. In this chapter, I try to show what the right kind of Christian difference might look like.

For my grandfather, church was a place, as it is for me. Specifically, it was Spruce Grove Methodist Church, a white, one-room, clapboard building set in the midst of a forest of huge evergreens and rhododendrons along the lower part of Mill Creek hollow. My grandparents were faithful members at Spruce Grove, and I often went with them to services in hopes of being invited for Sunday dinner. In those days, the difference church made for me, it made in spite of my efforts and intentions.

Because Spruce Grove was part of a four-congregation, rural "charge," there was preaching only one Sunday morning and one Sunday evening each month. The rest of the time, the faithful would gather and sing hymns from brown, dog-eared copies of *Heavenly Highway Hymns*. There would be a responsive reading of Scripture from the Sunday school lesson of the week, and then prayer for the members of the congregation. After prayer we were divided into groups according to age to cover the lesson, separated from one another by burlap curtains running along wires crisscrossing the sanctuary. In due course a bell would ring; and the congregation would regather to sing a final hymn and to await the benediction.

We were in church the evening my grandfather died. "Aunt" Edith Singleton was in the midst of praying the congregational prayer; she had just asked God to continue to be with my grandfather, when my aunt burst through the front door crying, "Something's wrong with Daddy! The hospital called and said something's wrong!" Immediately my grandmother rushed out and into a waiting car for the trip to Charleston, while the rest of the family went to her house to wait for news. A few hours later word arrived that he had died, and shortly after that the preacher arrived with my grandmother.

We gathered later that evening on the porch to tell stories about my grandfather and offer one another whatever consolation we could. The preacher had remained with us, and he was asked by my grandmother to say a few words and to pray for all of us. Before he prayed, the preacher recalled a conversation he had had with my grandfather prior to the surgery: He had asked my grandfather whether things were "right between him and the Lord." My grandfather had replied to that question affirmatively, and the preacher told us we could be assured that he was at that moment in a better place.

I suppose I took—and continue to take—a good deal of comfort in that assurance. The prospect of someday seeing my grandfather again is an exceedingly pleasant one that is perfectly consistent with the best of the Christian tradition. At the same time, however, I have come to believe that there was something missing in the way all of us related my grandfather's faith to his sickness and his death. Christian faith should have more to do with sickness and healing than what happens when something goes wrong in the operating room. Yet, the Christian community generally has failed to say what that "more" should be. The church has for the most part accepted unquestioningly the role given it by a Cartesian modernity, which says that religion is rightly concerned with the immaterial soul and not with the material body—and with the life to come, rather than this life. As a consequence, Christians have been unable to say what difference their peculiar practices and commitments might make with respect to the care of the sick.

In this chapter I address and refute the ways Christians have accepted or adapted to the Cartesian assumption by articulating an ontology of the human body and its goods based upon some of the most fundamental convictions of orthodox Christianity. I do this by showing first how the goods of the body shape, and are shaped by, the Christian account of the goods of life, and this because the body's *ontology* is shaped by that account. The theological body is formed, I suggest, by the social practices of baptism and Eucharist; these same practices also form the basis for the theological body's politics and hence for its ethics. The topics with which I deal here may at times seem to be unrelated to the concerns of Chapters 1 and 2, but as I hope to show, the body is in fact as much the concern of theology as of medicine. In this sense, a theological account of the body represents a point of convergence between these two practices and thus becomes the basis for a discussion of a Christian ethics of the healing arts.

## The Ends of Medicine and of Life

> Medicine does not consider the interest of medicine, but the interest of the body.
>
> —Plato, *The Republic*

The most cursory review of the history of medicine suggests that long before Plato's Socrates associated the practice of medicine with the "interest of the body," it was widely assumed that the *telos* of medicine was the restoration and maintenance of health. Health has been (and continues to be) regarded as a nearly universal human desire, one requisite to the pursuit of other kinds of human flourishing. This requisite suggests there is a distinct relationship between the proper goals of medical practice and the pursuit of a good life.[1] The terms of that relationship must, however, be specified clearly. They depend, as I have suggested previously, on particular accounts of health and of the good life, accounts that are not in their material content quite so self-evident or universal as they may seem at first.

As I suggested in Chapter 1, the very concept "health" may be understood and defined from more than one perspective. The broad positivism

characterizing much of modern medicine has meant that a highly individualized, pathocentric account of health has for some time dominated contemporary medical thinking; many of us, shaped as we are by medical discourse, have come in this sense to share the macabre sensibilities of one of
the characters from Flannery O'Connor's wonderful short story, "Good
Country People," a story about a woman who "had a special fondness for
the details of secret infections, hidden deformities . . . Of diseases, she pre-
ferred the lingering or incurable."[2] We have reached a point, in other
words, where we have become unable to speak of the body or its goods
without doing so in the technical language of sickness and disease.[3]

This development is hardly surprising. To claim an understanding of
what constitutes the health of an organism is to claim an understanding of
its true normative existence, what philosophers have typically referred to as
its *ontology*. If one understands the body's ontology to be given by the
physical and natural sciences alone, as modern medicine tends to, then one
is left to understand health in those same essential terms. Health in this
view is nothing more—or less—than a certain level of bodily function in the
absence of pathology. Yet, as Rick Carlson points out, this kind of positivist
understanding of the body, which is linked closely to the machine
metaphor, is problematic, inasmuch as it "assumes that human beings and
nature are competitors and hence that human survival is dependent on control and manipulation of nature. This is also the premise of modern medicine. Disease and sickness are losses to nature; they occur when the body
has been invaded by agents of disease."[4]

I showed in Chapter 1 that such a reductionist account of the body and
its goods works to isolate the person from her world and from those with
whom she shares her life. A more interesting, not to mention more accurate, account of health, I said, is one that takes into consideration the dy-
namic interrelationship of person and world and the interdependence of the
goods of the body and the goods of life.[5] Such an account is by no means
independent of or contrary to the physical and natural sciences. It simply
acknowledges that there are other, equally powerful ways of knowing the
truth about the body and its goods, and that these ways suggest, in the
words of Wendell Berry, that "community—in the fullest sense: a place and
all its creatures—is the smallest unit of health and that to speak of the
health of an isolated individual is a contradiction in terms."[6]

This does not mean that it is not helpful, and indeed almost always important, for medicine to be able to speak of the physiological health of an
individual person, or that an understanding of that person's health—or lack

of health, as the case may be—will not be partly or even largely pathocentric and determined by criteria derived from the basic medical sciences. It does mean, however, that the physical health of a person may be *finally* considered only in relationship to the goods of her life as she and those to whom she is morally bound have come to understand them. Physical health is necessarily both subordinate to and dependent upon those deliberatively-arrived-at understandings of what is for her a good life.

To say that physical health is a good *subordinate* to other goods is simply to say that physical health is not the greatest among the human goods, that it is not in the end a good to be pursued for its own sake. Accounts of the body derived solely from the medical sciences have nothing to say about whether there might be human goods beyond those of the physical body; these things are seen as matters of personal choice only peripherally related to physical health.[7] If in fact the good is whatever I say it is, my only concern with health is that the disposition of my body not interfere with my life plan.[8] In this sense health is perhaps peripherally, but not directly, subordinate to other goods.

Christian theology, however, has a good deal to say about the relationship of physical health to other human goods. A theological account of the world presumes that the creation is completely and thoroughly purposeful and that finally, in the words of Thomas Aquinas, "the end is the measure of things ordered to the end."[9] This means that although there may be several legitimate human ends, those ends must be ordered properly one to another and especially to the ultimate end, the one thing pursued and apprehended for its own sake.[10] Physical health is in this scheme an admittedly important human good, but it cannot be regarded as the ultimate human good. Women and men, notes Aquinas, are "ordered to something else as an end, since man is not the supreme good. Hence it is impossible that the ultimate end of man's reason will be the preservation of the [physical] human being."[11] Christianity thus holds that it is possible to be physically healthy without living well, or to live well in the relative absence of physical health.

But is not enough to say that health is subordinate to other ends of life in a hierarchy of goods. The goods of the body are not simply subordinate to the other goods in the hierarchy but also *dependent* upon these other goods for their definition. Aquinas explains that for all humans there is an ultimate end, something all persons desire for its own sake. That ultimate end is human flourishing.[12] Yet the Christian tradition, he adds, has never held that each person was free to choose what would allow him or her to flourish; true flourishing is based in a *universal* material content. Only a certain kind of friendship with God can provide real flourishing: "Ultimate and perfect happiness can only be in the vision of the divine essence. To make this evident, two points must be noted. First, man is not perfectly happy as long as something remains for him to desire and seek; second, the perfection of a power is judged in terms of its object . . . Perfection will be had by . . . union with God as an object."[13]

It is especially significant that Aquinas did not think of this union with God as any sort of disembodied mysticism. Rather, the happiness that comes from friendship with God is a kind of moral activity, and moral activity has to do with human life as an embodied creature living in relationship with other embodied creatures. "Since it is natural to the soul to be united to the body," he said, "the perfection of the soul cannot exclude the natural perfection of the body."[14] And because the body is interconnected with and interdependent upon other bodies, happiness—and by extension the pursuit of the good of the body—also requires "the help of friends" who are united in their pursuit of the good.[15] Because I am a body created by God, the way I understand my body's goods is inseparable from the way I understand what it means to be one who is created and redeemed by God's love, which calls me to be in friendship with others who are so created and redeemed.

It is interesting to contrast the relationally constituted, teleological account of the body I have offered here with the modern understanding of the body I introduced in Chapter 1. In the modern world the suggestion that friendship with God might be integral to health and healing is practically absurd for two reasons. First, modernity purports to know with some certainty what health is, based upon scientific knowledge of the body. In this regard theology is thought to have nothing important to say to science about what constitutes physical health. And second, there is a strong positivist tendency in modernity that says matters not disclosed by science are by definition unknowable, at least in the true, falsifiable, scientific sense of knowing something. Thus, as Leon Kass notes, science tells us that "we cannot *know* what we most need to know, namely, which way of life or form of regime is better or best and why."[16]

Modernity's agnosticism with regard to the existence of a best way of life relates in part to the popularity and convenience of the machine metaphor of the body in both its materialist and dualist forms.[17] Whether the self is the completely unrestrained, immaterial mind of Descartes inhabiting a reductively material, passive body, or simply the random product of a complex series of electrochemical reactions, there is no *good* reason to commend one way of life—and hence one use of the body—over another. The modern body is the genuinely private property of the autonomous agent, who is free to do with it what she will so long as that doing does not interfere with the freedom of others.

An explicitly theological account of the lived human body stands in strong opposition to such views. In some sense, the theological perspective may in fact be understood as having developed *in response* to these views. A theological account of the lived body understands that the reification of personal autonomy *first* emerged as a kind of existential reaction to the strong monism that was inherent in certain strands of ancient Greek philosophy.[18] As John Zizioulas points out, for the pre-Socratic Greeks, all real being was bound completely to its original source, such that

> being constitutes in the final analysis a unity in spite of the multiplicity of existent things because concrete existent things finally trace their being back to their necessary relationship and "kinship" with the "one" being, and because consequently every "differentiation" or "accidence" must be somehow regarded as a tendency towards "non-being," a deterioration of or "fall" from being.[19]

Genuine being thus precluded any notion of personal freedom or of real personhood. To the extent that one was a person, one had added something to—or perhaps it would be more appropriate to say one had taken something away from—her being; personhood was a *prosopon*, a mask, rather than one's *hypostasis*, or true substance.[20] The two concepts could not be confused; to do so would dissolve the essential unity of being in the monistic cosmos.

These conceptions of person and ontology are polar opposites of what has come to be recognized as the dominant "modern" view, which equates the two notions and which maintains that absolute individual autonomy is the real essence of human being. This modern account, however, also has its origins in Greek philosophy. Zizioulas argues that the transformation from the former to the latter resulted from a subtle shift in thinking, one which

> consists in a twofold thesis: (a) The person is no longer an adjunct to a being, a category which we *add* to a concrete hypostasis. *It is itself the hypostasis of being.* (b) Entities no longer trace their being to being itself—that is, being is not an absolute category in itself—but to the person, to precisely that which *constitutes* being, that is, enables entities to be entities. In other words from an adjunct to a being (a kind of mask) the person becomes the being itself and is

simultaneously—a most significant point—*the constitutive element* (the "principle or "cause") of beings.[21]

This equation of person with being, however, creates for the person a twofold existential crisis. The hypostatized person discovers herself as an autonomous agent, what Zizioulas calls "a *concrete, unique and unrepeatable* entity."[22] She resists all attempts to relativize her autonomy, for these are relativizations of her very identity as a unique person.[23] Yet in the end she finds herself unavoidably confronted by two such profound relativizations. The first of these is the relativization of autonomy attached to the apparent necessity of her existence. If freedom is autonomous choice, then the acceptance of existence as necessary constitutes a threat to that autonomy.[24] Zizioulas notes that

> Dostoevsky poses this great problem in a startling manner in *The Possessed*. There Kirilov says: 'Every man who desires to attain total freedom must be bold enough to put an end to his life. . . . This is the ultimate limit of freedom; this is all; there is nothing beyond this. Whoever dares to commit suicide becomes God. Everyone can do this and so bring the existence of God to an end, and then there will be absolutely nothing.'[25]

Dostoevsky helps us see that from the perspective of radical autonomy, the alternative to a seemingly necessary existence is death. But death is the equally relativizing obliteration of the person. "Death for a person means ceasing to love and to be loved, ceasing to be unique and unrepeatable, whereas life for the person means the survival of the uniqueness of its hypostasis, which is affirmed and maintained by love."[26]

Autonomous existence is thus inherently tragic, in that it presents to the person the very real threat of nihilism. Apart from a substantive account of how and amidst what kinds of relationships I am supposed to live, I am constrained only by my own desires. As a modern, autonomous subject, I discover that I am the master, but of a lonely fate. In comparison to such a fate, other, less complete relativizations of autonomous personhood seem tame; the politics of modernity are in this sense not quite so threatening. I find that I am willing to accept constraints on my autonomy after all:

> Indeed every claim to absolute freedom is always countered by the argument that its realization would lead to chaos. The concept of "law," as much in its ethical as in its juridical sense, always presupposes some limitation to personal freedom in the name of "order" and "harmony," the need for symbiosis with others. Thus "the other" becomes a threat to the person, its "hell" and its

"fall," to recall the words of Sartre. Once again the concept of the person leads human existence to an impasse: humanism proves unable to affirm personhood.[27]

A plausible solution to this dilemma requires an alternative account of the ontology of the body. If it is the case that a person's "natural" biological existence is constituted by her conception and birth, then it is also the case that the "natural" end of that existence is death, which is tragic because it represents the end of the individual person's biological hypostasis and what Zizioulas says are her "two basic components, eros and the body."[28] Zizioulas aptly sums up the dilemma:

> Man as a biological hypostasis is intrinsically a tragic figure. He is born as a result of an ecstatic fact—erotic love—but this fact is interwoven with an ontological necessity and therefore lacks ontological freedom. He is born as a *hypostatic* fact, as a body, but this fact is interwoven with individuality and with death. . . . His body is the tragic instrument which leads to communion with others. . . . But at the same time it is the 'mask' of hypocrisy, the fortress of individualism, the vehicle of the final separation, death.[29]

For this tragedy to be overcome, two conditions must be satisfied. First, the integrity of both the body and of the ecstatic impulse must be preserved, for they are the twin loci of genuine human personhood. Second, the hypostasis of the individual must be reconstituted in such a way that eros and the body remain but are no longer finally the loci of death and of fragmentation.[30] The impulse toward freedom as absolute autonomy must be transformed so that the alienation of the person from the other is overcome, and so that "in the context of personhood *otherness* is incompatible with *division*."[31] These conditions are met by Christian theology and its account of the lived human body.

## A Theological Ontology of the Body

> Wretched man that I am! Who will rescue me from this body of death? Thanks be to God for Jesus Christ our Lord! (Romans 7:24–25)[32]

A turn to theology represents neither an abandonment nor a deprecation of the human body. To the contrary, it is theological discourse, anchored firmly in the materiality of a good creation, that provides a proper understanding of women and men as integral parts of that creation. The body, according to the Christian tradition, is not a cage to be escaped through death. Rather, it is the very locus of God's saving activity and the means by which divine grace is communicated to the human person.[33] Christian orthodoxy knows nothing of the Cartesian dualism that characterizes so many popular understandings of the relationship of soul to body; in the Christian tradition, men and women, although always being more than their bodies, are never properly *less* than their bodies. Here we are brought back to Aquinas, who reminds us that in the Christian understanding, the soul can never be properly understood to exist apart from the body.

Geoffrey Wainwright engages the temptation to dualism that has always threatened Christian theological discourse:

> If our bodies are not us, then we are not responsible in and for them; and that irresponsibility may assume the character either of license or, indeed, of withdrawal. The same phenomenon occurred in the gnosticism of the second century. Saint Irenaeus countered its threat to Christianity by retelling the authentic biblical tale of the divine Word's history *ad extra* as the single sweep of universal creation, the making of humankind, the incarnation in Jesus the Christ, the constitution of the church, the institution and practice of the sacraments, and the awaited resurrection of the body.[34]

At the center of both Eastern and Western Christianity's multiple affirmations of the physical body lies the incarnation of the divine *logos* expressed in the human life, death, and resurrection of Jesus Christ. Hence Aquinas says:

> Indeed among divine works . . . nothing can be thought of which is more marvelous than this divine accomplishment: that the true God, the Son of God, should become true man. And because among them all it is most marvelous, it follows that that toward faith in this particular marvel all other miracles are ordered, since "that which is greatest in any genus seems to be the cause of the others."[35]

The incarnation is thus not inconsistent with God's redemptive activity elsewhere in history; the Christian God is and in a sense has always been "fleshy."[36]

That God's self-revelation has throughout the history of God's saving acts been *consistently* material and *frequently* corporeal points to the fact that in the incarnation Jesus' body was essentially and ordinarily human. The real incarnation of the Word of God in a truly and completely human body is a prominent theme in the Johannine literature of the New Testament; for the author of 1 John, a central measure of orthodoxy was assent to the claim that "Jesus Christ has come in the flesh" (*Iēsoūn Christon en sarki elēluthota*), where the flesh in question had been so real to the author and his contemporaries that he made a point of saying, "we have looked at [it] and touched [it] with our hands."[37] Moreover, the material accessibility of Jesus' body is true not simply of the man Jesus up to the time of his death but also of the resurrected body of Christ and the body of Christ present in the Eucharist.[38]

A wonderfully rich multiplication of meanings thus attends theological discourse about the body.[39] In theological discourse, Wendell Berry's implicitly theological claim that the body is an extraordinarily permeable entity that is, simply by virtue of its being a *body*, linked inextricably to other bodies gains a marvelous explicitness; when we say the word "body" theologically, we cannot distinguish in an *absolute* way whether we mean our own human bodies, Jesus' human body, Christ's bodily presence in the elements of the Eucharist, or the social body called church.[40] It becomes impossible to refer to one without at the same time (at the very least) alluding to the others. As Edward Schillebeeckx explains, "Jesus as man and Messiah is unthinkable without his redemptive community."[41] Thus "the administration of a sacrament, being an ecclesial action, though it concerns the recipient personally never concerns him alone"; it also, in some sense, concerns all other recipients—past, present, and future—as well as the giver of the sacrament, Christ himself.[42]

Christianity knows nothing of the isolated individual; a theological ontology of the body encompasses not only the Christian person but also her world, and especially the bodies of those to whom she is bound by membership in the gathered Christian community. Our very understanding of the body's normative being is determined by those social practices that constitute our membership in the body of Christ.[43] Thus a Christian may at various times in her life be well or be sick, but she is never well or sick in isolation from her fellow Christians.

## Baptism and Eucharist: Generating and Re-membering the Theological Body

Do you not know that all of us who have been baptized into Christ Jesus were baptized into his death? Therefore we have been buried with him by baptism into death, so that, just as Christ was raised from the dead by the glory of the Father, so too we might walk in newness of life. For if we have been united with him in a death like his, we will certainly be united with him in a resurrection like his. We know that our old self was crucified with him so that the body of sin might be destroyed, and we might no longer be enslaved to sin. For whoever has died is freed from sin. But if we have died with Christ, we believe that we will also live with him. We know that Christ, being raised from the dead, will never die again; death no longer has dominion over him. The death he died, he died to sin, once for all; but the life he lives, he lives to God. So you also must consider yourselves dead to sin and alive to God in Christ Jesus. (Romans 6:3–11)

Because there is one bread, we who are many are one body, for we all partake of the one bread. (1 Corinthians 10:17)

Now you are the body of Christ, and individually members of it. (1 Corinthians 12:27)

It is no longer I who live, but Christ who lives in me. And the life I now live in the flesh I live by faith in the Son of God, who loved me and gave himself for me. (Galatians 2:20)

Baptism and Eucharist have from the beginning been the two social practices that are constitutive not just of the Church's self-understanding and of its theological dogma but of its understanding of what it means for a Christian to live as a body.[44] Geoffrey Wainwright explains that the performance of these two sacramental practices is and rightly always has been socially constitutive of the church. "Baptism," he says, "is the sacrament of entry into a new set of family relationships," whereas Eucharist is understood as a "particularly creative moment in the liturgy for human fellowship."[45] These claims about the socially constitutive aspects of baptism and Eucharist are, however, only part of the story. They do not fully account for the significance of baptism and Eucharist in constituting the theological body; for there is, as I have already suggested, no clear distinction between normative existence (i.e., ontology) and social constitution.[46]

## Baptism as the Transformation of Being

Baptism is thus neither simply a rite of initiation into a new society nor a practical moral placeholder (though it is both of these); it is also an event constitutive of a transformed human body. Through baptism the body of the person is transformed into a new and different kind of entity. Hence Zizioulas notes that just "as the conception and birth of a man constitute his biological hypostasis, so baptism leads to a new mode of existence, to a regeneration, and consequently to a new hypostasis."[47] The individual who goes into the water is buried there, and in her place arises a new person whose body is from that point joined at the level of being to the crucified and resurrected Christ and his body.[48] As Karl Barth says, baptism "does not merely signify eternal reality, but is eternal reality, because it points significantly beyond its own concreteness."[49] Baptism is thus the means by which the tragedy of a purely biological hypostasis may be escaped; baptism transforms, rather than destroys or flees from, that which uniquely makes the person who she is: namely, her body. Both the inevitability of death and the determinism of biological necessity are transformed by the person's being joined to Christ, who represents in *his* body, as Barth says, "an ontological reality which does not suffer from [fallen] createdness."[50] To partake of this transformation of being, according to Zizioulas, is what it means to be genuinely a person: .

> The perfect man is consequently only he who is authentically a person, that is, he who subsists, who possesses a "mode of existence" which is constituted as being, *in precisely the manner in which God also subsists as being*—in the language of human existence this is what being a "hypostatic union" signifies.
>
> Christology consequently is the proclamation to man that his nature can be "assumed" and hypostatized in a manner free from the ontological necessity of his biological hypostasis, which, as we have seen, leads to the tragedy of individualism and death. Thanks to Christ man can henceforth himself "subsist," can affirm his existence as personal not on the basis of the immutable laws of nature, but on the basis of a relationship with God which is identified with what Christ in freedom and love possesses as Son of God with the Father. This adoption of man by God, the identification of his hypostasis with the hypostasis of the Son of God, is the essence of baptism.[51]

To exist as God exists is to have one's being constituted as being-in-relation. Just as relationality is not a characteristic of God added to God's being, but is rather constitutive of that being, so does relationality become constitutive of the baptized Christian's being.[52] Hence Zizioulas can say that "*to be* and *to be in relation* becomes identical. For someone or something to *be*, two things are simultaneously needed: being itself *(hypostasis)* and *being in relation* (i.e., being a person)."[53] At its most fundamental level, Christian existence is thus what Zizioulas calls *ecclesial* existence, "because, in fact, if one should ask, 'How do we see this new biological hypostasis of man realized in history?' the reply would be, 'In the Church.'"[54]

## Baptism Sustained in Eucharist:
## My Body Becomes Christ's Body

John Howard Yoder remarks that the creation of the new society called church is "the primary narrative meaning of baptism" and that this meaning is effected "by inducting all kinds of people into the *same* people."[55] The creation of the church as a new society, then, is not distinct from the fundamental reconstitution of the individuals baptized into the church *or* from the establishment of Christ's redemptive presence to the world in and through his ecclesial body. "Thus," as Zizioulas says, "the Church becomes Christ Himself in human existence, but also every member of the Church becomes Christ and Church."[56] This interweaving of Christ with members of the church is above all significant because of what happens to the baptized person's body: it is "liberated from individualism and egocentricity and becomes a supreme expression of *community*—the Body of Christ, the body of the Church, the body of the eucharist."[57]

Eucharist therefore is the second indispensable body-forming activity of Christian worship.[58] It is, as Harmon Smith says, in a sense the "essential means which God provides for us to participate in his life."[59] Eucharist is also the means by which the Christian person's body is ritually re-membered as part of the body of Christ.[60] Because the body is the focus of discourse surrounding the Eucharist, it is in that discourse that the polyvalence of the word—and of the reality it is used to signify—becomes especially rich. Consider, for example, the *epiklesis* of the United Methodist eucharistic liturgy, in which the presider says:

> Pour out your Holy Spirit on us gathered here,
> and on these gifts of bread and wine.
> Make them be for us the body and blood of Christ,
> that we might be for the world the body of Christ,
> redeemed by his blood.[61]

Eucharist is a distinctly *eschatological* event, not just because it is an anticipation of the yet-to-be fully realized consummation of the reign of God (although it certainly is that), but also because it establishes among the baptized a radically new way of life, the politics of the kingdom of God.[62] As a political event, the Eucharist consists first and foremost in the what the Orthodox call the *synaxis*, the gathering together of the baptized, so that, as Alexander Schmemann puts it, "we can see an obvious, undoubted triunity of the *assembly*, the *eucharist* and the *Church*."[63] This gathering of the baptized is not to be understood as a meeting of a voluntary association of individuals but as an act that both displays and constitutes Christian being as being-in-relationship. God's agency and the agency of the gathered community in the eucharistic celebration are therefore, from the outside, not radically distinguishable.[64] Community is, theologically speaking, an ontological category more fundamental than biology, and hence more fundamental than family, race, gender, or class.[65] Schmemann puts it this way:

> When I say that I am going to church, it means I am going into the assembly of the faithful in order, together with them, to *constitute the Church*, in order to be what I became on the day of my baptism—a *member*, in the fullest, absolute meaning of the term, of the body of Christ. "You are the body of Christ and individually members of it," says the apostle (1 Cor 12:27). I go to manifest and realize my membership, to manifest and witness before God and the world the mystery of the kingdom of God, which already "has come in power."[66]

The inseparability of the Eucharist from the politics of the new creation requires the church to have a fundamentally ascetic character. Asceticism represents not a denial or repudiation of the materiality and corporeality of creation but a proper reclaiming of those attributes *as* God's good creatures. As Zizioulas says, Christianity "accepts the biological nature but wishes to hypostatize it in a non-biological way, to endow it with real being, to give it a true ontology, that is, eternal life."[67]

We are returned, then, in our consideration of the Eucharist to the striking centrality of materiality and corporeality in Christian discourse. God acts in and through the actions of the assembled human community to establish the catholic unity of the body of Christ, where "catholic" refers simply to "the *wholeness* and *fullness* and *totality* of the body of Christ 'exactly as' . . . it is portrayed in the eucharistic community."[68] God's action in the eucharistic assembly is densely material and is hence an action taken "from inside our own existence, as part of creation."[69] The assembled members' actions—what they do with their bodies—can therefore be said to make a real difference. Such actions relate concretely to the members' pursuit of the greatest of human goods.

Consider the exhortations of Cyril, the fourth-century bishop of Jerusalem, to his community's catechumens with regard to the act of welcoming one another with a kiss prior to the eucharistic meal, understood throughout the history of the church as representing both the unity of the Christian body and the reconciling love of God for the world: "Then the deacon cries aloud, RECEIVE YE ONE ANOTHER; AND LET US KISS ONE ANOTHER. Think not that this kiss ranks with those given in public by common friends. It is not such: this kiss blends souls one with another, and solicits for them entire forgiveness. Therefore this kiss is the sign that our souls are mingled together, and have banished all remembrance of wrongs."[70]

The love present in the kiss has an ontological character, as Schmemann suggests when he says of the church that it is

> a union of love—or, as Khomiakov puts it, 'love as an organism'—not only in the sense that her members are united by love, but above all in that through this love she manifests Christ and his love to the world, she witnesses to him and loves and saves the world through the love of Christ. In the *fallen* world, the mission of the Church, as salvation, is to manifest the world as regenerated by Christ.[71]

Cyril is thus rightly concerned with the disposition of believers toward the body in the celebration of the Eucharist. Later in the same lecture, Cyril offers instruction concerning the handling of the bread and wine of the eucharistic meal, linking the manner of that handling to the unity of the body in much the same way he does in his remarks on the kiss of peace:

> Approaching, therefore, come not with thy wrists extended, or thy fingers open; but make thy left hand as if a throne for thy right, which is on the eve of receiving the King. And having hollowed thy palm, receive the Body of Christ, saying after it, Amen. Then after thou hast with carefulness hallowed thine eyes by the touch of the Holy Body, partake thereof; giving heed lest thou lose any of it; for what thou losest is a loss to thee as if it were to thine own members. . . .
>
> Then after having partaken of the Body of Christ, approach also to the Cup of His Blood; not stretching forth thine hands, but bending and saying in the way of worship and reverence, Amen, be thou hallowed by partaking also of the Blood of Christ. And while the moisture is still upon thy lips, touching it with thine hands, hallow both thine eyes and brow and the other senses.[72]

The bishop's concern that his charges behave correctly in the eucharistic assembly lest they profane its celebration does not negate the fact that the wholeness of the body remains at the same time the work of God. The wholeness of the body is a wholeness of flesh and blood, but it is a wholeness of flesh and blood established "from above."[73] It is a wholeness that comes from an imitation of God's life, but an imitation that is established and enabled by God's prior saving work in and through the members' bodies. As Schmemann notes, "The word 'unity' is divine because in the experience of Christian faith it is *referred* above all to God himself, to the revelation of divine life as unity and of unity as the content and fullness of divine life. God revealed himself in his triunity and triunity as his life, and this means as the source and principle of all life, as truly the life of life."[74]

There is thus no disparity in saying that the wholeness of the body is the work of God *and* that it is a function of the corporate social practices of its members. There is a harmony here, a notion of the cooperative work of God and church, which Schmemann argues is the very essence of faith.[75] Faith is not a religious feeling, he explains, but a particular disposition toward the Other:

> Faith is always and above all a *meeting* with the Other, conversion to the Other, the reception of him as "the way, the truth, and the life," love for him and the desire for total unity with him such that "it is no longer I who live, but Christ who lives in me" (Gal 2:20). And because faith is always directed to the Other, it is man's exodus from the limits of his "I," a radical change of his interrelations above all within himself.[76]

Because faith effects in the believer a certain disposition toward God, it also effects in her a certain disposition toward herself and other persons, a disposition that is displayed in a very concrete way by the politics of the body of Christ.

## The Politics and Goods of the Theological Body

> You are the Body of Christ; this is to say, in you and through you the method and work of the incarnation must go forward. You are to be taken, you are to be consecrated, broken and distributed, that you may become the means of grace and vehicles of eternal charity.
> —Saint Augustine

Everything about being Christian—including being ill as a Christian or caring as a Christian for someone who is ill—has to do with being connected to others.[77] The baptismal and eucharistic presence of God that constitute the Christian theological body is displayed concretely *in and to the world* by the common life of that body's members, a life I refer to here as *politics*. Because the body's ontology is constituted by God's presence, its goods are established and its politics determined by God's being, which is, as I have said above, first of all being-in-relationship or being as Trinity. "The expression 'God is love' (1 John 4:16)," says Zizioulas, "signifies that God 'subsists' as Trinity, that is as person and not as substance. Love is not an emanation or 'property' of the substance of God . . . but is *constitutive* of His substance, i.e., that which makes God what He is, the one God."[78]

God's presence to the theological body is thus the work of the entire god-head. The body is Christ's, and it is first a concrete, visible community established in history through and by the life, death, and resurrection of the man, Jesus of Nazareth. But Jesus, according to the Christian tradition, was the incarnate *logos* of the triune God. Consequently, even from the perspective of the Gospel narratives he "cannot be conceived in Himself as an individual."[79] Rather, as the Son of God he exists as a person for whom being *is* communion.[80] Moreover, Christ's being-in-relation is not simply a being-in-relation to the other persons of the godhead, within the "immanent" Trinity, but also a being-in-relation with those who are baptized into his body.[81] Christ subsists, in other words, in relation with the church, and he does so by the power of the Holy Spirit, who effects that subsistence. This is why the body of Christ is not *only* a metaphor describing those persons who gather in Jesus' name. As Zizioulas says,

> the Holy Spirit is not one who *aids* us in bridging the distance between Christ and ourselves, but he is the person of the Trinity who actually realizes in history that which we call Christ, this absolute relational entity, our Savior . . . . The Holy Spirit, in making real the Christ-event in history, makes real *at the same time* Christ's personal existence as a body or community.[82]

If Jesus Christ continues by the power of the Spirit to be present to the world *bodily* in and through the church, this means that the politics of the body are constituted not simply by an abstract or speculative ideal of divine relationality but also by a concrete way of being displayed in history by Jesus of Nazareth and the community he called into existence. So when Paul says in 1 Corinthians 12:4–7 that the members of the church are the body of Christ, called and enabled by God to live together in such a way as to promote the body's unity—its "common good"—he understands that common good to attain its material specification from something, or rather from someone, historically concrete.[83] The good of the members (and of their bodies) cannot properly be spoken of apart from the good of the community, which derives from the life of God. This is what Paul is getting at when he says in 1 Corinthians 12:12–13: "For just as the body is one and has many members, and all the members of the body, though many, are one body, so it is with Christ. For in the one Spirit we were all baptized into one body—Jews or Greeks, slaves or free—and we were all made to drink one Spirit."

Because the theological body derives its existence from the life of God, its politics have (at least) three particular material attributes. These attributes, which are the basis of the Christian practices surrounding the care of the sick that I attempt to develop in chapter 4, are distinguishable but fundamentally inseparable. The first of them is a "christoformity," which characterizes the members' lives, and especially their disposition toward their own and one another's inexplicable or undeserved suffering. The second is an interdependence of members that harmonizes the perfect ontological unity of the body of Christ with the perfect ontological difference of the bodies of its members. The third, finally, is the understanding that human weakness, fragility, and humble service are, in the body of Christ, symbols of authority.

## *Christoform Service in and to Suffering*

The first task of displaying the politics of the theological body is to show that the "body of Christ" addressed by Paul in his correspondence is the same community called into existence by Jesus of Nazareth. To say that the politics of the body are derived from and determined by the life of God is to say first of all that they are derived from and determined by Jesus Christ, who Paul says is the head (*kephalē*) of the body.[84] "There is no ministry in the Church," Zizioulas remarks, "other than Christ's ministry."[85] Christ's ministry, however, is inescapably social and political, as even a cursory reading of the synoptic Gospels shows. The politics of the Christian body are the politics of Jesus and his disciples; faith in Christ is inherently social and political, and this in a specific way.[86] Because the church is called to be the normative locus of Jesus' ministry in this age, the life of the church may not be correctly understood apart from the life of Jesus, as Jurgen Moltmann suggests:

> Faith in Christ can no longer be separated from ethics. The recognition that Christ alone is the Redeemer and Lord cannot be restricted to faith. It must take in the whole of life. . . . The *solus Christus* of the Reformers cannot be normative merely for the doctrine of faith. It must be the rule for ethics too, for *solus Christus* also means *totus Christus*—the whole Christ for the whole of life, as the second thesis of the Barmen Theological Declaration of 1934 says. But this means that Christology and christopraxis become one, so that a total, holistic knowledge of Christ puts its stamp not only on the mind and the

heart, but on the whole life of the community of Christ; and it also means that Christ is *perceived and known* not only with the mind and heart, but through the experience and practice of the whole of life.[87]

The focus of Jesus' preaching, ministry, and life was the kingdom of God, meaning the call to follow Jesus was and is a call to citizenship in that kingdom. Citizenship in the kingdom is neither an abstract existential ideal nor a utopian expectation for the distant future, but the active participation of those called by Jesus in the imminent establishment of a new political order. In his "Nazarene discourse" (Luke 4:16–30), Jesus reads from the prophet Isaiah and proclaims the coming of "the year of the Lord's favor," announcing to those present, "Today this Scripture has been fulfilled in your hearing." John Yoder remarks that although a certain difficulty attends specifying the exact sense in which Jesus believed that scripture from Isaiah was fulfilled on that day, "what the event was supposed to be is clear: it is a visible socio-political, economic restructuring of relations among the people of God, achieved by his intervention in the person of Jesus as the one Anointed and endued with the Spirit."[88]

There is thus a fundamental continuity between the life of God, the kingdom of God, and the body of Christ, such that Jesus' life and teachings—and especially his teachings about the kingdom—become a primary means by which we are to understand the politics of the body. It is not insignificant, Yoder notes, that in the face of a steadily rising tide of opposition following his controversial proclamation at Nazareth, Jesus responded by gathering a community of disciples: "To organized opposition he responds with the formal founding of a new social reality. New teachings are no threat, as long as the teacher stands alone; a movement, extending his personality in both time and space, presenting an alternative to the structures that were there before, challenges the system as no mere words ever could."[89]

Jesus' gathering of disciples is morally significant because it is the means by which he *bodily* reproduces himself and his ministry in and to the world. Here Jesus' teachings are inseparable from his example.[90] Two related pedagogical concepts have been used with some consistency in the Christian tradition to describe the disciple's relation to Jesus. The first of these is "discipleship," which Yoder says centers "upon the noun 'disciple' and the verb 'follow after' or 'learn.' The image is spatial: The Israelites 'following after' the pillar of cloud; a prophet or a rabbi or Jesus being followed around Palestine by his pupils."[91] The second concept is "imitation." Here, Yoder notes, "the imagery is more structural or perhaps mystical; it affirms an inner or formal parallelism of character or intent beneath the similar behavior."[92] These two concepts, asserts Yoder, although not precisely interchangeable, are both rooted in the Levitical holiness code and the exhortation, "Be holy, for I [YHWH] am holy." The common origin of the two concepts thus makes it appropriate to see them as functionally interchangeable.[93]

The Gospel accounts of Jesus' life with the community display a trajectory toward one specific event in that life that has normative implications for his followers. In the face of intensifying opposition to his ministry, Jesus predicted that his own fate would be to suffer and die on an imperial cross, and that the disciples would, if they were faithful to the kingdom in which Jesus had taught them to live, be likely to experience a comparable fate.[94] Moltmann argues that following Jesus in the way of the cross is properly the truest meaning of Christian faith:

> The gospels intentionally direct the gaze of Christians away from the experiences of the risen Christ and the Holy Spirit back to the earthly Jesus and his way to the cross. They represent faith as a call to follow Jesus. The call to follow him (Mark 8.31–38 par.) is associated with Jesus' proclamation of suffering. To follow Jesus always means to deny oneself and to take 'his cross' on oneself."[95]

The exhortation to those called by Jesus, as well as to the masses attracted to him because of his teaching or his miracles, was consistent: "Take up your cross and follow me." Christian faith is cruciform; the call to follow Jesus is a call to the cross, a call, as Stanley Hauerwas says, to see in Jesus' cross "the summary of his whole life."[96] Hauerwas continues: "You cannot know who Jesus is after the resurrection unless you have learned to follow Jesus during his life. His life and crucifixion are necessary to purge us, like his disciples and adversaries had to be purged, of false notions about what kind of kingdom Jesus has brought."[97] It is in the cross, Hauerwas says elsewhere, that we can see "the truth of the kingdom."[98]

Care must be taken at this point: On the one hand, the cross must not be turned into a universal cipher for all human suffering or even for all Christian suffering. Yoder explicitly rejects this tendency in contemporary Protestantism:

> The cross of Christ was not an inexplicable or chance event, which happened to strike him, like illness or accident. To accept the cross as his destiny, to move toward it and even to provoke it, when he could well have done other-

wise, was Jesus' constantly reiterated free choice; and he warns his disciples lest their embarking on the same path be less conscious of its costs (Luke 14:25–33). The cross of Calvary was not a difficult family situation, not a frustration of visions of personal fulfillment, a crushing debt or a nagging in-law; it was the political, legally to be expected result of a moral clash with the powers ruling his society.[99]

On the other hand, it is wrong to particularize Christ's suffering service to such an extent that that it can serve as a model for discipleship only when Christians are being terrorized by the state. Such thinking, it seems to me, discounts the possibility that the Church's experience of worshiping a crucified God can make intelligible the immense suffering of all kinds that is characteristic of the best of lives in a fallen creation. This is not to say that every trivial inconvenience ought to be reinterpreted as a form of cross-bearing; it is to say merely that Jesus' suffering has a moral and theological significance beyond its being a consequence of state terror. Hauerwas is especially helpful here:

> Any truthful account of the Christian life cannot exclude suffering as integral to that life. Yet it is important that this not become an invitation to make suffering an end in itself or to acquiesce to kinds of suffering that can and should be alleviated. Admittedly, this is not an easy distinction to make in theory or in practice, but it is the kind of distinction that must be hammered out by the common wisdom of people who worship the God found on the cross of Jesus of Nazareth.[100]

So although Yoder is certainly correct to insist that the cross is first and foremost an instrument of state terror utilized against political insurrectionists—like Jesus and his followers—his view of the cross is too constrained, in that it fails to show how Jesus' willingness to suffer the cross was characteristic not simply of his attitude toward the idolatrous state but also of the whole of his life as a servant to a fallen world, a life whose purpose was to display the redemptive love of the triune God for that world. What is most *theologically* significant about Christ's life, in other words, was the *performance* of suffering service he demonstrated on the cross.[101] This, it seems to me, is at least part of the argument Paul is making in his use of the Christ hymn in Philippians 2:6–11. Christ Jesus

> though he was in the form
> of God,
> did not regard equality with

God
as something to be exploited,
but emptied himself,
taking the form of a slave,
being born in human likeness.
And being found in human form,
he humbled himself
and became obedient to the
point of death—
even death on a cross.

Therefore God also highly
exalted him and gave him the name
that is above every name,
so that at the name of Jesus
every knee should bend,
in heaven and on earth and
under the earth,
and every tongue should confess
that Jesus Christ is Lord,
to the glory of God the Father.

Paul employs this hymn, thought to be originally a liturgically established hymn of praise to Jesus, to say that Jesus' entire life, and *especially* his death on the cross, is for Christians morally normative, not only because Christians are exhorted to imitate Jesus but also because they have been made members of his body—called, as Paul says later in Philippians, "to the sharing (*koinonia*) of his sufferings" (Philippians 3:10).[102]

So it is not incidental that the author of the Christ hymn explicates Jesus' *kenosis* ("he emptied himself") in terms of Christ's *first* becoming human, *then* becoming a slave, and *finally* becoming obedient to death on a cross. Christ, who had existed in the form of God (*morphē theou*), has taken the form of a slave (*morphēn doulou*) and been subjected by his own obedience to death on a cross (*thanatou de staurou*). This parallelism of divinity and slavery is a shocking one. In the Roman Empire, crucifixion was the *summum supplicum*, the "extreme punishment," typically reserved for certain classes of people: the poor, traitors, aliens, and notorious criminals. The particular gruesomeness of the cross made it an especially effective instrument of state terror and a powerful deterrent to popular uprising. Most significantly, however, the cross was understood as the *servile supplicum*, the "slave's punishment," which is to say that it served consistently as the means by which troublesome slaves were executed.[103]

Given the role of the cross in the Roman Empire, the juxtaposed images of slavery and crucifixion in the hymn would have been seen by first-century Christians to interweave almost seamlessly. What would have come as a surprise would be the further juxtaposition of those images with that of Christ's divinity.[104] That particular part of the hymn, properly understood, creates what Steven Kraftchick refers to as an "ontological flash" in which "the determinate being is involved in self-contradiction, that is, by being in contrast to something else. Thus a being's understanding contains within itself its own negation."[105] The Christian God is a God who became for the world a crucified slave, and Christians are to be for the world imitators of that God, particularly in their common life.

None of this means that there is a precise correlation between Christ's suffering and Christian suffering. The cross does not in any clear sense *explain* suffering; indeed, I am persuaded that most of the suffering we witness or experience will remain absolutely inexplicable. Yet Jesus' performance of suffering service, seen most clearly in the cross, offers Christians the opportunity to make some of their suffering and some of their service to the suffering among them an expression of discipleship. In this sense Christian suffering may be understood as analogous (in a limited way) to Christ's suffering, for suffering tends to be an excruciatingly isolating experience. Often when we suffer we are incredibly frustrated by the fact that we feel unable to *express* exactly what we are experiencing to those with whom we share our lives. And when someone close to us suffers, we are isolated from them by the fact of the inexpressibility of their suffering.[106] In the midst of suffering the pursuit of a good life fades into the background and seems impossible, if not irrelevant. Yet I am persuaded that this need not be the case.

The bodies in and through which we and those close to us suffer are of the same kind as the body assumed by Jesus, the body scourged and crucified. The pain—and the sense of isolation—that our bodies experience when we suffer has been experienced before in the body of Jesus. Through our baptism, moreover, God has acted to make all of us a part of that body, creating the possibility of really sharing one another's suffering. Just as Jesus' suffering was ultimately not to his benefit, but rather to the benefit of those to whom he was sent, so can our suffering and our sharing in the sufferings of others in the body be seen as to the benefit of those with whom we share our lives—which is to say that the ways we are sick and the ways we behave toward those in our midst who are sick may be shaped by our understanding of Jesus and his suffering. As Paul says in 1 Corinthians 12:26, "When one member suffers, all suffer together with it." As Hauerwas suggests:

> There is no reason why even the suffering we undergo from illness, suffering that seems to have no good reason to exist, cannot be made part of the telos of our service to one another in and outside the Christian community. For example, the very willingness of those who are suffering from illness to be in the presence of the well is a form of service. Suffering and pain make us vulnerable, and often we try to protect ourselves by attempting to be "self-sufficient." The willingness to be present as well as to accept the assistance of others when we need help is a gift we give one another. The trick, of course, is to be the kind of community in which such a gift does not become the occasion for manipulating each other, for trying to obtain through our weakness what we cannot get others to give us voluntarily.[107]

An important distinction needs to be made here. Suffering, no matter what the cause, is not a gift to the sufferer or to anyone else and should not be sought. What *can* be understood as a gift (as well as a virtue), however, is the *way*—and with whom—we suffer when suffering is for whatever reason unavoidable; our *performance* of suffering is what ultimately matters. What *may* be understood as a gift is our willingness to be present to and for one another in various ways during less than happy and even horrific circumstances. This is genuinely possible, however, only when we understand ourselves as bound to one another on the level of being-in-relation that membership in the body of Christ makes possible. Hauerwas is certainly correct to suggest that this sort of presence is in some sense something we must will and is therefore susceptible to distortion. Yet that willing is possible only because of God's prior redemptive activity, by which individual members are made into the one body. When my sister or brother suffers, I am *in fact* suffering along with them, and when I suffer, they are *in fact* suffering along with me. And whichever of these situations might be the case, all parties involved may be assured that it is the responsibility of the entire body to bear that suffering in whatever way it can.

## Unity and Difference

The cross of Christ is therefore important not simply because it offers the possibility for the redemption of suffering but also because it is the basis of the communion that constitutes the body. Zizioulas argues that Christ's *kenosis* is significant and is to be imitated not because the goal of the Christian life is suffering but because the goal of the Christian life is perfect communion with God and with those with whom we have been called into membership in Christ's one body:

> Communion with the other requires the experience of the cross. Unless we sacrifice our own will and subject it to the will of the other, repeating in ourselves what our Lord did in Gethsemane in relation to the will of his Father, we cannot in history reflect properly the communion and otherness that we see in the triune God. Since the Son of God, moved to meet the other, his creation—by emptying himself through the kenosis of the incarnation—the 'kenotic' way is the only one that befits the Christian in his or her communion with the other—be it God or the neighbor. In this 'kenotic' approach to the other, communion is not determined in any way by the qualities that he or she might or might not possess. In accepting the sinner, Christ applied to communion the Trinitarian model. . . . The other is not to be identified by his or her qualities, but by the sheer fact that he or she is, and is himself or herself. We cannot discriminate between those who are and those who are not 'worthy' of our acceptance. This is what the Christological model of communion with the other requires.[108]

A kenotically based understanding of communion is of course radically different from, not to mention inconsistent with, typical forms of social life in the modern world. In modernity, it is supposed that before she is anything else, the other is one from whom I am fundamentally alienated, a potential enemy from whom I must be protected.[109] Difference in the contemporary world is perceived as a fundamental threat to being; the other is dangerous simply because she is unlike me, because her life is not mine, and because she calls into question my mastery of my world.[110] Those relationships into which we do enter in modernity are typically conceived in contractual terms and are entered into on the basis of mutual self-interest and for the preservation of order.[111] Hence nearly any laying aside of self-interest is regarded not as constitutive of being but as a supererogatory act that could just as easily have gone justifiably undone.

Zizioulas suggests that such widespread alienation of persons from one another is the consequence of a distinctly theological problem.[112] In the fallen world, he says, "difference becomes division" and "distinction becomes distance":

> *Diaphora* (difference) must be maintained, for it is good. *Diairesis* (division) is a perversion of diaphora, and is bad. The same is true of *diastasis* (distance)

which amounts to *diaspasis* (decomposition), and hence death. All this is true, as St. Gregory of Nyssa had already observed, to the *diastema* (= space, in the sense of distance both of space and time) that characterizes creation *ex nihilo*. Morality is tied up with createdness out of nothing, and it is this that the rejection of the Other, God—and of the other in any sense—amounts to.[113]

Christian *koinonia* provides a solution to the destructive divisions characteristic of life in a fallen world. Here the call to moral action merges with the fact of God's redemptive work, as Zizioulas explains: "If the Church wants to be faithful to her true self, she must try to mirror the communion and otherness that exists in the triune God."[114] This mirroring requires that the church be a community constituted not just by baptism and Eucharist but also by repentance, which is not simply sorrow, but also a turning away from the status quo to a radically new way of life together. The body need not and indeed may not be divided against itself.

This is Paul's main point in his Corinthian correspondence and especially in 1 Corinthians, where the theological claim at the end of that letter's salutation—"God is faithful; by him you were called into the fellowship of his Son, Jesus Christ our Lord" (1:9)—is followed immediately by an exhortation for the body's members to live so as to mirror that calling: "Now I appeal to you, brothers and sisters, by the name of our Lord Jesus Christ, that all of you be in agreement and that there be no divisions among you, but that you be united in the same mind and the same purpose" (1:10).[115] Divisions in the body are incompatible with the redemptive work of God by which the body has been created.[116]

This exhortation to unity is but one small part of Paul's version of a broad rhetorical strategy frequently used by writers in the first-century Greco-Roman world, the rhetoric of concord, or *homonoia*, which was intended to promote unity within the political community being addressed.[117] Martin notes that Paul's language in 1 Corinthians is often "borrowed directly from Greek homonoia speeches, and his rhetorical strategy of urging the Corinthians to do what is beneficial and what will make for the common advantage, rather than exercising their complete autonomy, is that of homonoia speeches."[118]

One of the common devices employed in the rhetoric of concord was to compare the community to the human body and to suggest that anything upsetting the "normal" order of things could be likened to an illness.[119] Of particular significance in the rhetoric of concord was the assumption that the political body was properly constituted by a hierarchical social order—characterized especially by distinct economic or class divisions—and that

the most common illness attacking that body was caused by division resulting from the abandonment or neglect of that hierarchy.[120] The rhetoric of
concord was thus predictably conservative, advocating what Martin refers
to as a "benevolent patriarchalism . . . geared to maintaining class structure
by advocating only *moderate* exploitation of the lower class."[121]

Paul's rhetoric in 1 Corinthians differs significantly from the classical
rhetoric of concord at this very point. His language is in one sense still hierarchical, but rather than serving as a defense of the ruling position of the
upper class, Paul actually employs it against the assertion of privilege by the
wealthy and powerful within the body of Christ.[122] This is an especially important move theologically because the language of 1 Corinthians is otherwise so consistent with classical *homonoia* rhetoric. Since being trained in
rhetoric was probably understood to indicate relatively high social standing, the obviously well-educated Paul would have been expected, at least by
those acquainted with customary uses of the rhetoric of concord, to under-
gird the usual order of things for his own benefit and for the benefit of his
upper-class peers.[123] Yet this is quite the opposite of the position he takes.

Paul's admonitions to the higher socioeconomic strata of the Corinthian
church are, from the perspective of conservative Greco-Roman politics,
subversive, if not revolutionary. He goes against the typical logic of concord by arguing that the upper classes—which he refers to as the
"Strong"—are creating divisions in the body by the exercise of their normal
cultural privileges. As a means of serving their lower-class sisters and brothers, he urges them to surrender those privileges.[124] To help substantiate his
argument, he holds himself up as an example: Though he is the founder of
the Corinthian church and an apostle through whom God has worked consistently and effectively, neither he nor any other leader deserves particular
allegiance or special treatment, especially when that treatment results in the
division of the body.[125]

Here Paul's use of the language of the physical body and its unity becomes especially important. Martin argues that an emphasis on radical individual autonomy linked to a general deprecation of materiality—especially of the physical body—was common to certain of the popular
philosophical movements of the first-century Greco-Roman world. This
way of thinking, moreover, was evidently characteristic of the Strong party
in the Corinthian church.[126] Their familiarity with these philosophical
themes both flowed from and served to defend their social position in
Corinthian culture and, they believed, in the church: They were apparently
of the opinion that the ways they used their bodies and their material goods

were theologically of little or no consequence, particularly to the other, weaker members of the church. But Paul argues that this is not at all the case. The body and its unity, he explains, are central to the message of the gospel.

Paul's concern for the unity of the body is demonstrated in several places in 1 Corinthians, perhaps most clearly in his discourse concerning the affect of division on the eucharistic assembly (1 Corinthians 11:17–34). The Corinthian church evidently celebrated the Eucharist in concert with a common meal, which proved to be an occasion for schism.[127] Martin explains:

> Paul speaks of those who "have not" (*hoi mē echontas*, 11:22) as opposed to those who "have" things like houses in which to eat and drink their fill. This recalls the way Greek rhetoric often referred to the two main classes of rich and poor. In the church the "haves" (*hoi echontes*) arrived early (with more control over their time, they could arrive at the meetings well before any laborers, who owed their days to their employers or masters) and began, at their own leisure, the common meal, which probably included at some point a more formal breaking of bread and sharing of wine commemorating the death of Jesus. Thus they were being filled, perhaps even getting drunk, while others, as Paul says, were "going hungry" (11:21).[128]

This way of proceeding with a common meal was not atypical of dinner parties in the first-century Greco-Roman world; the way those events were customarily conducted served intentionally to reinforce the class distinctions common to that culture.[129] It is therefore not surprising that the Strong at Corinth expected the assembly of believers to be conducted in a similar manner.[130] Paul's concern for the unity of the body challenges their assumptions, instructing them to change their behavior (11:33–34) for explicitly theological reasons. The transferal of the economy of the Greco-Roman dinner party into the eucharistic assembly is wrong, he says, because it represents a failure in "discerning the body" (11:29).[131]

What the Strong failed to realize, in other words, was that the "body of Christ" in the bread of communion and the political "body" gathered for the common meal were ontologically identical, and that the bodies of the members constituted, and were constituted by, their participation in the assembly. For the gathered community to behave in a manner inconsistent with the theologically established fact that the body was Christ's was thus not simply a gross distortion of the gospel but a corruption of that common body.

In what comes as a shocking pronouncement to contemporary readers, Paul links physical sickness and death among the members to the community's failure to discern the body (11:30). We are left to wonder whether Paul regards such physical ailments as the direct result of God's disciplinary agency or as simply the consequence of neglecting the ontological unity of the theological body; but the one thing that is absolutely clear is that Paul takes the interconnectedness of the body and its members' bodies extremely seriously.[132] This is a significant point to keep in mind when proceeding directly from Paul's concerns for a unified eucharistic assembly to his extensive elaboration on the *polis*-as-body theme in chapter 12, where he explains that "just as the body is one . . . and all the members of the body, though many, are one body, so it is with Christ" (12:12). There seems to be a fundamental sense in which Paul intends that these words be taken as more than "just" an analogy.

It is significant, however, that the strong unity of the body of which Paul speaks consists neither in uniformity nor egalitarianism. The rich variety of the human personality *and* the human body are preserved. There is in the body of Christ a rich diversity of members, first of all because there is a fundamental diversity in the trinitarian life of God. Paul argues that this diversity is displayed ideally by the body's common life, explaining in 12:4–6 that "there are varieties of gifts, but the same Spirit; and there are varieties of services, but the same Lord; and there are varieties of activities, but it is the same God who activates all of them in everyone." The body of Christ is diverse because the triune God whose being constitutes that body is diverse.[133]

Zizioulas suggests that the diversity inherent in God's triune being carries at least three implications for the social life of the body of Christ. First, he says, "otherness is constitutive of unity and not consequent upon it. God is not first one and then three, but simultaneously One and Three." Because God's unity is constituted by diversity, "otherness is not a threat to unity, but a *sine qua non* condition of it."[134] There can thus *be* no effective Christian unity without difference, since, as Paul explains, "the body does not consist of one member but of many. If the foot would say, 'Because I am not a hand, I do not belong to the body,' that would not make it any less a part of the body. And if the ear would say, 'Because I am not an eye, I do not belong to the body,' that would not make it any less a part of the body" (12:14–16).

Second, Zizioulas explains that within the Trinity "otherness is absolute. The Father, the Son and the Spirit are absolutely *different* (*diaphora*, none of them being subject to confusion with the other two)."[135] When difference is seen as essential to flourishing, the violent tendency to colonize the other—to make it less of a threat, either by making it more like me or by ignoring it altogether—is transformed into an extraordinary appreciation and a thankfulness that the other is *not* like me. In 12:17–19 Paul elucidates this point by asking the Corinthians to imagine a body without difference: "If the whole body were an eye, where would the hearing be? If the whole body were hearing, where would the sense of smell be? But as it is, God arranged the members of the body, each one of them, as he chose. If all were a single member, where would the body be?"

Finally, says Zizioulas, "and most significantly, otherness is not moral or psychological, but ontological."[136] The differences between members of the body are not simply roles adopted in one situation or another (though such adoptions might well occur); they are constitutive of who those members are for all time. In other words, certain differences that exist between members of the body are irreducible—and necessarily so, for the good of the body *and* of its members. Difference represents not a threat to individual autonomy but the possibility of a gift of wholeness through interdependence. As a member of the body, I discover that the other's difference is a difference I cannot do without. Consequently, explains Paul, "there are many members, but one body. The eye cannot say to the hand, 'I have no need of you,' nor again the head to the feet, 'I have no need of you'" (12:20–21). It is not simply suffering that is shared within the body but the solution to suffering, as well.

### Weakness as Authority

The irreducible diversity of the body exists not for the sake of diversity itself but for the sake of the body. A member is not who she is for her own sake alone but for the sake of the body and its other members, as well. The multiplication of differences that makes the body function as it should is not infinite; diversity is not at all the assurance of an infinitely atomistic universal autonomy. There remains in the body a kind of hierarchy of members, a hierarchy rooted in the example of the suffering servant Jesus and displayed in the body's regard for its weakest members. Paul's admonitions for the Strong party in Corinth to surrender its normal social privileges for the sake of the body are thus rooted not simply in abstract ideals of justice nor in a pragmatic exhortation for unity but in a particular theological worldview. Martin explains:

Paul wants to place two different worlds in opposition to one another: the world of Greco-Roman rhetoric and status, with its attendant upper-class ideology, and a somewhat hidden world of apocalyptic reality proclaimed in the gospel of Christ, which has its own, alternative system of values and status attribution, which in some sense "mirrors" the values of "this world" but in another sense counters and overturns those values.[137]

Hence in 1 Corinthians 12:22–25, as Paul proceeds with his discourse on the body, he explains that it is not *simply* the case that difference in itself is important for the wholeness of the body:

On the contrary, the members of the body that seem to be weaker are indispensable, and those members of the body that we think less honorable we clothe with greater honor, and our less respectable members are treated with more respect; whereas our more respectable members do not need this. But God has so arranged the body, giving the greater honor to the inferior member.

The normal conservative logic of concord is subverted by the logic of the gospel, which gives the *true* hierarchy of the theological body.[138] Those typically regarded as weak therefore have an authority that is demonstrated in the way they teach—and in the ways they allow—the rest of the body to care for them and meet their particular needs. In that caring the true nature of the body is displayed, as Paul concludes: "There may be no dissension within the body, but the members may have the same care for one another. If one member suffers, all suffer together with it; if one member is honored, all rejoice together with it" (12:25b–26). The unsatisfactory alternatives inherent in individualism—colonizing violence and isolating tolerance—are avoided, while the difference of the members is preserved.

## The Theological Body Is a Social Ethic

A certain picture of the Christian life as a social process flows from this politics of the theological body. This process, moreover, has a direct bearing on the way the members of the body are to care for one another's health and answer questions about whether and how to utilize the manifold resources of the modern medical establishment in that care. The gathered body is formed by its worship, by its corporate participation in and reenactment of the story of the life, death, and resurrection of Jesus of Nazareth. But what it means for that body to be Christ's *here and now* can be specified in principle only to a certain extent.[139] For the most part, such specifications emerge as the consequence of deliberative "practical moral reasoning," which Yoder says is the process by which "people make particular choices which are illuminated by their general faith commitments, but which need to be worked through by detailed here-and-now thought processes."[140] Practical moral reasoning is a corporate process that takes place in the assembly of the members and proceeds by the assumption that the members are committed to the common authority of the gospel, an authority that is displayed in and through one another according to a certain participatory model.

Practical moral reasoning is thus a kind of moral problem-solving that acknowledges that the solution to a moral problem belongs not to the individual but to the community. It presumes that the church is living as a counter-cultural community in varying degrees of tension with the world and its institutions and that conflicts will periodically arise between the *ethos* of the community and that of the world, conflicts that may be adequately resolved only when the voice of every member is heard and weighed. Hence the body's diversity is crucial to its morality, which requires for its sustenance voices of prophecy, memory, and practical wisdom, as well as particularly strong examples of faithfulness to the community's ideal.[141]

Yoder relates the process of resolving these conflicts to the "rule of Christ" or the "power of the keys" in Matthew 18:15–20, where Jesus grants to the disciples both the means and the authority to resolve these conflicts when they threaten to divide the community:

> We have here then a kind of situation ethics, i.e., a procedure for doing practical moral reasoning, in a context of conflict, right in the situation where divergent views are being lived out in such a way as to cause offense. This rejects a rigid or automatic casuistic deduction on one hand and individualism or pluralism on the other. The obedience of the brother or sister is my business.[142]

The fact that this kind of reasoning is done in such a "context of conflict" suggests that it is guided by a sense of what might be called "constrained disagreement."[143] MacIntyre explains that "when a tradition is in good order it is always partially constituted by an argument about the goods the pursuit of which gives to that tradition its particular point and purpose." A living tradition is, in fact, nothing less than a "socially embodied argument" about what constitutes a good life for its members.[144]

The notion that practical moral reasoning within the church takes the form of constrained disagreement does not contradict what I have said above, however, about the material specificity of the politics and goods of the theological body. Practical moral reasoning presumes that the conversation taking place within the body of Christ will be guided by a profoundly christoform unity, a unity that comes from the extension of the body backward in time to the community of Jesus and his disciples and that continues to be grounded in and formed by the sacramental practices of (at least) baptism and Eucharist.[145] It is imperative that the life, death, and resurrection of Jesus remain in some sense the norm to which the Christian conversation aspires.[146] This requires the community to remain vigilant about the uncritical acceptance of the moral logic of the world. As Yoder says: "Only from within the community of resurrection confession is the cruciformity of the cosmos a key rather than a scandal."[147]

It is this "cruciformity of the cosmos" that must shape the ways in which Christians are sick and the ways in which they care for the sick in their midst. It is the community, in all its rich yet fragile diversity, that is and that must be the body of Christ, whose liturgical practices serve both to cultivate the virtues necessary for Christians to be faithful to God and to achieve the Good of friendship with God in the midst of sickness and death.

# 4

# BEYOND BIOETHICS

## Caring for Christ's Body

### *What My Teacher Could Not Teach Me*

All good human work remembers its history.
—Wendell Berry, *What Are People For?*

Writing this book has quite obviously given me a good deal of time to think carefully about my grandfather's last days. I suppose it has been something of a cathartic experience for me, even though I still cannot say for sure why I always have found and probably always will find his death so disturbing. Perhaps it is because he was never permitted time to be really ill, never given an indication that his death was imminent, and because those of us who loved him were never permitted time to care for him in his illness. To the very end there were few indications that he had a fatal illness, and virtually no sign that he needed special care of any sort. We had to take it on blind faith that he needed the surgery his physicians recommended. It is true that he did not feel as well as he once had, but for the most part he seemed as able as ever. On the day before he died he rose at the usual time, dressed in his usual clothes, ate his usual breakfast, and went to a usual day's work in the hay meadow. I spent most of that morning following him around the fields, loading hay bales onto the wagon he towed behind his tractor. Then the phone rang, and my grandmother called him in from the field; he went to the hospital, had surgery, and died. Just like that, or so it seemed.

Yet if all I can say about my grandfather's death is that it was tragic because it was sudden and unexpected, I have said nothing at all of interest to anyone. People die suddenly and unexpectedly all the time, not because there is something wrong with their care but because that is simply the way things are in this fallen creation. And certainly I cannot say in good faith that his death would have been better if only it had taken place at home and had been characterized by suffering and misery.

Perhaps, however, his death was finally a tragedy not because it was death, nor because it was sudden, but because it was so horribly inconsistent with his life, a life given to land and kin. If this is the case, then his death was tragic because it stole him from me and the rest of his family and friends without giving him or us a chance to say good-bye properly. It was a tragedy because he was taken away from us, not by his death but by the mode of his death. He died alone, in a hospital, miles from home. His deathbed was a solitary one, a fact that is regrettable most of all because it meant that this great man who had taught me so many good things was kept from teaching me anything about how to die.

In my grandfather's case, in part because of the nature of his illness and its proper treatment and in part because of the way medical resources were distributed in that place and time, things probably could not have happened differently. Nonetheless, it would be a mistake to be fatalistic and passive about the way sickness, death, and healing occur and are dealt with in the contemporary world. There are better and worse ways of being ill and of caring for the ill, and in what follows I will say what I believe are some of the better ways for Christians.

Here I try to show what sort of concrete moral practices flow from the theological account of the body I developed in the previous chapter. I do this by entering into conversation with what has come to be known as "virtue theory." There is a logic to this approach: I suggested in the first chapter and argued explicitly in the third that every ontology of the body is constituted by the social practices of particular communities. (The theological ontology of the body developed in the previous chapter, for instance, is based upon the existence of the social practices of baptism and Eucharist within the church.) In a similar manner, virtue ethics proceeds from the assumption that social practices also play a role in the formation of human moral agency.

Accordingly, I begin this chapter by bringing ancient and contemporary virtue theory into conversation with recent work in moral psychology, moral philosophy, and the philosophy of mind in order to suggest a consistent relationship between moral agency, habits, and social practices. Such an account, I suggest, closely follows the presumption that morality is not so much about making discrete decisions about what to do as it is about the formation of our bodies as we live in certain kinds of relationships with others. I then proceed to discuss the notion of virtue in general and Christian moral virtue in particular, showing how Christian virtue may be formed and informed by the liturgical practices of the body of Christ.

The concerns of the previous chapter are especially relevant at this point. As I will show, what Aquinas refers to as the theological virtues—and here I am thinking especially of the virtue of charity, or friendship with God—are in fact those peculiar characteristics of the body of Christ that bind the members to one another in a way that actually makes them one body, characteristics that are defined in and conveyed through the liturgical practices of the church.

Based on this account of liturgical practices, I then attempt to explicate a constellation of explicitly Christian virtues surrounding the care of the sick, suggesting that Christians, by virtue of their membership in the body of Christ, ought to be sick and care for the sick in their midst in ways determined by that membership. There are, in other words, theologically virtuous ways of being ill, of dying, and of caring for the ill and dying, ways that faithfully display to the world the reality of the Word made flesh.

Perhaps a word to the wise reader is in order here. The reader will undoubtedly find that parts of this chapter have a character different from the others, in that they are considerably less polemical and somewhat less analytic. This is in part because my intent here is to engage in a conversation about, rather than provide a definitive answer to, the questions with which I began this book. However, the primary reason for the different nature of this chapter is that I am dealing here—and this is especially true of my discussions of the relationship of the liturgy to virtue and to bioethics—with matters that largely evade analysis and that may only be shown. Consequently, I try to provide examples, as well as descriptions, of what it might mean for Christians to be faithful in sickness and death and in the care of those who are sick and dying.

## *Learning to Do What Comes Unnaturally: Agency, Habit, and Virtue*

In Chapter 2 I suggested that if the discipline of ethics was to be of any practical significance, it would be because it taught us how to live well, how to make certain kinds of practical choices about how to pursue the goods of life in given situations. Such choices, however, are not just a matter of some abstract, rational, autonomous subject choosing from among a range of presented options. A high level of rationality *as such* is neither a sufficient nor perhaps even a necessary condition for doing and being good.

For in order consistently to choose the good, a person must first be *trained* to choose well, a process that engages and forms her at every level of being, meaning that it engages and forms her *body*. In Book Two of his *Nicomachean Ethics*, Aristotle remarks that the moral choices we make are functions of our dispositions, and that "our moral dispositions are formed as a result of the corresponding activities."[1] Character, in other words, both forms and is formed by right action.

Another way of putting this is to say that questions about whether and how we are to go about living morally are to a significant extent questions about our personal *identities*. Questions about what I should do in a particular situation are in fact questions about who I am. Most philosophical treatments of the matter of personal identity have focused, says Owen Flanagan, "on two related questions. First, there is the metaphysical question of what makes some individual the same or virtually the same over time. Second, there is the epistemological question of what criteria are used to identify and reidentify an individual over time."[2] An account of identity that adequately explains moral development, however, must be "thicker" than this, in that it must be able to describe how a person's moral agency is formed over time to enable her to act in ways consistent with her own (and her community's) notions of what is good.[3]

The classical modern answer to the question of identity and agency derives largely from the thinking of Descartes and holds that the *self* is identifiable with the inward and immaterial mind. As such, the self is essential, unassailable, and at every moment perfectly free to choose from among an infinite number of possibilities. In spite of obvious difficulties with the Cartesian account, first pointed out by Gilbert Ryle in his 1949 book The *Concept of Mind*, this answer has endured—especially on what might be referred to as a popular level—to the present day.[4] Its appeal, suggests Flanagan, is largely due to the fact that it provides a clear, precise defense of free and stable human agency, which is thought to be important in light of the apparent alternative:

> It seems as if I dissolve as an agent, if I am not the prime mover, myself unmoved, of my thoughts and actions, if *I* do not exist, or do not exist as a genuine agent, then I am simply a cog in some grand cosmic accident, one that produces an illusion in the space "I" occupy. So I am nothing, the cosmos is a surd, and my life is not mine at all. As such it can have no meaning for me who is not, and who does nothing.[5]

This fear—that the alternative to the essential Cartesian self is blunt determinism or nihilist meaninglessness—is bolstered by a cluster of "postmodern" critiques of the modern position. These critiques argue that human subjectivity is simply a consequence of the convergence of various kinds of contingencies. Because every aspect of human life is so radically contingent, these critiques say, there in fact *is* no real human agency. The self is for all intents and purposes nothing more than an illusion—albeit a very convincing one—created by the convergence of different kinds of forces.[6] According to Flanagan, however, the valid observations these arguments present about the contingent nature of human identity and agency do not lead necessarily to the dissolution of responsible moral agency:

> Continuity and connectedness matter, not strict identity. . . . Before and after we gain powers of self-authorship we express ourselves in ways particular situations call upon us to be. But even supposing I am nothing more than some package of socially responsive roles, I am still something rather than nothing. So the argument hardly establishes the death of the subject; it simply makes the subject a social construction all the way down. But houses are completely constructed, and they exist. Being constructed hardly makes something into nothing. Usually it is the other way around.[7]

What Flanagan's position indicates is that the significant question for moral discourse is not *whether* we can continue to think of humans as responsible moral agents who can be praised or blamed for their actions, but rather *how* we ought to think about the way responsible moral agency is developed. The suggestion that moral agency and personal identity are both formed largely by the convergence of contingencies of time, place, and practice implies that choice and identity are in fact fundamentally intertwined, that, as Ruth Anna Putnam explains, "choosing what to do . . . is choosing who one is going to be." Putnam goes on to say that the relationship between identity and choice suggests, moreover, that identity is not just formed in times of moral crisis: "One's character and one's ends play crucial roles in one's moral life not only at times of difficult choice but also during tranquil periods."[8] Not just some but *all* of my decisions help make me who I am.

The fact that the discrete decisions one makes about her way of life have a cumulative effect on the development of her character means that a person is, in a "thick" sense, both the agent and the patient of her identity *and* her way of life. In spite of the radically contingent nature of her existence she is one person, whose "oneness" is the product of a multitude of contingencies held together by what Flanagan calls a "narrative connectedness." Narrative connectedness, he explains, is simply the ability "to tell some sort of coherent story" about one's life.[9] Flanagan's position resonates with that of Alasdair MacIntyre, who argues in *After Virtue* that "man is in his actions and practice, as well as in his fictions, essentially a story-telling animal." MacIntyre notes that storytelling is central to the moral enterprise not simply because humans tell and listen to stories but also because, "I can only answer the question 'What am I to do?' if I can answer the prior question 'Of what story or stories do I find myself a part?'"[10] Moreover, explains MacIntyre, the act of characterizing some given human behavior as morally good or bad is always a matter of "placing a particular episode in the context of a set of narrative histories, histories both of the individuals concerned and of the settings in which they act and suffer."[11] Such settings, he explains, are invariably constituted by the social practices of tradition-bearing communities, those "socially embodied argument[s]" about what constitutes a good life for women and men.[12]

MacIntyre, it seems to me, makes an important point that Flanagan does not, which is that the particular narratives within which I locate my life make a great deal of difference for whether my life can be characterized as morally significant. For Flanagan, what matters is *that* I can conceive of my life as taking the form of a story that means something *to me*. He believes, in other words, that it is possible for one to *choose* a narrative that helps make sense of one's life. I follow MacIntyre in disagreeing with this assumption. In fact, our lives make sense because we find ourselves made part of the stories of others who are on a quest to reach a particular moral *telos*. In any case, Flanagan and MacIntyre seem to agree that personal identity and the moral life are narrative and material in form and thus dependent on some kind of habituation; both offer, in other words, a non-reductive, *materialist* account of moral agency.

Flanagan argues that the capacity to narrate one's life coherently and meaningfully does not require a high degree of introspection or reflectiveness. For the self conceived as a morally significant "center of narrative gravity," he says, nothing more is required than "a *subjective sense* of an *invigorating sameness and continuity*."[13] Such a sense, he suggests, can be practically unconscious. What matters is not that a detailed list of sophisticated reasons can be given for acting in one way rather than another, but that the actions taken are important ones for the actor, that they are, in other words, consistent with the narratives through which she has come to identify herself as a particular kind of person of whom particular things are expected.[14]

The question that arises here is how, if not through the exercise of some sort of pure reason, this sense of "important actions" is developed. Virtue theory and the psychology of mind converge by answering that one way strong, consistent moral agency is developed is through the cultivation of certain kinds of embodied habits.[15] According to Thomas Aquinas, the most thorough Christian expositor of a moral philosophy rooted in the notion of virtue, habits are among the most fundamental "principles of human acts."[16] Aristotle, whose moral philosophy Aquinas follows closely, argues that "it is incumbent on us to control the character of our activities, since on the quality of these depends the quality of our dispositions. It is therefore not of small moment whether we are trained . . . in one set of habits rather than another."[17] Good habits are morally indispensable because they help us live consistently along a particular trajectory toward particular ends. They help us, in other words, to embody those ways of life suggested by the stories into which we find ourselves drawn.

Ruth Anna Putnam suggests that "a well-established routine becomes a habit, and a firm habit will, in novel circumstances, establish a new routine. What routines and habits do for us is this: they obviate the necessity to decide at every moment what to do next; they provide an easy explanation for a host of actions."[18] Though habits are scarcely in themselves reasons to live or to act, they tend to strengthen, rather than diminish, a life's sense of meaning and purposefulness; this is an especially significant point for Aquinas, who argues not only that we should do good but that we should also *enjoy* doing good, and that the delight attending doing good can be acquired only through habituation.[19]

Habits, says Aquinas, are acquired dispositions that form us "all the way down"—at the level of the body, the will, and the intellect.[20] Because we are both patients and agents of our actions and are made up, as Aquinas puts it, of "both an active and passive principle,"[21] these dispositions are inescapable aspects of consistent human agency. For "by repeated acts, a quality is formed in the passive and moved power, and this quality is called a habit."[22] Because we are complex creatures who are continually acting and being acted upon by a multitude of forces, habits require for their development the consistent repetition of specific habituating acts that form our bodies in particular ways; without these acts, Aquinas seems to say, we cannot hope to develop the dispositions requisite to living well.[23]

Habits are of course not valuable in themselves but because they dispose the agent toward particular valuable ends. *Virtue* is the name given to habits that dispose the agent toward good ends: Aquinas explains that a virtue, as a kind of a habit, is the "perfection of a power," where "power" is the human capacity to act purposefully toward a specific, worthwhile end.[24] Of course, for a habit to be called a virtue in any final sense, the end in question must be an absolutely good one. Aquinas remarks that genuine virtue is "a good quality of the mind, by which we live rightly, of which no one can make bad use, which God works in us without us."[25]

Aquinas means for this definition of virtue to be comprehensive, insofar as he intends it to account for the various ways in which (what he categorizes as) intellectual, moral, and theological virtue is developed and displayed as a person moves toward her final end.[26] Lest we get the mistaken idea that once we settle into a particular routine we are morally assured of success, it is important that we consider here the many ways in which Aquinas believes we can go wrong *in spite of* the presence of good habits. Habits are necessary, yet they are also fragile; "habits of virtue are lost by sinning," he notes, and "virtues come into being and are lost through contrary acts."[27] There is always the chance that we may commit such contrary acts, since judgment is so significant a component of moral activity and "a habit of virtue or vice is corrupted by the judgment of reason whenever it moves contrary to such virtue or vice."[28] The most thoroughly habituated person retains the freedom to make bad judgments about what to do in a particular situation, which suggests the importance of the moral-intellectual virtue of practical moral reasoning.[29]

For Aquinas the intellectual virtue of practical moral reasoning, which he calls prudence, is indispensable. Prudence, he explains, is "right reasoning about what is to be done."[30] Although prudence is a distinct intellectual virtue, it operates at the intersection of the intellectual virtues of wisdom, science, and understanding and the cardinal moral virtues of justice, temperance, and fortitude.[31] Prudence assumes the presence of a certain measure of "moral virtue, which rectifies the appetite."[32] Yet, the moral virtues cannot operate properly without prudence, for the moral virtues, which habitually order a person's desires toward the good, are not automatic; their exercise requires a *measure* of deliberation and choice. "Hence," Aquinas claims, "prudence is a virtue that is necessary to lead a good life."[33]

But neither prudence nor the moral virtues are finally sufficient for what Aquinas would regard as a completely good life. Good judgment must be accompanied by the development of a disposition to desire and pursue the right things. And because for Aquinas the one thing that is to be desired and pursued above all others is friendship with God, the virtues finally have an irrevocably theological component. This is not to say that for Aquinas there is no virtue that is not *explicitly* theological. To the contrary, he speaks at some length about the virtues of those outside the Christian tradition. Certain of these virtues he calls political, and they exist presumably as the consequence of the fact that the entire creation—including moral communities outside the church—belongs to and is in some sense ordered by God. Moreover, Aquinas identifies certain virtues that exist "between" the political virtues and the theological virtues and that are not explicitly theological in their derivation. These he calls the purifying virtues and the perfect virtues. The purifying virtues are displayed in the lives of "those who are on the way and tending toward a likeness of what is divine," whereas the perfect virtues are evident in the lives of those who have gone farther than their peers in the quest for the good.[34]

There is a point, however, at which complete virtue cannot be attained and developed except through the distinct and particular work of God. This is true first of all, says Aquinas, because "the exemplar of [all] human virtue must preexist in God," but also because all human activity is properly ordered to the final end of friendship with God, an end that requires for its achievement God's gracious assistance in the form of the infused moral virtues and the theological virtues of faith, hope, and charity.[35] Of course, the God who for Aquinas infuses these virtues is not a philosophically derived unmoved mover but a God who is known only through that story and those practices that reenact the drama of God's saving activity in and through Israel, Jesus, and the church.

Consequently, it seems reasonable to suggest that when God acts to form the character of a person through the infusion of theological and moral virtue, God's agency is mediated by the church: that community whose practices have been responsible for the transmission and reenactment of God's story. This is the argument I develop in what follows, as I continue a line of thought begun in Chapter 3: The liturgical practices of the gathered community are an important means by which the virtues are given to and displayed in the life of the Christian.

### From Virtue to Liturgy and Back Again

> What was visible in Christ has now passed over into the sacraments of the Church.
>
> —Leo I

No one, Christian or otherwise, becomes good alone. Virtue requires for its development the work of a particular sort of community whose social practices form the lives of its members. Implicit in Aristotle's arguments

concerning virtue in his *Nicomachean Ethics* is the assertion that virtue requires for its development and sustenance a political community composed
of groups of friends devoted to training one another to live well.[36] The
practices of such communities act to sustain the narrative traditions that
form their members' identity and offer them reasons to live in one way
rather than another. "To enter into a practice," remarks MacIntyre, "is to
enter into a relationship not only with its contemporary practitioners, but
also with those whose achievements extended the reach of the practice to
its present point. It is thus the achievement, and *a fortiori* the authority, of
a tradition which I then confront and from which I have to learn."[37]

The claim that God "works in us without us" in order to infuse certain
moral and theological virtues is not a dismissal of the centrality of social
practices for the formation of character. It is rather a specification of *which*
community and *which* practices attend the moral development of that people who are called to imitate the holiness of their God. The church, in other
words, is precisely that traditioned community through whose practices the
Christian virtues are developed. Through their regular participation in the
*liturgy*, which is first of all (but not only) the ritual public worship of the
gathered community, Christians enter into those relationships that train
and enable them to live well as the body of Christ.[38]

I use the term "liturgy" here in the broadest sense of the word to refer
first of all to what Christians do when they gather but also to the way they
live as Christians when they go out into the world. In the sense that they
gather for a prescribed form of worship and then go into the world in mission, Protestants from the Free Church and other traditions are as "liturgical" as Roman Catholics or the Orthodox. This does not mean, however,
that there are not good and bad or better and worse liturgies. Indeed, as I
hope to show in what follows, I believe that a good deal of the failure of
Christians to live distinctive lives is due to the fact that the liturgies of our
churches have been revised and reduced in ways that render them incapable
of forming us well.

It is "in worship," claims Aidan Nichols, that "our Christian selves are
formed."[39] The Christian life is in this sense, according to Vigen Guroian,
"the achievement *of a community* in struggle with and in mission to the
world. Such an ethic," he goes on to say, "will not long prosper as mere
personal habit or sentiment."[40] Rather, it requires the full force of those
long-standing practices that teach and enable the church to make God's
story their own. Guroian explains: "Tradition is transmitted and becomes
normative for Christian living not only through preaching, doctrine, and

theological discourse, but also through the prayer and worship of Christians. Liturgy provides a vital link between Christian tradition and ethics, shaping their communal meaning and rendering the truth of the Christian faith persuasive."[41]

What Christian worship has to do with Christian virtue is suggested by Aquinas, who, in a concise summary of the relationship between acquired and infused virtue, explains:

> All virtues, intellectual and moral, which are acquired by our actions, proceed from certain natural principles which pre-exist in us, as we have said. In place of these natural principles, God has bestowed on us theological virtues whereby we are ordered to a supernatural end, as we have also said. Hence it was necessary that *other habits*, corresponding proportionally to the theological virtues, be caused in us by God which are related to the theological virtues as the moral and intellectual virtues are to the natural principles of virtues.[42]

Aquinas seems to indicate both a continuity and a discontinuity between those moral virtues acquired through the life of "natural" communities and those moral and theological virtues infused by God. The discontinuity is of course the presumed proximity of God's agency in the formation of the human agent; in the case of the infused virtues, God is a much more immediate agent than in the moral virtues acquired through habituation. Yet, Aquinas does not necessarily indicate that God is in some mystical sense the *absolutely* immediate agent for the acquisition of these virtues. For he indicates—and here is the continuity—that God uses "other habits" to effect the infusion of theological virtue.[43]

The seemingly radical disparity between moral virtue acquired through habituation and moral and theological virtue acquired through infusion by God thus dissolves to a certain extent if we understand the liturgy to be the primary modality for the bestowal of all virtues on the Christian. The practices of the liturgy are, one might say, the locus of those "other habits . . . caused in us by God" of which Aquinas speaks. Guroian indicates something like this in suggesting that as members of a counter-cultural community that is called to live and act both over against and in service to the world, "Christians must remind themselves that their identity and morality are grounded . . . in those distinctive practices of the church through which it constitutes itself and remembers, not only in word and thought but in action, the truth it confesses regarding the lordship of Jesus Christ."[44]

The significance of liturgical practices as ritualized social activities that actually form the body of the person participating in them to be and behave in one way rather than another cannot be overestimated here. Catherine Bell suggests, in language echoing Paul's rhetoric from 1 Corinthians, that such practices not only form the body of the person participating in them but also are constitutive of the *social* body that is the bearer and transmitter of those particular practices.[45] I am, it turns out, formed by the practices of my community, and my right participation in those practices is part of what sustains the community's existence. "Ritualization," Bell explains, "produces this ritualized body through the interaction of the body with a structured and structuring environment."[46] This claim bears directly on the point I have made above, that is, well-developed moral agency need not be equated with a thorough rational analysis about what is to be done. The logic of ritual, says Bell, "is embodied in the physical movements of the body and thereby lodged beyond the grasp of consciousness and articulation."[47]

The performance of the liturgy is thus an especially intense locus of Christian body-forming activity. "Sacraments," James White reminds us, are socialized rituals that "involve both words and actions." He continues:

> If, by words, we speak to each other in God's name, in the sacraments we often *touch each other in God's name.* We act for God in acting to each other. At the heart of several sacraments is the laying on of hands, through which power, blessing, or authority is conveyed. . . . Our worship is full of hands: giving the peace, baptizing, pronouncing benediction, giving the body and blood of the Lord, uniting the hands of lovers, sprinkling a coffin with dust. We touch each other, and we handle bread, a cup, water, and oil.[48]

These actions, White says, form the body of Christ not simply by virtue of their own force but also because they are the means by which God acts in our lives; for

> human beings do not act alone in them. These sign-acts are important actions because through them Christians experience God's self giving. Our human actions are needed to give visible form, to make incarnate the divine action. Because our humanity needs actions as outward and visible signs of self-giving, God gives us sacraments so that we can know that which is inward and spiritual. It is no different from knowing our neighbor through his or her actions. God gives Godself through actions, too. As with words, the Holy Spirit works through the actions that the Christian community performs in God's name.[49]

In other words, the church becomes Christ's body and its members Christ's representatives—that is, his *apostoloi*—to the world first of all because of God's grace, a grace that is made available normatively to the church in and through those particular, repeated human acts that compose the Christian liturgy. The church gathers to worship in God's name with both the hope and the promise of becoming increasingly closer friends of God. It is in this gathering that God makes all virtue available to the church, as God gives to the gathered faithful the gift-virtue of charity, that perfect love of God that is the form of the virtues.[50] "All the moral virtues," Aquinas explains, "are infused together with charity."[51] Charity is thus *both* a gracious gift and a skill to be developed; it is, as Paul Wadell says, "the power or skill to make good on the promise of grace, to sustain and deepen that love that is our life."[52]

Charity moves us from self-absorption to absorption with God and with one another.[53] As such, says Wadell, it is the "soul of the Christian paradox, for charity is the love which demands ourself, but it is also the love which promises a self. In friendship with God we give ourself away, we surrender to the Spirit, and in that surrender our most exquisite individuality is secured, for we become what God in perfect love has always wanted us to be."[54]

Through charity and in friendship with God, we discover that a significant part of what God has made us to be is, in Paul's words, "members one of another." The essence of a Christian ethics centered in the gift of charity, it turns out, is discovered, developed, and displayed in certain kinds of relationships with others. Wadell explains:

> If morality originates in this encounter with another whose presence demands recognition, and whose presence is experienced as a call to come out of ourself in response, then . . . all genuine moral response is "other-directed" or "other-centered." There is a specific direction to moral behavior, a movement away from oneself to another. The explicit dynamic of morality is to become part of a world larger than our own through love. This is possible when we respond in trust and affirmation to all the others who come our way. Morality works for the liberation of ourselves, but such liberation can only come from others, and ultimately from God. We are freed from the prison of self-centeredness, from the weary stratagems of egoism and fear, when we accept the invitation of another to be a part of their world.[55]

The liturgy is replete with words and gestures that move us beyond ourselves toward God and one another: the greeting ("The Lord be with you . . . and also with you."); the peace ("Peace be with you . . . and also with you"); the prayers of confession and of the people; and especially the Eucharist, with all its rich language about the oneness of the body—all involve our being together not simply *with* but also *for* one another. These various liturgical acts are thus the means by which we are trained to be the kind of people who are capable of genuine friendship with God and with one another. In the liturgy we learn that there is no proper separation of the way we profess to love God from the way we are called to love our neighbor, that, as Harmon Smith points out, "Christian worship, rightly understood, means to display life in submission to and conformity with God's holiness and righteousness."[56]

Thus we learn *in* the liturgy *that* the liturgy is not simply a repeated event in the life of a gathering community but a continuation of the peculiar way of life created in and by that gathering. "*Liturgy,*" Smith reminds us, "*is everything the church offers to God in the name of Jesus.*"[57] Geoffrey Wainwright explains that the church has always recognized this fact:

> The notion of "imitating" in daily life what is done in the liturgy is by no means confined to the ministerial priesthood. Several prayers at Mass during the Easter season in particular carry the idea through for the entire assembly of the faithful. Thus it is prayed on Easter Monday that the baptized may "keep in their lives to the sacrament they have received in faith"; on the Friday in the first week of Easter, that "we may imitate and achieve what we celebrate and profess"; on the second Sunday of Easter, that the paschal sacrament "may live for ever in our hearts and minds"; and on the final Saturday of the season, that "we who have celebrated the Easter ceremonies may hold fast to them in life and conduct."[58]

All of life thus may in a sense be liturgical, in that all of life is potentially an opportunity for Christians to display the virtues, which are nothing less than the skills necessary to make visible in their body God's redemptive love for the creation. And at no time are we given more significant opportunities to display that redemptive love than when we are sick or dying or when we seek to care for the sick and dying we discover among us.

## An Excursus on Virtue and Medicine

One of the more promising recent developments in bioethics has been the discipline's willingness to enter into conversation with virtue ethics. That entry, however, has not been without equivocation. For example, the most recent edition of Beauchamp and Childress's *Principles of Biomedical Ethics* grants a place to virtue ethics near the book's end, where they remark that "what counts most in the moral life is not consistent adherence to principles and rules, but reliable character, moral good sense, and emotional responsiveness."[59] The authors do not, however, consider how their presumption of the essential liberal self of modernity might in fact preclude any serious consideration of virtue ethics. By making virtue an afterthought they have made it an impossibility.

A more serious and comprehensive attempt at a virtue-based bioethics is offered by Edmund Pellegrino and David Thomasma in their book, *The Virtues in Medical Practice*. By making virtue the centerpiece of their work they avoid the problems confronting Beauchamp and Childress, whose efforts to make virtue ethics a part of their principle-based work are characterized by Pellegrino and Thomasma as "less than successful" because they fail to consider the virtue of prudence and its relationship both to the other virtues and to obligation-based ethical theories.[60]

*The Virtues in Medical Practice* is characterized by the same strengths and weaknesses as the authors' more foundational work, which I reviewed in Chapter 2—which is to say that in the end their otherwise remarkable work simply shows too much faith in medicine itself as a moral discourse capable of sustaining the kinds of serious moral practices they envision. Because they are concerned, it seems, only with "a set of virtues entailed in being a good physician,"[61] they are unable to consider how the care of the sick might—and perhaps must—be one well-integrated part of the life of an entire community. Pellegrino and Thomasma are, on the one hand, certainly correct to argue that medicine "is at heart a moral enterprise." On the other hand, they are wrong to suggest that medicine's moral seriousness ipso facto makes all of its practitioners members of a common "moral community . . . bound together by a common moral purpose."[62]

Pellegrino and Thomasma come close to admitting as much. Noting the profound social transformation undergone by medicine in recent years, they say in near despair:

> We do not know how the medical profession will resolve this dilemma. Many physicians still want to remain faithful to the primacy of the patient's welfare and the idea of a profession. Others see no reason why physicians should be held to a higher standard of conduct than anyone else. What is most distressing is the pervasive conviction that the citadel of ethics has already fallen, that it is no longer possible to be an ethical physician, and that the only choices are capitulation, accommodation, or early retirement, with warnings to one's children not to enter the fallen city. Those who would resist feel powerless, alone, and abandoned by the profession. They justifiably complain that others cannot expect them to be sacrificial lambs trying to reverse the inimical forces arrayed against traditional medical ethics today.[63]

These concerns are altogether justifiable. Perhaps the most significant thing about them is the insight they offer into the impossibility of sustaining a moral life outside the practices of a moral community. In another era, medicine might have been such a community. However, it is clearly not one in this era. In the modern world the moral practice of medicine requires not simply virtuous physicians but virtuous patients, as well. And neither physicians nor patients can hope to be virtuous apart from membership in a strong community with a particular narrative tradition and accompanying practices that can train them to be good.

## Christian Virtues Surrounding the Care of the Sick

> Before others and above all, special care must be taken of the ill so they may be looked after, as Christ, "I was sick, and you visited Me"; and "What you did for one of these, My least brothers, you did for Me" (Matt 25:36, 40). The sick must remember they are being taken care of for the honor of God. They must not distress the brothers who care for them with unreasonable demands. Nevertheless, these demands should be suffered patiently, since a greater reward is obtained from them.
>
> —The Rule of St. Benedict, Chapter 36

The ancient *Rule* of the Benedictine monastic order devotes an entire chapter to the care—and to the conduct—of the sick. The particular instructions given in there are in themselves fairly unremarkable. The well who are charged with caring for the sick are reminded that the sick are important to God and that their care is a worthy and virtuous enterprise. The sick are reminded that there are better and worse ways of being ill and that they should embody the better ones. And some fairly common-sense advice is given concerning the practical conduct of the care offered, regarding diet, hygiene, and so forth. Nothing here seems especially imaginative or innovative or even Christian, with one exception. The care given and received is to be given and received "as Christ," who is thought, according to the Scripture, to be especially present in the lives of the sick.

When we read these instructions in the context of the entire *Rule* and its most basic assertions, what this means becomes somewhat clearer. The Benedictine *Rule* presumes above all that the human *summum bonnum* of friendship with and service to God is best carried out in and through the common life of a liturgical community whose members understand themselves as belonging to one another.[64] In such a community, caring for the sick among the members is but one of the conditions of that service. Thus the rule does not ask what kind of persons are required to care for the sick "as [for] Christ." The answer to that question is embodied in the daily lives of those living together and following the *Rule*. The kind of persons required to care for the sick "as Christ" are those formed by the practices of the *Rule*.

The Benedictines were of course well aware of the significance of the *Rule* in making them the persons they were; for the material conditions in which they lived made it continually apparent. They shared a highly regimented common life in remote monasteries, a life characterized by hard work and by significant measures of daily prayer and confession, study, and gathered worship. In such a setting, where membership in the same body of Christ was not simply an ideal aspiration or a theological truth but an inescapable fact of daily existence, the cultivation of the virtues would scarcely require a second thought. Thus the *Rule* is perhaps more remarkable for what it does not say than for what it says about the care of the sick.

What the *Rule* does not say but does presume about the sick and their care is that such care, if it is to be done "as to Christ," requires first of all the virtue of charity, that form of all virtues that binds the members to one another *as* the body of Christ. The presence of charity makes possible the full presence of the cardinal moral virtues of courage, temperance, justice, and prudence, all of which are required if the members of the body are to "suffer together" and to "have the same care for one another." Those living according to the *Rule* would have known this and understood themselves to be in the process of being trained in charity by the practices of the liturgy as interpreted in the *Rule*.

But the situation for most contemporary Christians is markedly different from that of those early Benedictines. Neither Benedictine monasticism nor other less cloistered forms of intentional community are real options for most of us. The very way the modern world is structured tends in a multitude of ways to alienate us from one another rather than to unite us, a truth that is displayed nowhere more starkly than in the modern practices of health care. Christian virtue, in such a context, comes hard. This does not mean, however, that Christian virtue and the community required for its development are irrelevant or optional for those of us who live in the contemporary culture. The baptism shared by Christians continues to bind them as members of the same body of Christ with the same obligations to one another as those shared by the ancient Benedictines. The virtues developed in and displayed through the gathered body are as significant now as they were then; caring for the sick still requires courage, temperance, justice, prudence, and especially charity. Only the context is different.

The contemporary context requires Christians to cultivate specific virtues that are especially resistant to the atomizing and alienating forces of modern culture. The Christian virtues attending the care of the sick and dying derive, as do all the virtues, from the theological virtue of charity. Such virtues presume the presence of the cardinal moral virtues, but they go beyond these in their specificity to display to the modern world God's intentions for the body and for the body of Christ. These virtues must shape and be shaped by the lives of both patients and caregivers. They must be developed and displayed wherever and in whatever measure is possible as gestures of resistance and of witness to the violent, alienating practices of the modern world.

## Virtues for Patients: Dependence and Constancy and Why They Matter

The very notion of virtuous patients is either inimical or irrelevant for most of modern medicine and modern bioethics, which have portrayed themselves as being concerned almost exclusively with the actions of professional caregivers. The very word "patient" suggests, especially in the modern context, a certain passivity and abandonment of agency in deference to the expertise of the caregiver—a passivity and abandonment that are indeed to some extent appropriate, given the way that certain serious illnesses and injuries debilitate us and render us incapable of acting. Yet, notes Alasdair MacIntyre,

> what is significant is the relatively small difference between the way in which physicians assume responsibility for patients in these latter types of case (where everyone would agree that *someone* must assume responsibility) and their assumption of responsibility for and over patients who suffer from a variety of aches, pains, swellings, fevers, and bruises, but who are in no way incapacitated from the exercise of responsibility according to our ordinary nonmedical criteria. Traditionally, the patient puts himself in the doctor's hands.[65]

But clearly illness need not be an entirely passive endeavor in most cases. There are better and worse ways of being sick, and the *performance* of illness matters a great deal in a community's pursuit of its common good and the goods of its members. Patients have a potentially profound effect on their caregivers, as well as on those others to whom their illness requires them to be present. Christians in particular must learn to be sick well; for the virtuous performance of illness provides gestures of both resistance and witness to a world characterized by loneliness and isolation.

Patients need to cultivate certain virtues first of all as gestures of resistance. The practice of medicine in this day has been reduced almost completely to a contractualism in which, says MacIntyre, "traditional medical authority cannot be vindicated" on any widespread basis.[66] There is no reason, given the contemporary situation of medicine among strangers, for a Christian patient who has significant, tradition-dependent ideas about the human good (or any other patient with such tradition-dependent ideas) to trust that those ideas will be taken seriously by a system that will in short order treat her as a collection of diseased parts.[67] In such a world, Christian patients must assert their own agency in order to keep their bodies from being severed from the body of Christ.[68] Such agency, if it is to be faithful and effective, requires the cultivation of certain virtues.

The cultivation of virtues among patients is, however, not just a matter of developing practices of resistance toward a hostile world. Christian patients must also embody virtue for the sake of witness, not simply for their own benefit but also for the benefit of the body of Christ and ultimately for the benefit of the world. At the conclusion of "Patients as Agents," MacIntyre makes a gesture in this direction:

> What is possible is to work with those with whom one does share sufficient beliefs to rescue and to recreate authority within communities that will break with the pluralist ethos. . . . In medicine it means working for a variety of new forms of medical community, each with its own shared moral allegiance. Within these the notion of authority could again begin to find context and content.[69]

Two closely related virtues, which I shall call dependence and constancy, provide this sort of content for Christians in the modern context.

*Dependence: Letting the Body Be the Body.* "Dependence" is how I name the virtue of letting oneself be cared for as a member of the body of Christ. Dependence is much more than being a "good patient" who arrives for appointments and pays fees on time, who does not complain, and who has unlimited trust in her caregiver's expertise; for given the contractual nature of modern medical practice, a "good patient" is nothing more than an autonomous individual who keeps one half of a financial contract.[70] And the very nature of contracts precludes the need for virtue on behalf of the patient; she is simply purchasing a service. The virtue of dependence is much more than that.

Another, perhaps more helpful way of describing dependence is to say that it is the virtue by which a person is able to let the body be the body. Being a body, as I have shown in previous chapters, entails being connected to—and frequently dependent on—other bodies. It is finally our bodies, especially our sick bodies, that remind us we are not and cannot be fully autonomous or self-sufficient. We need the care of others, and never more than when we are sick. Yet it is not simply the *fact* of care that is important but also the way we understand what is happening when we are being cared for. When Paul says in 1 Corinthians 12:25 that the body has been so arranged by God that "the members may have the same care for one another," he is not simply reminding his readers that as members of the body of Christ they are required to care for one another; they must also *allow* themselves to be cared for in a certain way as a simple function of the integrity of the body. And it is this latter skill, the skill of being cared for as a matter of course, that is not easily attained.

The very notion of "care" implies that there must be a recipient of that care, a person "cared for."[71] Being cared for well is a skill that must be developed, a virtue that must be cultivated. To place ourselves in a position of dependence and receptivity and to receive care as a member of the same body as the caregiver requires that we understand care in an absolutely non-contractual way. The tendency to justify the care being received by paying for it, and hence making it part of a contractual economy in which remuneration and care are inseparable from one another, must be resisted. For paying, when understood as an action of the same order as caregiving, transforms the relationship into something other than an interaction between members of the body of Christ.[72]

Making exchange *constitutive* of the caring relationship suggests that the person cared for has value and contributes to the relationship with the caregiver only to the extent that her being cared for is a temporary status into which she has descended and from which she will soon enough escape. Insofar as this sort of transience is attached to being cared for, what the person cared for gives to the caregiver has to do only with who the person cared for is before and after the caring is done (i.e., a partner in a contractual exchange) and nothing to do with her status as a dependent. Such a notion of care violates the very integrity of the body of Christ, in which dependence and interdependence are constitutive of the body.

Thus on a broader level what I am speaking of here is quite simply the fundamental difference between Christianity and capitalism. John Milbank accounts for the antipathy between the Christian account of human existence and the highly individualized capitalist account, which he says

> in its most innate tendency precludes community. This is because (let us remind ourselves), it makes the prime purpose of society as a whole and also of individuals to be one of accumulation of abstract wealth, or of power-to-do-things in general, and rigorously subordinates any desire to do anything concrete in particular, including the formation of social relationships.[73]

Milbank goes on to point out that in the Christian understanding, on the other hand,

> a thing exchanged is not a commodity, but a gift, and it is not *alienated* from the giver but expresses his personality, so that the giver *is* in the gift, he *goes with* the gift. Precisely for this reason a *return* on the gift is always due to the giver, unlike our modern 'free gift'. Yet this gift is still a gift and not a commodity subject to contract, because it returns in a slightly different form at a not quite predictable time, bearing with it also the subjectivity of the counter-giver.[74]

The fact that both a person's state of being dependent and the care offered to her in light of that dependence may be viewed as gifts does not mean that the dependence associated with illness *is not* or *should not* normally be a temporary state. Insofar as illness in itself is *not* a good and health and healing *are* goods, the dependence associated with illness should not be something Christians seek for its own sake. But when Christians are sick, for however long, they must be willing and able genuinely to *live in that moment* in a state of dependence on the other members of the body. In doing so they are both exercising their proper authority as "weaker members" and placing themselves under the authority of the rest of the body.[75]

What it means for the weak or dependent members to possess and to exercise authority becomes clearer when we reread 1 Corinthians 12 in the particular context of caring and being cared for when sick. Paul says in verse 14 that "the body does not consist of one member but of many," and he then goes on to illustrate the interdependence that constitutes the Body *as* the Body. In the context of caring for the sick and the virtue of dependence, Paul might have gone on to say, in verses 15–18, something like this:

> If a person who is sick or who has an injury and is unable to get out of bed would say, "Because I am not well and able to care for myself, I am not an im-

portant part of the body," that would not make her any less a part of the community. And if a person who is sick and unable to work would say, "Because I
cannot pay my bills and fend for myself I am not part of this body," that
would not make her any less a part of the community. And if a person who is
too sick to care for her children would say, "Because I am unable to take care
of my kids I am not really a significant part of this body," that would not make
her any less a part of the community. After all, if we were all absolutely self-
sufficient and independent and able to pay for professionals and institutions to
handle things for us whenever something went wrong, what would be the need
for a community at all? How would the world ever understand anything about
what it means to be a Christian? And why would God have made us part of a
body? The point is that God *has* made us members of one body, and part of
what that means is that when we are sick and need help, we should not be
ashamed to receive that help *from the body*. I know this is not easy to do and
that it violates our pride and our senses of independence, but we must learn to
do it for the sake of our witness. We are, after all, really a *body*.

*Constancy: Being Sick and Dying As We Have Lived.*   There is a profound
sense in which certain aspects of our entire lives may be seen as prepara-
tions for dying. "Constancy" is the name I give to the virtue that disposes a
person who has lived her life well, as a faithful member of the body of
Christ, to be sick and to die in a manner consistent with that life. Constancy is the virtue that makes it possible for a person to experience an af-
firmative outcome for Rilke's poetic prayer:

> God, give us each our own death
> the dying that proceeds
> from each of our lives:
> the way we loved,
> the meanings we made,
> our need.[76]

Aristotle might say that a person who possesses the skill to die in a way
that proceeds from their life is one who *clearly* has lived well, one who
*clearly* has achieved real happiness, or *eudaimonia;* for as Stanley Hauerwas notes, "according to Aristotle, it seems that happiness comes not during, but at the end of our life—thus the fear of untimely death. Happiness is
the characteristic of those who live in a manner such that the end of their
life confirms the way they have lived. ... The happy person, thus, is one
who can claim their death as their own."[77] The virtue of constancy there-

fore has to do not only with the end of life but with its entirety. Put in more explicitly theological terms, we can say that the virtue of constancy is the skill necessary to make sense of our lives—to ourselves and to others—at the time of our deaths. Hauerwas explains: "Fundamental to Christian convictions is the assurance that anyone who has followed the way of life we call Christianity will be able to look back on their life and say, 'I would not have it otherwise.' And to say this is the happiest thing anyone can say, if they say it truthfully and without self-deception."[78]

Because Christians are made part of the one body of Christ, the skills needed to die well can be acquired and displayed only as we make it a point to let the virtuous dying be present to us so that we might learn from them how to die. Indeed, the community *requires* the presence of the dying if its integrity is to be preserved. This presence, however, is made extraordinarily difficult by the social and, especially, the medical practices of modernity, which seek to avoid or to control death and to segregate the dead and dying from the rest of us. Ray Anderson observes:

> We no longer think about the dead, we think about dying. The dead are removed from us surreptitiously. One moment there is the dying, under the care of licensed professionals who grant us occasional intrusions into the process. The next moment, there is an empty bed, an empty room, and no further need to make the anxious visit to the hospital. The one who is now dead has disappeared, under the care of licensed professionals, and only emerges for a fleeting moment, if at all, as an artifact in the liturgical drama supervised by a team of professional caretakers.[79]

Death thus takes on a surreal quality for most contemporary Americans, and the notion of a good death or a faithful death becomes an absurdity, as Anderson suggests:

> In a report to the American Academy of Pediatrics in 1971, we were told that by the time a child in the United States reaches the age of 14 he or she can be expected to have seen, on average, 18,000 people killed on television! Yet, these same children will live, on average, for the next 40 years without experiencing the death or loss of an immediate family member. And even then, they will be shielded from the death so that the living will disappear instantly, almost like the sudden departure of a character in a television drama.[80]

Modernity renders death unnatural, that is, as something that is radically discontinuous with the rest of life. Hence we see a multifaceted "professionalization" of death, as dealing with it is increasingly left to those who have been designated experts. A significant amount of energy and resources are expended to develop increasingly elaborate and increasingly desperate life-extending technologies, ranging from xenografting to artificial organs, as the end of life increasingly falls solely within the purview of the health care industry.[81] Thus the seeming paradox between the drive to extend individual life at all costs and the growing and increasingly heated debate over the propriety of various types of physician-assisted suicide is in fact no paradox at all; both views represent a desire to control death, a shift toward an increasingly instrumental understanding of our bodies, and a transfer of authority from the wisdom of the traditional community to the expertise of the professional—a transfer that extends through the moment of death to the very way we deal with the bodies of those who have died. The traditional practices of sitting up with the dead and of the family wake have given way to the polished (and expensive) funeral parlor "viewing." Funerals are no longer held in churches but in generic funeral home chapels. And burials have been moved from traditional family or church-based cemeteries to private ones, where the professionally embalmed and made-up body of the deceased is placed in a metal casket in a leak-proof vault in a grave that is the final, absurd extension of our contemporary fetish over private property.[82]

These practices, and the (mis)understanding of death undergirding them, lie in sharp distinction to the Christian understanding of death. The best of the Christian tradition does not simply claim that the biological fact of death as the end of our lives in this world is itself in some way "unnatural"; rather, as Anderson explains, Christianity properly understands death as "that which belongs to one's natural life."[83] What may be rightly said of Christianity is that it sees the experience of death *as judgment* and as the *final terminus of human existence* as being attributable to the sinfulness of a fallen creation. Here Anderson follows Karl Barth, who, he notes, "has given the most definitive answer to the question concerning death and human nature":

> Our finite being, argues Barth, belongs to our original God-given nature and is not the result of sin. Barth, in effect, makes a critical distinction between "dying" and "death." The experience of dying is intrinsic to our created human nature. Human nature is not potentially oriented to immortality (Erickson), nor driven by some inner principle towards death as a "final decision" which relates us to God (Rahner).[84]

The Christian understanding of death begins with the fact that God's judgment of the creation has already taken place in the life, death, and resurrection of Jesus of Nazareth. An appreciation of the gospel assurance that through baptism we also share in the resurrection from the dead thus becomes a central tenet for recapturing the Christian practice of dying well. The fact of Christ's resurrection and the promise of final resurrection enables us to live with the fact that we are by nature finite and dependent. The doctrine of the resurrection allows us to understand death as properly belonging to human creatureliness without at the same time experiencing death as a final, negative judgment of our lives. As Anderson argues, because of the resurrection of Jesus of Nazareth and the gospel promise that humanity has a share in that resurrection, death

> no longer has the power to plunge human beings into a destiny of their own making. This power has been nullified and the "sting of death" has been removed. The means by which death has been nullified in its power to bring condemnation has not been achieved by appealing to a motive of love in God more worthy of praise than his wrath; rather, His wrath has been felt totally and unmediated in the midst of His love. The love of God in Jesus Christ cannot be known without also coming near to the terrible judgment and condemnation of God on the cross.[85]

Thus, concludes Anderson: "Death has not been canceled and replaced with something else; rather, the time of the human person as represented by Jesus of Nazareth has been extended through death, so that death no longer is the boundary of finiteness and the history of the human person."[86]

This truth must be made real to the Christian community through the conduct of practices that give definite material content to the notion of *euthanasia*, which means, literally, "good death."[87] The first step in the recreation of the reality of a good death is for the body of Christ to allow a space in its midst for death and for those who are dying. The creation of this space requires first of all that the Church reclaims death from the modern spheres of individual autonomy and professional expertise and makes it once again the province of the communal wisdom of the body of Christ.[88] Before we can say how we ought to die, we may first have to say how we should not die, as Edward Abbey has said, albeit perhaps with a bit of overstatement: "*Not* in snowy whiteness under arc light and klieg lights and direct television hookup. No never under clinical smells and sterilized medical eyes cool with detail calculated needle-prolonged agonizing, stiff and starchy in the white monastic cell, no."[89]

Anderson concurs with this sentiment and goes well beyond it in search of a positive alternative:

It is clear that the human environment of dying was itself a casualty of the modernization of medicine and health care. We cannot go back, ever again, to that earlier state of the art where the limits of life preservation were reached without breaking out of the boundaries of family love and care. The humanization of dying must not be viewed as an attempt to sentimentalize dying, nor should our concern for the recovery of the human environment of dying be motivated by nostalgia.[90]

Anderson's concerns about the impossibility of "going back" to a family-based way of dying are legitimate, insofar as modern life has rendered the geographic proximity of the extended family permanently a thing of the past. But the body of Christ has never been dependent upon the ties of biological family. It is a baptismally *reconstituted* family with the liturgical resources to resist the modern institutionalization of death. The Church's catholicity means that its integrity is not altogether dependent upon geography. Thus, we can say, at least, that the material possibility still exists for the body of Christ to cultivate the virtue of constancy in death, the virtue that allows the community to learn from the sick and dying and to benefit from their presence; for "we all," says Anderson, "some day," will die. But we prepare for the truth of that experience when we have created a life in community with those who will not conceal the truth from us at the very last.[91]

*Dependence and Constancy on Display: The Life and Death of Flannery O'Connor.*   To this point I have not been terribly specific about how the virtues of dependence and constancy might be cultivated through the liturgical practices of the body of Christ. One reason for this is that I am skeptical on theological and philosophical grounds about the possibility of making such specifications in the abstract; doing so would seem to indicate that certain practices are the uncomplicated efficient *causes* of certain virtues, a position that I wish to avoid. Yet there is another, simpler reason for my failure. I simply do not know how to *say* how the liturgy might form these virtues. I believe that I can, however, show something of what those virtues look like as they are acquired and displayed over the course of one extraordinary life.

Flannery O'Connor was born in Savannah in 1925 and raised in nearby Milledgeville, Georgia. O'Connor attended Georgia College and the University of Iowa Writer's Workshop, graduating in 1947. She developed into a serious and dedicated writer who authored numerous books and short stories, nearly all of which were set in the southern United States and many of which were disturbing and even macabre stories about grotesque characters. In 1950 she became seriously ill and was told she suffered from a chronic, autoimmune collagen disease called lupus erythematosis. She was, in the years following that diagnosis, seriously debilitated and frequently ill, up to the time of her death in 1964 at the age of 38.[92] Her life and her work during that period reflect something of the virtues of dependence and constancy.

Her work is at once deeply disturbing and theologically insightful, two characteristics she understood to be closely related. In a 1960 essay entitled "The Grotesque in Southern Fiction," she remarked:

> Whenever I'm asked why Southern writers particularly have a penchant for writing about freaks, I say it is because we are still able to recognize one. To be able to recognize a freak, you have to have some conception of the whole man, and in the South the general conception of man is still, in the main, theological. . . . I think it is safe to say that while the South is hardly Christ-centered, it is most certainly Christ-haunted.[93]

The life of Flannery O'Connor was more than Christ-haunted, however. Above all else, her life and her vocation as a writer were both firmly rooted in her Catholic Christianity. "I write the way I do," she explained, "because and only because I am a Catholic. I feel that if I were not a Catholic, I would have no reason to write, no reason to see, no reason ever to feel horrified or even to enjoy anything."[94] Her faith appears to have been neither overly pious nor excessively emotional; being Christian, she believed, was nothing other than living a life in communion with others, such that one arrived at a particular understanding of life and its goods. Her view was that this life was to be lived always as a passionate quest for God, who she believed to be the greatest Good.[95] "Always," she reflected, "you renounce a lesser good for a greater; the opposite is what sin is."[96] This is a telling statement, indicating that Flannery O'Connor saw life in this world itself as something good, as something neither to be fled nor to be loved and grasped for its own sake. Her belief in the finite nature of this life gave her a particular understanding of what was going on in her frequently ailing body. She once wrote to a friend:

> I am always astonished at the emphasis the Church puts on the body. It is not the soul she says will rise but the body, glorified. I have always thought that purity was the most mysterious of the virtues, but it occurs to me that it would never have entered the human consciousness to conceive of purity if we were not to look forward to a resurrection of the body, which will be flesh and spirit

united in peace, in the way they were in Christ. The resurrection of Christ seems the high point in the law of nature.[97]

She seems to have meant that it is through this lens of Christ's bodily resurrection that all other truth, including the truth about our bodies, must be understood and interpreted. She wrote to that same friend, who had expressed doubt concerning the believability of certain aspects of the Christian narrative:

> For you it may be a matter of not being able to accept what you call a suspension of the laws of the flesh and the physical, but for my part I think that when I know what the laws of the flesh and the physical really are, then I will know what God is. We know them as we see them, not as God sees them. For me it is the virgin birth, the Incarnation, the resurrection which are the true laws of the flesh and the physical. Death, decay, destruction are the suspension of these laws.[98]

What is especially remarkable about all this is O'Connor's insight into *why* she saw the world in the way she did. Hers was a life formed above all by participation in the liturgy as a member of Christ's body, something she seems to have understood deeply. In this sense individual piety was of little use to her, especially in comparison to the worship of the Church, which she believed was "the only thing that is going to make the terrible world we are coming to endurable; the only thing that makes the Church endurable is that it is the Body of Christ and that on this we are fed."[99] In another letter to the same friend, she remarks that

> the individual in the Church is, no matter how worthless himself, a part of the Body of Christ and a participator in the Redemption. There is no blueprint that the Church gives for understanding this. . . . I distrust pious phrases, particularly when they issue from my mouth. I try militantly never to be affected by the pious language of the faithful but it is always coming out when you least expect it. In contrast to the pious language of the faithful, the liturgy is beautifully flat.[100]

What O'Connor means here by the flatness of the liturgy is somewhat clearer when seen from the perspective of her understanding of the role of habits in the formation of all of life. She was in this respect deeply influenced by Aquinas and by more contemporary expositors of Aquinas like Etienne Gilson and Jacques Maritain, to whom she referred frequently in her correspondence and from whom she learned, says her friend Sally

Fitzgerald, "'the habit of being,' an excellence not only of action but of interior disposition and activity that increasingly reflected the object, the being which specified it, and was itself reflected in what she did and said." [101] By participating regularly—meaning *habitually*—in the liturgy, the center of which she rightly understood to be the Eucharist, which is the community's participation in the body of Christ, O'Connor formed the dispositions that enabled her to face sickness and to die in a manner consistent with the way she sought to live her life.[102]

Being formed in such a way by the liturgy enabled her to see her illness as one of the innumerable contingencies of human life, contingencies that have the capacity to effect either good or evil. "I have never been anywhere," she remarked, "except sick. In a sense sickness is a place, more instructive than a long trip to Europe, and it's always a place where there's no company, where nobody can follow."[103] There is in much of her correspondence a sense that she had accepted her illness and the limitations accompanying it, a sense that life goes on through, and not simply around or apart from, illness. "I have enough energy to write with," she said shortly after becoming sick, "and as that is all I have any business doing anyhow, I can with one eye squinted take it all as a blessing. What you have to measure out, you come to observe closer, or so I tell myself."[104]

As it became increasingly apparent that hers was an illness from which there would be no recovery, O'Connor continued to look to the liturgy and to her friends as sources of strength. She continued, as she always had, to carry on a vigorous correspondence with several people. In spite of the fact that she was obviously suffering a good deal, the content and tone of those letters is neither self-pitying nor maudlin.[105] She mentioned in passing in a letter to a friend that she had received the "now-called Sacrament of the Sick. Once known as Extreme Unction," an indication that she and those around her had faced the fact that her death was imminent.[106] Yet what is most striking about these final letters is that they continue, in the midst of all her suffering and sadness, to express a profound concern with the connections she had established with others through the years.[107] It is these connections that are the central theme of a prayer she sent in a letter to a friend just two weeks before she died, a prayer that gives splendid expression to the life of one formed by the virtues of dependence and constancy.

O Raphael, lead us toward those we are waiting for, those who are waiting for us: Raphael, Angel of happy meeting, lead us by the hand toward those we are looking for. May all our movements be guided by your light and transfigured by your joy.

Angel, guide of Tobias, lay the request we now address to you at the feet of Him whose unveiled Face you are privileged to gaze. Lonely and tired, crushed by the separations and sorrows of life, we feel the need of calling you and of pleading for the protection of your wings, so that we may not be as strangers in the province of joy, all ignorant of the concerns of our country. Remember the weak, you who are strong, you whose home lies beyond the region of thunder, in a land that is always peaceful, always serene and bright with the resplendent glory of God.[108]

Flannery O'Connor's participation in the body of Christ formed in her the skills she needed to live and die well and to teach others about those skills. She possessed an amazing, theologically formed insight about living and dying well, an insight that I will continue to unfold in a moment, after I have introduced the virtues that caregivers need to possess.

## Virtues for Caregivers: Hospitality and Presence

There is a sense in which it is simply impossible to distinguish clearly between the virtues for patients and those for caregivers. It is not simply that one cannot exist in any complete sense without the other but that as members of one Body, those who give care and those who receive it are continually and mutually interdependent in ways that are indescribably complex. We can, however, make distinctions between those who are sick and those who are not; hence it is possible to say that virtuous caregivers can and indeed must be available to the sick, whether or not the sick are virtuous, just as virtuous patients can and must be disposed in a certain way toward those around them, regardless of whether they are being cared for by virtuous people. The virtues of hospitality and presence are in this sense the relatively more active corollaries to the patient virtues of dependence and constancy.

Those schooled in and by the practices of modernity are likely to find the virtues of hospitality and presence especially anachronistic, seeing them as belonging to a past time in which ways of life that included those sorts of behaviors were unfortunately necessary. Modern life is, as I have argued in Chapters 1 and 3, inextricably linked to and formed by the practices of a capitalist political economy that trains us to value, more than anything else, efficiency. The modern understanding of what it means to have a division of labor and the rise of the expert/specialist are themselves rooted in capitalism's esteem for efficiency; indeed, as Neil Postman has pointed out, the final dissolution of traditional ways of understanding what it meant to be part of a community formed by bonds of mutual understanding (in favor of what he refers to as a "technological theology") may well be traced to the emergence of management science and the professional manager, who is the "scientist" of efficiency.[109]

Hospitality and presence are the very antitheses of efficiency because they are constitutive of a way of life that demands that a great deal of time be spent in a decidedly inefficient way. It is and probably always will be easier—and certainly more efficient—to care for one another through professionals and institutions, to hire someone else to be with our sick and our dying. And indeed, there often will be good reasons to do this, inasmuch as there are kinds of medical care that can be offered *only* in this context. Yet professional and institutional care should not be permitted, as it so often is, to drift over into an abandonment (even a temporary one) of the sick and dying. The integrity of the body of Christ demands this.

Hospitality and presence are in fact not readily separable. Formally, at least, it can be said that hospitality is the name given to the virtue that enables us to welcome others into our lives, whereas presence is an expression of our willingness to enter into and share the lives of others. In this sense these virtues represent our willingness to share our bodies and our sustenance with one another. There is a long tradition of these practices in the Christian faith, and within that tradition they are more or less simply assumed to be part of the common life of the church. In this day, however, they must be treated as virtues that are acquired through training, for they are no longer integral parts of our lives.

The Christian account of hospitality is based in the understanding that a sacred or sacramental bond exists between guest and host.[110] In this sense the hospitality tradition has a strong continuity with Paul's rhetoric of the body in 1 Corinthians; having been made part of God's new, all-inclusive humanity in Christ, Christians are obligated to open their lives to the lives of others as members of that new humanity.[111] But this tradition does not simply originate with the rise of Christianity; it also has a strong historical foundation in the Jewish practice of welcoming the stranger into one's home, a practice rooted in Abraham's exemplification of hospitality to the mysterious strangers at Mamre and in the experience of Israel's nomadic existence in the wilderness, between their exodus from Egypt and their entering into and seizing of the Land of Promise.[112]

And of course a radicalization of the Jewish notion of hospitality was an especially integral part of the life and teachings of Jesus himself, who spent much of his time eating and drinking with "sinners and tax gatherers" and indicated that his followers should do likewise. Hospitality was so significant a part of Jesus' eschatological vision of the new creation that he indicated that those who took time to care for the sick were in fact making a profound expression of their love for God: "Truly I tell you," he remarks in Matthew 25:40, "just as you did it to one of the least of these who are members of my family, you did it to me."[113]

*Characteristics of the Virtues of Care.*   There are, it seems, at least three important characteristics of the virtues of hospitality and presence, three things that will be discovered by those who seek to acquire them: Hospitality and presence are time-consuming; they are difficult; and they are at once dangerous and surprising.

The first thing we discover about being hospitably present to the sick and dying is that it takes *time*. Hospitality and presence are not solutions to problems, at least not in any immediate, causal sense. They are not based in method or technique. They are almost totally non-instrumental, sometimes to the point of seeming frivolous. Hospitality and presence value the sick and dying for who they are *in the midst of* their experience of illness, rather than for who they once were or who they may eventually become. In this sense, the exercise of these virtues gives rather than takes time, for it enables us to genuinely live in the reality of time present.[114]

Jean Vanier, the founder and director of the L'Arche communities, where non-disabled members live together in community with those with mental disabilities, expresses the importance of such a non-instrumental approach to caring for those who are especially dependent on their caregivers:

> L'Arche is special, in the sense that we are trying to live in community with people who are mentally handicapped. Certainly we want to help them grow and reach the greatest independence possible. But before "doing for them," we want to "be with them." The particular suffering of the person who is mentally handicapped, as of all marginal people, is a feeling of being excluded, worthless and unloved. It is through everyday life in community and the love that must be incarnate in this, that handicapped people can begin to discover that they have a value, that they are loved and so lovable.[115]

What Vanier says about being with persons who are mentally retarded is just as true of being with those who are ill, especially for those who are ill for extended periods of time. Illness is in itself isolating, and this isolation threatens the sick person's personal integrity, their sense that they have significance *as a sick person*. Being hospitably present to the sick is the first step to overcoming this sense of isolation and insignificance; it makes real to the ill person that when "one member suffers, all suffer together with it" (1 Corinthians 12:26). But, as Vanier notes, the development of such a caring presence requires the investment of time:

> Individual growth toward love and wisdom is slow. A community's growth is even slower. Members of a community have to be friends of time. They have to learn that many things will resolve themselves if they are given enough time. It can be a great mistake to want, in the name of clarity and truth, to push things too quickly to a resolution. Some people enjoy confrontation and highlighting divisions. This is not always healthy. It is better to be a friend of time. But clearly too, people should not pretend that problems don't exist by refusing to listen to the rumblings of the discontent; they must be aware of the tensions.[116]

If we are to become such "friends of time" we must learn that such work will disrupt our lives precisely to the extent that we are captured by the frenetic pace of the modern world and its god, efficiency. Everything about this old, fallen creation pushes us away from one another and presses us to pay others to care for our sick friends and family in institutional settings. This is especially a product of the modern political economy. We are trained to believe that a good life is acquired by competitive hard work, by the acquisition of private property and private wealth. Such acquisitions leave no space for habitual generosity, and especially no space for generosity with what we typically think of as our private time or space. Hospitality and presence are in this sense difficult because they challenge our understandings of what it means to have a good life. Time taken to be with others is time given away, time that cannot be spent acquiring wealth, property, and status. And space genuinely shared with others is no longer private space.[117] Taking time and sharing space means being a member of the body, in that it means becoming materially dependent on others or allowing others to become materially dependent on us.

Such dependence is of course dangerous, though it can also be joyfully surprising. It is dangerous in that it reveals to us that as Christians we are not yet what we say we are. Vanier remarks that "many communities are founded on dreams and fine words; there is much talk about love, truth, and peace."[118] Yet those words are tested by fire when we try to act on them through our presence to the sick and the dying. For the sick and the dying are like those with mental disabilities: they "are demanding. Their cries are the cries of truth because they sense the emptiness of many of our words; they can see the gap between what we say and what we live."[119] This sort of exposure, not to mention the demands of the sick themselves, is threatening and pushes us to withdraw from those for whom we are called to care. But to so withdraw is to transform ourselves and our communities into something other than the body of Christ.

There is an incredible tendency in the offering of our presence to another person, a tendency to be surprised by what they are capable of doing for us. We often find that just when we think that it is we who are offering hospitality by welcoming them into our presence, it is in fact they who are being hospitable. John Koenig points out that this reversal is present in the narratives of the New Testament:

> In many of the encounters with strangers recorded by our New Testament witnesses the roles of guest and host tend to reverse themselves or break down altogether. This potential for fluidity is contained within the Greek language itself, for the noun *xenos* denotes simultaneously a guest, a host, or a stranger, while the verb *xenizeion* means "receive as a guest" but also "surprise" and hence "present someone or something as strange." Correspondingly, *philoxenia*, the term used for hospitality in the New Testament, refers literally not to a love of strangers *per se* but to a delight in the whole guest-host relationship, in the mysterious reversals and gains for all parties which may take place.[120]

It is here, finally, in this surprising reversal, that we discover the impossibility of distinguishing radically between caregiver and the person cared for. The relationship is not so objective as to be able to make that distinction; it is organic, in that it becomes for all concerned a purely natural expression of membership in the body. In this sense the first step of acquiring virtue is in fact, as both Aristotle and Aquinas suggest, a matter of taking time to act virtuous. For when we make time to be with the sick, we find that we are trained, like the assistants working in the L'Arche communities, to live differently. As Vanier explains:

> Things have to go at a pace which can welcome their least expression. . . . So the assistants have to be the more attentive to the many non-verbal communications, and this adds greatly to their ability to welcome the whole person. They become increasingly people of welcome and compassion. The slower rhythm and even the presence of the handicapped people makes me slow down, switch off my efficiency motor, rest and recognize the presence of God. The poorest people have an extraordinary power to heal the wounds in our hearts. If we welcome them, they nourish us.[121]

*Hospitality and Presence Exemplified: Caring for Mary Ann.*   In order to display examples of hospitality and presence, I return now to my earlier conversation with the life of Flannery O'Connor. I want to look carefully at a particular episode in that life—a story within her story, if you will—one through which she discovered herself amazingly transformed by a group of people possessed of these skills.

In the spring of 1960 O'Connor received a letter from a community of Dominican nuns in nearby Atlanta. Their vocation, she learned, was to provide care for terminally ill cancer patients who could not afford other, more conventional options. The occasion of the letter was a somewhat strange one: The sisters wanted O'Connor to write a book, possibly a novel, about one of their former patients, a recently dead twelve-year-old girl named Mary Ann whose story, they believed, bore telling.[122]

O'Connor's initial reaction to the request was skeptical. She had reservations about the literary merits of the project itself and especially about the notion that she should write it. Her initial temptation seems to have been to refuse the request, although her resolve in that direction was not especially strong.[123] In an April letter to one of her close friends she expressed her general skepticism toward the project; at the same time, however, she noted that there was something compelling about the idea. "What interests me in it," she explains, "is simply the mystery, the agony that is given in strange ways to children."[124]

In the end, O'Connor declined the request to author the book but did agree to edit a memoir if the nuns were inclined to write one. One of the things that seems to have swayed her was the impression she obtained of the girl by looking at a photograph the sisters had enclosed:

> It showed a little girl in her First Communion dress and veil. She was sitting on a bench, holding something I could not make out. Her small face was straight and bright on one side. The other side was protuberant, the eye was bandaged, the nose and mouth crowded slightly out of place. The child looked out at her observer with an obvious happiness and composure. I continued to gaze at the picture long after I had thought to be finished with it.[125]

The story of the book's writing and publication is from that point fairly unremarkable. A manuscript was, to O'Connor's surprise, eventually produced, edited, and finally published.[126] From a literary standpoint, she remarks, it was not especially well done, having "everything about the writing to make the professional writer groan."[127] At the same time, however, the whole process seemed to have had a considerable impact on Flannery O'Connor herself, as she found her life increasingly connected to the lives of the sisters and their patients. One of the things she had previously known about the order was that they were founded by the daughter of Nathaniel Hawthorne. As she found herself increasingly drawn into reading Hawthorne's work, she began to discover surprising connections between his story and her own. Hawthorne, it seems, understood and conveyed to his daughter through his writing something about what it meant to be with the sick, especially that it was a chore that frequently tested the limits of the caregiver's capacity for charity but that must nonetheless be embraced.

> In *Our Old Home*, Hawthorne tells about a fastidious gentleman who, while going through a Liverpool workhouse, was followed by a wretched and rheumy child, so awful-looking that he could not decide what sex it was. The child followed him about until it decided to put itself in front of him in a mute appeal to be held. The fastidious gentleman, after a pause that was significant for himself, picked it up and held it. Hawthorne comments upon this: "Nevertheless, it could be no easy thing for him to do, he being a person burdened with more than an Englishman's customary reserve, shy of actual human beings, afflicted with a peculiar distaste for whatever was ugly, and, furthermore, accustomed to that habit of observation from an insulated standpoint which is said (but I hope erroneously) to have the tendency of putting ice in the blood."[128]

O'Connor goes on to explain that this fictional account had its basis in facts that Hawthorne did not include in *Our Old Home*. It turns out that Hawthorne, as his family discovered when his personal notebooks were published after his death, had undergone an experience remarkably similar to that of the "fastidious gentleman" in his fictional work. Of that factual episode, Hawthorne remarked that it "was as if God had promised the child this favor on my behalf, and that I must needs fulfill the contract. . . . I should never have forgiven myself," his journal entry concludes, "if I had repelled its advances."[129]

The effect of her father's account of this incident on Rose Hawthorne was so profound that she once said that these "were the greatest words her father ever wrote."[130] The truth of this claim is borne out by the way she spent her life. "She discovered," O'Connor writes, "much that he sought, and fulfilled in a practical way the hidden desires of his life. The ice in the blood which he feared, and which this very fear preserved him from, was turned by her into a warmth which initiated action. . . . She charged ahead, secure in the path his truthfulness had outlined for her."[131]

O'Connor's introduction to the book crafted by the nuns seems less concerned with the story of Mary Ann's remarkable life and death than it is with the Sisters who cared for her and in that caring made her life and her death possible by their own "warmth which initiated action":

> She and the Sisters who had taught her had fashioned from her unfinished face the material of her death. The creative action of the Christian's life is to prepare his death in Christ. It is a continuous action in which this world's goods are utilized to the fullest, both positive gifts and what Pere Teilhard de Chardin calls "passive diminishments." Mary Ann's diminishment was extreme, but she was equipped by natural intelligence and by a suitable education, not simply to endure it, but to build upon it. She was an extraordinarily rich little girl.[132]

What Flannery O'Connor finally discovered was that she shared with the Sisters, albeit in a very different fashion, the vocation of being surrounded by and embracing the grotesque, a discovery essential to those who would welcome and be with the sick and dying:

> This opened up for me also a new perspective on the grotesque. Most of us have learned to be dispassionate about evil, to look it in the face and find, as often as not, our own grinning reflections with which we do not argue, but good is another matter. Few have stared at that long enough to accept the fact that its face too is grotesque, that in us the good is something under construction. The modes of evil usually receive worthy expression. The modes of good have to be satisfied with a cliché or a smoothing-down that will often soften their real look. When we look into the face of good, we are liable to see a face like Mary Ann's, full of promise.[133]

Her point here is that the way we are driven in this world to understand what is good—that is, what we should desire for ourselves and for others—is a sanitized and often dangerously empty substitute for the real thing. When confronted with a face—with a body—like Mary Ann's, we are driven to ask why that face exists and what might be done to keep others like it from existing in the future, rather than to be with that face and to do the hard work of cherishing it and learning from it and making it part of our lives. The question of whether faces such as Mary Anne's should be welcomed and embraced in the name of Christ or eliminated in the name of relieving suffering, O'Connor believes, is at root a theological one. The latter alternative translates, she suggests, into the tendency of this age "to use the suffering of children to discredit the goodness of God, and once you have discredited his goodness, you are done with him."[134] Having dispensed with God, suggests O'Connor, we think of ourselves as free to get serious about eliminating the evil represented by broken bodies like Mary Ann's, to engage in what O'Connor names "cutting down on human imperfection." What we fail to realize, however, is that in our efforts we "are making headway also on the raw material of the good." Care for the sake of care is thus marginalized as a proper *telos* of medicine. We continue to feel sorry for those with incurable illnesses or horrific deformities, but we frame those sentiments in language that is firmly oriented toward a future in which such feelings will be unnecessary because such deformities will have been eliminated. And of such a future, O'Connor had this to say:

> In this popular pity, we mark our gain in sensibility and our loss in vision. If other ages felt less, they saw more, even though they saw with the blind, prophetical, unsentimental eye of acceptance, which is to say, of faith. In the absence of this faith now, we govern by tenderness. It is a tenderness which, long since cut off from the person of Christ, is wrapped in theory. When tenderness is detached from the source of tenderness, its logical outcome is terror. It ends in forced-labor camps and in the fumes of the gas chamber.[135]

The lesson O'Connor would have us learn from the story of Mary Anne is that we may avoid the horror of such a tenderness only as we develop the virtues requisite to being with the sick and the dying—no matter how grotesque they may appear to us. "The action by which charity grows invisibly among us," she says, "entwining the living and the dead, is called by the Church the Communion of Saints. It is a communion created upon human imperfection, created from what we make of our grotesque state."[136]

## *Healing: A Virtue for Vocational Caregivers*

Most of what I have written to this point has purposely resisted the dominant working assumption of modern bioethics, which is that the discipline of bioethics ought to be concerned first and foremost with helping professional caregivers make morally difficult decisions on behalf of their patients. I have suggested, to the contrary, that morally well-formed patients who are part of strong, supportive communities will in many cases render the specialist-decisionist model of bioethics irrelevant. My assumption of that position should not be taken, however, as an indication that the moral disposition of the vocational caregiver—whether she is a physician, a nurse, or a therapist—is incidental to the care of the sick and the dying. In the ideal context I have tried to envision here, the skills and the character of the vocational caregiver are just as important to the caregiving enterprise as are the dispositions of the patient and her community. In fact, the character and actions of the caregiver and of the patient cannot and should not be separated, a position toward which I have been moving from the beginning. For surely the professional who cares for the sick as a vocation, ought to possess at least the same kinds of virtues as those who offer care as a part of their daily lives.

The more specific questions to be engaged here are, "What sort of people should become—or be permitted to become—vocational caregivers, and what kinds of care are morally appropriate for them to offer to their patients?"[137] These are of course questions that modern biomedicine has been reluctant to ask in any detail, inasmuch as that discipline prefers to think of itself as an enterprise whose authority lies more in its allegedly value-neutral expertise than in its inherently moral practices of caring.[138] Yet, if what I have said about the relationship between character, social practices, and moral action is at all true, these are questions that remain central to the entire enterprise of moral medicine. Let me now engage them through the particular lens of the Christian practice of healing.

*Healing in the Christian Tradition.*   Because Christians have always understood our bodies to be good and essential to our existence, we have also always understood sickness and death to be relative deprivations of good, and health and life to be relative goods. Therefore Christianity has always been concerned with healing the sick and has always understood that healing, in whatever form, to be a gift from God and a demonstration of God's compassionate, redemptive concern for creation.[139]

Christian accounts of healing are rooted in the example of Jesus, whose miracles of healing, as Karen Westerfield-Tucker reminds us, were understood by the New Testament authors to "witness to his identity as Messiah and proclaim, as effective signs, the advent of the new age (e.g., Matt. 9:35; 11:4–5; Luke 11:20; John 20:31)."[140] As the manifest presence of the new age of God's reign, Jesus was the incarnation of God's compassion toward all of creation and especially toward women and men. Matthew 9:35–36 suggests, as part of a discourse that links Jesus' ministry of healing directly to the proclamation of the gospel of the kingdom, that *compassion (splanchnizomai)*, the ability to feel the sufferings of another at the deepest level, was at the center of Jesus' ministry: "Then Jesus went about all the cities and villages, teaching in their synagogues and proclaiming the good news of the kingdom, and curing every disease and every sickness. When he saw the crowds, he had compassion for them, because they were harassed and helpless, like sheep without a shepherd."

The Christian tradition embodied in the liturgical life of the church often has seen healing, like the rest of God's redemptive activity in creation, as mediated materially through the agency of other persons. In his enumeration of some of the many gifts that contribute to the integrity of the Body in 1 Corinthians 12:28, Paul suggests that there are likely to be in the body of Christ members who have been graced with this gift and who are expected to exercise it for the common good of building up the Church's witness to the goodness and the redemptive power of God.

The healing practices of the church have typically centered around the exhortation found in James 5:14–16, which reads:

> Are any among you sick? They should call for the elders of the church and have them pray over them, anointing them with oil in the name of the Lord. The prayer of faith will save the sick, and the Lord will raise them up; and anyone who has committed sins will be forgiven. Therefore confess your sins to one another, and pray for one another, so that you may be healed. The prayer of the righteous is effective and powerful.[141]

Ritualized liturgical services of healing based on this text have typically included not only prayer but also, in keeping with the admonition of the Scriptures, the laying on of hands and the application of consecrated oil or some other medium representative of God's capacity and willingness to effect healing.[142] The prayer for the blessing of the oil in the earliest church was offered, according to Westerfield-Tucker, "immediately after the eucharistic prayer and indicates that the oil could be used internally or externally for the benefit of strength and health."[143] The proximity of the consecration of oil to the Eucharist is evocative of a sense that the health of the body of the Christian is finally inseparable from the health of the body of Christ, that the Christian's physical health and the common good of the community are intertwined.

From the earliest days of the church, liturgical practices of healing have belonged to an entire family of "corporal works of mercy" through which Christians have offered care of various sorts to both members and strangers with various physical and material needs. The inclusion of these liturgical practices within a broad understanding of care suggests that there should exist no sharp discontinuity between divine healing and medical healing.[144] Indeed, a theology of these liturgical practices of healing offers valuable insight into how one might answer questions about the character of vocational caregivers and the appropriateness of the various modalities of care they might offer. That the liturgy has frequently centered around a certain kind of person recognized by the community (an elder or a deacon or perhaps one having the gift of healing), who applies a certain substance with a certain kind of touch (consecrated oil with the laying on of hands or the signing of the cross on the forehead), is an interesting place to start a theological engagement with the techniques and practices of modern biomedicine.[145] To begin such an engagement here enables us to think analogously about what kinds of persons and what sorts of actions are appropriate to the moral practice of medicine.

*Healers and Healing.* It should be impossible to separate the moral disposition of the caregiver from the kinds of care she offers her patients. Technical proficiency is of course highly important, but that proficiency may not be separated from considered judgments as to whether or not some technique or another is *morally* appropriate, either in general or in a particular case. To make this claim is simply a specific way of saying that virtues are learned in and through community, that there is a unity of the virtues, that intellect and morality are linked by the virtue of prudence, and that technical proficiency in the absence of a well-developed character may be a dangerous thing indeed.

The vocational caregiver must possess first of all the capacity for compassion, the sense of somehow belonging to the patient and of sharing her concerns, her fears, and her expectations.[146] The significance of compassion suggests that medical care is at its best when caregiver and patient share a common life, at least in some way. However, there is a legitimate question as to whether this is any longer a possibility in the modern world. Wendell Berry states this question especially well when he asks: "How can adequate medical and health care, including disease prevention, be included in the structure and economy of a community? How, for example, can a community and its doctors be included in the same culture, the same knowledge, and the same fate, so that they will live as fellow citizens, sharing in a common wealth, members of one another?"[147]

By "community," Berry seems to mean first of all a group of people living in geographical proximity and economic interdependence with one another; the presumption is that such people will share a tradition-based, common way of life in which they will hold certain substantive goods in common. This is a splendid ideal, of course, but one that is becoming increasingly rare in the modern world. In the absence of such day-to-day geographic proximity and economic interdependence, I am suggesting that a shared faith, a shared baptism, and shared liturgical practices all serve to provide bases from which a satisfying answer might be given to Berry's question. Having these things in common *first of all* provides a means by which the kinds of physical and economic interdependence he seeks may eventually be achieved.

A Christian physician of course cannot and should not presume that her faith is shared by her patients, nor should she insist that this be the case. Regardless of the *patient's* belief—or lack thereof—the care offered by the Christian physician must be offered compassionately, meaning that it will be animated and guided by the virtue of *charity*.[148] Charity in caring vocationally for the sick consists neither in sentimentality nor in niceness, but in respect and hospitality—in the caregiver's welcoming of the patient into her world and in her willingness to enter into the patient's world in such a way that the patient becomes a meaningful partner in the caregiving enterprise. Charitable care takes time, time to listen to and even to learn from the patient; it allows, in other words, for the possibility that as the patient narrates her life and her illness, the physician, as well as the patient, will be transformed into someone better than they previously were.

If a physician or other caregiver wants to offer charitable care, she must be made to understand that such care may be offered only in an environment that allows the patient to be present as a moral agent. This may mean either that the primary locus of medical care must be relocated away from the hospital or medical center, or that the hospital or medical center must be radically reconceived and transformed into a place where expertise and technique are continuously made subordinate to charity. Berry articulates this need for reconception as he recalls the circumstances of his brother's recent hospitalization for coronary bypass surgery:

> In the hospital what I will call the world of love meets the world of efficiency—the world, that is, of specialization, machinery, and abstract procedure. Or rather, I should say that these two worlds come together in the hospital but do not meet. During those weeks when John was in the hospital, it seemed to me that he had come from the world of love and that the family members, neighbors, and friends who at various times were there with him came there to represent that world and to preserve his connection with it. It seemed to me that the hospital was another kind of world altogether.[149]

Where medical practice is concerned, any discussion about how efficiency—which in this case is but another name for technical expertise—
might be brought into and made subordinate to the world of charity must
deal with at least two issues, issues that I can only mention here. First, charity must confront and transform efficiency when efficiency claims that the
capitalist market and its attendant utilitarian logic are the most legitimate
vehicles for determining the particulars of care—of who receives care, and
how much, and of what kind. Here efficiency insists, employing an unapologetically utilitarian calculus, that the best care for the greatest number
will ultimately be provided if and only if the market is permitted to do its
work, if hospitals and insurance companies and medical suppliers are
owned by corporations and administered by managers whose primary
obligation is to stockholders. Care is commodified, and as a desirable commodity it consequently comes to be understood as scarce. Berry points out
that "this sort of logic is absolutely alien to the world of love. To the claim
that a certain drug or procedure would save 99 percent of all cancer patients or that a certain pollutant would be safe for 99 per cent of a population, love, unembarrassed, would respond, 'What about the one percent?'"[150]

Second, vocational care offered in charity is care that has come to terms
with the reality of death and with the intimate (albeit not necessary) connection that exists between sickness and death.[151] That so many of the in-
tractable difficulties in bioethics are located at the final margin of life is an
indication that much of contemporary biomedicine has yet to come to
terms with death. Once again Berry's response is priceless:

> And yet love must confront death, and accept it, and learn from it. Only in
> confronting death can earthly love learn its true extent, its immortality. Any
> definition of health that is not silly must include death. The world of love in-
> cludes death, suffers it, and triumphs over it. The world of efficiency is de-
> feated by death; at death, all its instruments and procedures stop. The world of
> love continues, and of this grief is the proof.[152]

Care flowing from the virtue of charity is care, finally, that understands
that knowledge and expertise and efficiency alone, though necessary, are
never sufficient. As important as they are, and as legitimate as their place is
in the contemporary practice of medicine, they are not enough.

Berry concludes his essay by relating an episode from his brother's hospitalization. As he and his brother's wife and other family members waited
impatiently to hear the results of the procedure, they were finally greeted by

two nurses who informed them that the surgery had gone well but that it had not been without its difficulties. The reports they brought disturbed Berry's sister-in-law, and the nurses sought to console her:

> The two young women attempted to reassure her, mainly by repeating things they had already said. And then there was a long moment when they just looked at her. It was such a look as parents sometimes give a sick or suffering child, when they themselves have begun to need the comfort they are trying to give.
>     And the one of the nurses said, "Do you need a hug?"
>     "Yes," Carol said.
>     And the nurse gave her a hug.
>     Which brings us to a starting place.[153]

Indeed it does. And perhaps it brings me to a place of ending, as well. For that finally may be all that can be said about the sorts of people who should become vocational caregivers—that they are the sort of people who understand that sometimes the best care is made complete by something as simple as a hug.

# AFTERWORD:
# AWAITING THE REDEMPTION
# OF OUR BODY—
# LIFE AND DEATH IN THE MEANTIME

> We know that the whole creation has been groaning in labor pains until now; and not only the creation, but we ourselves, who have the first fruits of the Spirit, groan inwardly while we wait for adoption, the redemption of our bodies. (Romans 8:22–23)

Nothing written here will be worth much to those who do not at least understand the significance of the v0irtue of patience. Much, indeed most, of what I have said in this book presupposes the importance of being willing and able to wait for the vindication of that peculiar way of life that holds, as John Yoder has said, that

> the triumph of the right, although it is assured, is sure because of the power of the resurrection and not because of any calculation of causes and effects, nor because of the inherently greater strength of the good guys. The relationship between the obedience of God's people and the triumph of God's cause is not a relationship of cause and effect but one of cross and resurrection.[1]

Yet such patience is neither passive nor self-deceptively content with the way things are. It acknowledges the reality of suffering and rests on the hope that things *will* one day be better than they now are. It simply holds that the fulfillment of that hope is in the hands of God.

In her remarkable novel, *Storming Heaven*, Denise Giardina tells the story of men and women from the mountains of Appalachia, of their lives and loves and their struggles against forces that would steal from them and destroy their lives and their land. I find *Storming Heaven* deeply moving, not simply because it is so beautifully written but also because the inhabitants of its pages are so familiar to me. The book's characters have an inexplicable love for the rugged mountain land they call home. They possess a deep sense of belonging to the land and to those with whom they share it. And they understand, partly because they live so closely with the land and with one another and partly because of the way the world has so cruelly reached out and struck them down, that any of the sweet happiness attained in this life of sadness and of sickness and death will almost certainly turn out to be fleeting and ephemeral.

Death is a constant companion to the characters in *Storming Heaven*. They forever are struggling to make sense of the suffering and the loss with which they are confronted. God is frequently evoked, not as an easy solution to a difficult problem but as a faithful partner in a seemingly unwinnable struggle. The dead in *Storming Heaven* are not content to rest in peace; their ghosts wander the once beautiful mountains, now scarred and neglected by the coal companies. Yet they wait, impatiently and restlessly and almost angrily for the last day, the day when they will, by the power of God, rise up whole, the day when the wrongs done to them and their homes will be made right. At the book's conclusion, one of the main characters thinks of her dead kinfolks as she stands before the family cemetery where her just-dead lover will soon be buried:

> I walked past the cemetery where Rondal would at last have a place of his own. The headstones did not stand in tidy rows on that slope beside Scary mountain. They were placed companionably, as people will sit together and talk—Aunt Jane beside Uncle Alec, Albion facing them under a spreading oak, Florrie's dead baby at his feet. The elements had already worn the names from the older stones and they leaned at gentle angles as though conferring with one another. Butterflies and honeybees tended the violets and sweet clover that grew over the graves. It was a tranquil place, but no one could ever imagine a quiet slumber for the dead in that earth. They are not a people made for eternal peace, and even if they were, the mountains would not let them rest. The mountains are conjurers, ancient spirits shaped by magic past time or remembered. The dead walk abroad in the shaded coves, or writhe in their graves, pushing up with strong arms and legs, waiting for the day.[2]

These words are for me evocative of another place in those same mountains, a place I visited recently on a trip back to West Virginia. On that trip I drove up a mountain hollow on a winding washboard road to visit my grandfather's Homeplace. I parked my truck alongside that road, scaled an adjacent barbed wire fence, and climbed the steep hill to the family cemetery where all my grandfather's kin are buried. And I stood there in that cemetery and imagined all of them pushing up with *their* strong arms and legs, waiting impatiently for that day, when there will be no more sickness, and no more death, and no more longing. And then, I walked back down the hill and returned to my life, taking their memory with me, and began trying again, perhaps a little more seriously, to be a faithful member of a people who will care for one another as we would care for Jesus himself as we wait for that day.

# NOTES

## Chapter 1

1. Stanley Hauerwas, "A Tale of Two Stories: On Being a Christian and a Texan," in *Christian Existence Today* (Durham, N.C.: Labyrinth, 1988), p. 29.

2. John Milbank, *Theology and Social Theory: Beyond Secular Reason* (Cambridge, Mass.: Basil Blackwell, 1990), p. 3.

3. As my preceding reference to Milbank indicates, I obviously believe that theology *does* make a difference. Yet, the direct relevance of theology to the ethical practice of medicine is hardly a foregone conclusion among moral philosophers and theologians. The majority of contemporary medical ethicists, including those with substantial theological concerns, seem to agree with James Gustafson, who said in the 1975 Pere Marquette Theology Lecture at Marquette University, published as *The Contributions of Theology to Medical Ethics* (Milwaukee, Wisc.: Marquette University Press, 1975), pp. 1–2: "A person whose primary field of interest is theology can contribute to literature about ethics and medicine without articulating the theological grounds for the arguments and judgments that are made. . . . Often to introduce theology becomes an unjustifiable reason for one's secular colleagues to discount what one might say about medical ethics."

The ongoing failure of Christian theology to provide an alternative account of medical practice is thus a significant part of what I am addressing here. In 1979, Alasdair MacIntyre issued a challenge about theology and medicine, saying: "What we ought to expect from contemporary theologians in the area of medical ethics: First—and without this everything else is uninteresting—we ought to expect a clear statement of what difference it makes to be a Jew or a Christian or a Moslem, rather than a secular thinker, in morality generally. Second . . . we need to hear a theological critique of secular morality and culture. Third, we want to be told what bearing what has been said under the two headings has on the specific problems which arise for modern medicine." See "Theology, Ethics, and the Ethics of Medicine and Health Care: Comments on Papers by Novak, Mouw, Roach, Cahill, and Hartt," *Journal of Medicine and Philosophy* 4 (1979), p. 435.

Of MacIntyre's challenge, Stanley Hauerwas and Charles Pinches remark: "Subsequent developments have made it clear that that issue did little to convince anyone that theology had or has anything distinctively important to say about these matters. MacIntyre challenges theologians to accent their differences, but in this time called modernity most theologians have attempted to downplay them. Their task has been to suggest that Christians believe pretty much what anyone would believe on reflection. For example, the call for theology to be a 'public' discourse seems carried by the urge to show that theological convictions do in fact measure up to standards of truthfulness generally recognized in liberal democratic societies. Only if theology meets these standards can Christians enter into the public arena without apology." From "Practicing Patience: How Christians Should Be Sick," in *Christians Among the Virtues*, (Notre Dame, Ind.: University of Notre Dame Press, 1997), pp. 211–212, n. 10.

4. Ivan Illich, *Medical Nemesis* (New York: Pantheon, 1976), p. 3; James P. Browder, *Elected Suffering: Toward a Theology for Medicine* (Ph.D. Dissertation at Duke University, Durham, NC, 1991), p. 8; see also, Edwin Pellegrino and David Thomasma, *A Philosophical Basis for Medical Practice* (New York: Oxford University Press, 1981), p. viii.

5. See Bryan S. Turner, *Regulating Bodies: Essays in Medical Sociology* (London: Routledge, 1992), pp. 18, 22.

6. Michael Walzer, *Spheres of Justice: A Defense of Pluralism and Equality* (New York: Basic Books, 1983), p. 87.

7. Walzer's point is well taken; however, he is wrong to assume that Christianity is unconcerned with the body or its goods, as I shall show presently. His presumptions about Christianity's view of the body are typically modern, in that they presume that the proper concerns of religion are with matters inward and eternal and, as Catherine Pickstock remarks, "detachable from a specific locus in ecclesial practices . . . compatible with any practices whatsoever." *After Writing: On the Liturgical Consummation of Philosophy* (Oxford: Blackwell, 1998), p. 154.

8. The whole notion of science as savior is amazingly complex, as Mary Midgley shows in her *Science as Salvation: A Modern Myth and Its Meaning* (New York: Routledge, 1992). My concern here is not to dismiss science or to suggest that it ought not to play a significant part in modern medical practice. Rather, I want to suggest that there has come to exist in the popular mind a broadly positivist sense that science and those practices (such as medicine) that are generally understood as "scientific" will very soon prove capable of solving the most difficult human problems.

9. Illich, *Medical Nemesis*, p. 252.

10. Ibid.

11. Gerald McKenny, *To Relieve the Human Condition: Bioethics, Technology, and the Body* (New York: SUNY Press, 1997), p. 2. McKenny refers to this imperative in modern medicine as the "Baconian project," a fit appellation, I think, given the role of Sir Francis Bacon in the modern philosophical project.

12. Eric J. Cassell, *The Nature of Suffering and the Goals of Medicine* (New York: Oxford University Press, 1991), p. vii.

13. Ibid., p. 30.

14. Illich, *Medical Nemesis*, pp. 252–253.

15. A. E. Clark-Kennedy, *The Art of Medicine in Relation to the Progress of Thought: A Lecture in the History of Science Course in the University of Cambridge* (London: Cambridge University Press, 1945), p. 44; cf. Illich, *Medical Nemesis,* pp. 45–47.

16. By "modernity" I mean to refer broadly to that constellation of political, philosophical, and scientific thought that emerged from the Enlightenment and has been institutionalized in the liberal bureaucratic state. I follow John Milbank for the most part in seeing the emergence of nominalism in the fourteenth century as being a significant force in the theological transition from medieval to modern thought; cf. Hauerwas and Pinches, "Practicing Patience," p. 210, n. 6, and McKenny, *To Relieve the Human Condition,* p. 15.

17. Alasdair MacIntyre, "Patients as Agents," in *Philosophical Medical Ethics: Its Nature and Significance,* ed. S. F. Spicker and H. T. Engelhardt (Dordrecht, Holland: D. Reidel Publishing, 1977), p. 199.

18. Alasdair MacIntyre, *After Virtue,* 2d ed. (Notre Dame, Ind.: University of Notre Dame Press, 1984), p. 6.

19. Ibid., p. 39.

20. John Rawls, "Justice as Fairness: Political Not Metaphysical," *Philosophy and Public Affairs* 14, no. 3, 1985, pp. 225, 240.

21. Ibid.

22. John Rawls, *A Theory of Justice* (Cambridge, Mass.: Belknap/Harvard University Press, 1971), pp. 92–93, emphasis mine.

23. See Illich, *Medical Nemesis,* p. 105. Avoiding death is especially important in a world where the pursuit of rational desire is the only good; one cannot pursue one's desires when one is dead.

24. See James A. Morone, "The Bureaucracy Empowered," in *The Politics of Health Care Reform: Lessons from the Past, Prospects for the Future,* ed. James Morone and Gary Belkin (Durham, N.C.: Duke University Press, 1994), pp. 148–164.

25. See Alasdair MacIntyre, "Medicine Aimed at the Care of Persons Rather Than What . . . ?" in Spicker and Engelhardt, *Philosophical Medical Ethics,* pp. 84–89.

26. See Susan Reverby and David Rosner, "Beyond the Great Doctors," in *Health Care in America: Essays in Social History* (Philadelphia: Temple University Press, 1979), pp. 3–16.

27. Gert Brieger, "The Historiography of Medicine," in *Companion Encyclopedia to the History of Medicine,* ed. Roy Porter and W. F. Bynum (New York: Routledge, 1993), p. 25.

28. Deborah Lupton, *Medicine as Culture: Illness, Disease and the Body in Western Societies* (London: Sage, 1994), p. 78.

29. Browder, *Elected Suffering,* p. 30; cf. S. I. M. Du Plessis, "Comte's Sociological Intent," in *The Compatibility of Science and Philosophy in France: 1840–1940*

(Cape Town, A. A. Balkema, 1972), p. 237, and Frederick Coppleston, *A History of Philosophy,* vol. 9, *Maine de Biran to Sartre* (New York: Doubleday, 1974), pp. 74f.

30. Coppleston, *A History of Philosophy,* p. 90, quoting Comte's *Cours de philosophie positive,* 2d ed. (Paris: 1864), vol. 1, p. 16.

31. Browder, *Elected Suffering,* p. 33.

32. Ibid., pp. 48, 50.

33. Henry E. Sigerist, *The Great Doctors: A Biographic History of Medicine* (Garden City, N.Y.: Doubleday, 1958), p. 387, italics mine.

34. Iago Galdston, *The Social and Historical Foundations of Modern Medicine* (New York: Bruner/Mazel, 1981), p. 5.

35. See Reverby and Rosner, "Beyond the Great Doctors," p. 5. The authors suggest that science has become the "dominant ideology and material base of medicine."

36. Clark-Kennedy, *The Art of Medicine,* p. 6.

37. Erwin H. Ackerknecht, *A Short History of Medicine* (Baltimore: Johns Hopkins Press, 1982), p. 170.

38. Ibid., pp. 79f., 103–104.

39. Ibid., p. 233. Iago Galdston notes: "Unquestionable, medicine has made great progress during the past two hundred years, to take an arbitrary period. It has gained enormously in precise knowledge. In many respects, both informationally and technically, it has become more exact. But that doesn't make it an exact science"; see *The Social and Historical Foundations of Modern Medicine,* p. 5.

40. Sherwin W. Nuland, *Doctors: The Biography of Medicine,* (New York: Vintage Books, 1988), pp. xx, 136. In all fairness to Nuland, his more recent book *How We Die* (New York: Alfred A. Knopf, 1993) is a good deal less scientistic; he says, for example that: "Between the lines of this book lies an unspoken plea for the resurrection of the family doctor. Each one of us needs a guide who knows *us* as well as he knows the pathways by which we can approach death" (p. 266). I find Nuland's plea quite appealing, albeit, given his earlier work, a bit naive; the restoration of the family physician would require nothing less than a social and cultural revolution in which the expectations placed on physicians by the public and the expectations physicians place on themselves and on their patients were altered significantly. Then again, it is arguably that sort of revolution that I propose in Chapter 4.

41. See Peter E. S. Freund and Meredith B. McGuire, *Health, Illness, and the Social Body: A Critical Sociology,* (Englewood Cliffs, N.J.: Prentice-Hall, 1991), pp. 5–6. The authors explain that *all* descriptions, including medical descriptions, are social constructions in the sense that some information is included in them and others is not. This point will be developed in considerably more depth below.

42. Illich, *Medical Nemesis,* p. 166.

43. Brieger notes on this point: "We can readily agree that by viewing disease and medicine as a whole, as socially constructed, we are widening our gaze upon the

development of medical knowledge and medical practices, but to claim, as François Delaporte does, that disease does not exist, and that what does exist is only practices, is to deny too much"; see "The Historiography of Medicine," p. 30; cf. Alasdair MacIntyre, *Whose Justice? Which Rationality?* (Notre Dame, Ind.: University of Notre Dame Press, 1988), p. 350. MacIntyre explains that this is the case for all discourse, saying that there is "no standing ground, no place for enquiry, no way to engage the practices of advancing, evaluating, accepting and rejecting reasoned argument apart from that which is provided by some particular tradition or another."

44. MacIntyre, *Whose Justice? Which Rationality?*, p. 350.

45. This does *not* mean, however, that critical rigor should be abandoned or that all accounts of the body must be regarded as equally truthful. Allowing for more than one true description does not necessarily open the door to a relativism in which *every* description must be regarded as equally true. MacIntyre deals quite well with this point in an interview in *Cogito 5*, no. 2 (1991), pp. 67–73.

46. Freund and McGuire, *Health, Illness, and the Social Body*, pp. 218–229. The five assumptions of the biomedical model identified are mind-body dualism, physical reductionism, specific etiology, the machine metaphor, and the body as an object of regimen and control.

47. Ibid., p. 226.

48. See, for example, Owen Flanagan, *The Science of the Mind* (Cambridge, Mass.: MIT Press, 1991), p. 1. Drew Leder, approaching the Cartesian problem from a phenomenological perspective, makes an interesting observation about the rather commonsensical nature of Cartesian dualism in his book, *The Absent Body* (Chicago: University of Chicago Press, 1990), where he says: "Far from being indigenous just to modern society, a certain telos toward disembodiment is an abiding strain of Western intellectual history. . . . The body has frequently been relegated to a secondary or oppositional role, while an incorporeal reason is valorized. . . . It is often assumed that this dualist paradigm is shaped by ontological commitments at the expense of attending to lived experience. However, I will argue against this view. I will suggest that experience plays a crucial role in encouraging and supporting Cartesian dualism. Specifically, I refer to experiences of bodily *absence*" (p. 3, italics original). Freund and McGuire make a complimentary point in their treatment of dualism and its influence on medical practice. Drawing on the work of Michel Foucault, they suggest that dualism in medicine has its *philosophical* roots in Cartesian thinking, but its *clinical* roots in the rise of clinical observation and pathological anatomy in medical practice in the eighteenth and nineteenth centuries; see *Health, Illness, and the Social Body*, p. 226.

49. René Descartes, *Discourse on Method and the Meditations*, trans. F. E. Suttcliffe (New York: Penguin, 1968), pp. 41, 43, 53–60.

50. Flanagan, *The Science of the Mind*, p. 9. Browder shows nicely how Cartesian doubt became a central tenet of the experimental medicine of Claude Bernard; see *Elected Suffering*, pp. 66–68, 87. His association of Bernard's method with that

of Descartes is consistent with W. M. Simon's article on Bernard in *The Encyclopedia of Philosophy*, ed. Paul Edwards (New York: Macmillan, 1967), vol. 1, p. 304.

51. Flanagan, *The Science of the Mind*, p. 7. Sarah Coakley points out that Descartes' later work is a good deal more nuanced than this, in that it does express some appreciation of the difficulties of a mind-body dualism: "Visions of the Self in Late Medieval Christianity: Some Cross Disciplinary Reflections" in *The Special Nature of Women?* (Special issue of *Concilium, vol.6)*, ed. Anne Carr and Elizabeth Schussler Fiorenza (Philadelphia: Trinity Press International, 1991), pp. 93–94. I am grateful to Stanley Hauerwas for bringing this article to my attention.

52. Immanuel Kant, *Foundations of the Metaphysics of Morals*, trans. Lewis Beck White (New York: Macmillan, 1989), p. 49.

53. MacIntyre, "Medicine Aimed at the Care of Persons," p. 90.

54. See Flanagan, *The Science of the Mind*, pp. 4, 11.

55. MacIntyre, "Medicine Aimed at the Care of Persons," p. 89.

56. See Freund and McGuire, *Health, Illness, and the Social Body*, p. 227.

57. Illich, *Medical Nemesis*, p. 160.

58. See MacIntyre, "Medicine Aimed at the Care of Persons," p. 90.

59. Arthur Kleinman, *The Illness Narratives: Suffering, Healing, and the Human Condition* (New York: Basic Books, 1988), pp. 130–131; cf. Freund and McGuire, *Health, Illness, and the Social Body*, pp. 154–155, and Rick Carlson, *The End of Medicine* (New York: John Wiley and Sons, 1975), p. 210, both of whom make these sorts of distinctions between the relatively active category "illness" and the more passive category "disease."

60. Kleinman, *The Illness Narratives*, pp. 132–134, first and third emphases mine. Kleinman says of the written record of this interaction, which is concerned only with Mrs. Flower's disease: "Gone from the record is Melissa Flowers as a sick person under great social pressure, worried and demoralized by difficult family problems."

61. Ibid., pp. 134–135.

62. Arthur Frank, *At the Will of the Body: Reflections on Illness* (Boston: Houghton Mifflin, 1991), pp. 50–51.

63. Bryan Turner remarks: "We can talk about having a body, being a body, and doing a body"; see *Regulating Bodies*, p. 16. I find this way of speaking about the experience of embodied living helpful, although, as I will show presently, not sufficient.

64. Frank, *At the Will of the Body*, pp. 8, 12. Illich makes a similar point, saying that this way of conceiving medicine is tantamount to "an idolatry of science" that "overlooks the fact that research conducted as if medicine were ordinary science, diagnosis conducted as if patients were specific cases and not autonomous persons, and therapy conducted by hygienic engineers are the three approaches which coalesce into the present endemic health-denial"; see *Medical Nemesis*, 252.

65. Turner, *Regulating Bodies*, p. 170.

66. Michael Polanyi, *The Tacit Dimension* (Gloucester, Mass.: Peter Smith, 1983), p. 29.

67. Descartes, p. 54.

68. Freund and McGuire, *Health, Illness, and the Social Body*, pp. 3–4.

69. Wendell Berry, "Health Is Membership," in *Another Turn of the Crank* (Washington, D.C.: Counterpoint, 1995), p. 89.

70. Freund and McGuire, *Health, Illness, and the Social Body*, p. 3.

71. Berry, "Health Is Membership," p. 88.

72. Ibid., p. 94.

73. Ibid., pp. 94–95.

74. Ibid.

75. Illich, *Medical Nemesis*, pp. 253f.

76. Lester King, *The Growth of Medical Thought* (Chicago, University of Chicago Press, 1963), p. 233.

77. For an excellent historical treatment of this transition, one to which I refer extensively below, see Michel Foucault, *The Order of Things* (New York: Vintage Books, 1973).

78. Robert James Hankinson, "The Growth of Medical Empiricism" in *Knowledge and the Scholarly Medical Traditions*, ed. Don Bates (Cambridge: Cambridge University Press, 1995), p. 61.

79. Ibid., p. 62.

80. Ibid., p. 69.

81. Galdston, *The Social and Historical Foundations of Modern Medicine*, p. 7.

82. Ibid., p. 19.

83. Ibid., pp. 31–32.

84. Milbank, *Theology and Social Theory*, p. 12.

85. Not insignificantly, as I shall show in the next section, this control of the *factum* extends especially to the control of the human body.

86. Milbank, *Theology and Social Theory*, p. 14.

87. See Milbank, *Theology and Social Theory*, pp. 20–22. Not insignificantly for the work of this book, Milbank explains that the voluntarism of the nominalists and Renaissance thinkers (including both the theologically heterodox Hobbes and the neo-pagan Machiavelli) was embodied and sustained in both spheres. He notes that "the Machiavellian secular . . . came to exist as the discovery of a new sort of *virtù* which could not be reconciled with the Christian virtues. If the Hobbesian field of power seems to be constructed by a perverse theology, then the Machiavellian field of power is constructed by a partial rejection of Christianity and appeal to an alternative *mythos*" (p. 21).

88. Paolo Rossi, *Francis Bacon: From Magic to Science*, trans. Sacha Rabinovitch, (Chicago: University of Chicago Press, 1968), pp. 1–35.

89. Ibid., p. 21, italics mine.

90. Galdston, *The Social and Historical Foundations of Modern Medicine*, p. 32; cf. Rossi, *Francis Bacon*, p. 36. My account of Bacon's work in what follows is heavily dependent on both Galdston and Rossi and is based on two factors: First,

Galdston places Bacon's work in a specifically *medical* context; that is, he shows how Bacon's thinking about the place of humans in their world and the purpose of their work has been assumed by modern medicine. Second, Rossi shows how Bacon's work is derivative in part from the nominalists, who suggested, as I've mentioned above, that what makes us human is our ability to exert our individual, autonomous will.

91. Rossi, *Francis Bacon,* p. 37.

92. Ibid.

93. Max Horkheimer and Theodor Adorno, *Dialectic of Enlightenment* (New York: Continuum, 1997), p. 3.

94. Rossi, *Francis Bacon,* p. 38. Rossi sees in Bacon's abandonment of "the rubbish and bother of the schoolmen" the development of a "logic of facts similar to the logic of those philosophers of the Enlightenment who were to see in Bacon their master" (p. 38). Charles Taylor, in *Sources of the Self* (Cambridge, Mass.: Harvard University Press, 1989), pp. 230–231, shows how Bacon's program was taken up and advanced beginning in the 1640s by the Puritans, who shared with Bacon a disdain for traditional authority combined with a desire to put philosophy to work making better the human estate.

95. See Rossi, *Francis Bacon,* p. 68. Rossi explains that Bacon saw Aristotle and his medieval appropriators as the principal enemies of the new philosophy. Bacon believed that "Aristotle's fruitless philosophy is the main obstacle to man's regaining of the prelapsarian bliss and control of the universe"; see *Francis Bacon,* p. 128.

96. Galdston, *The Social and Historical Foundations of Modern Medicine,* p. 21.

97. Berry, "Health Is Membership," p. 96.

98. See Milbank, *Theology and Social Theory,* p. 13.

99. Wendell Berry, *What Are People For?* (New York: North Point Press, 1990), p. 125.

100. MacIntyre, in *After Virtue,* pp. 6–35, shows how ethical "emotivism" is the product of that modern thinking that separates facts from values.

101. Ibid., p. 82. MacIntyre goes on to say of this division: "'Fact' becomes value-free, 'is' becomes a stranger to 'ought' and explanation, as well as evaluation, changes its character as a result of the divorce between 'is' and 'ought'" (p. 84).

102. Ibid., p. 58.

103. Ibid.

104. Ibid., p. 52.

105. Michael Polanyi, "Scientific Outlook: Its Sickness and Cure," *Science* 125 (March, 1957), p. 481.

106. Polanyi, *The Tacit Dimension,* p. 20.

107. Ibid., p. 4.

108. Polanyi, "Scientific Outlook," p. 482; cf. *Tacit Dimension,* p. 36: "Accordingly, the operations of a higher level cannot be accounted for by the laws governing its particulars forming the lower level. You cannot derive a vocabulary from pho-

netics; you cannot derive the grammar of a language from its vocabulary; a correct use of grammar does not account for good style; and a good style does not provide the content of a piece of prose. We may conclude then quite generally . . . that it is impossible to represent the organizing principles of a higher level by the laws governing its isolated particulars."

109. Polanyi, *Tacit Dimension*, p. 33.

110. MacIntyre, *After Virtue*, pp. 58–59.

111. See McKenny, *To Relieve the Human Condition*, p. 4.

112. Ibid., p. 33.

113. A classical contemporary statement of this position is Robert Nozick, *Anarchy, State, and Utopia* (New York: Harper Collins, 1974).

114. The classical expression of this view is, of course, Rawls, *A Theory of Justice*.

115. MacIntyre, *After Virtue*, p. 71.

116. Freund and McGuire, *Health, Illness, and the Social Body*, p. 228, italics mine.

117. For Foucault on this point see, *The Order of Things*, pp. 308, 312. I owe this way of putting this transition and the status of the subject in modernity to Romand Coles; see in particular, Romand Coles, *Self/Power/Other: Political Theory and Dialogical Ethics*. (Ithaca: Cornell University Press, 1992), p. 68. Note, Foucault uses the masculine "man" here; I shall henceforth use the more inclusive "human" or "modern subject" in its place, except where quoting directly.

118. Coles, *Self/Power/Other*, p. 68, italics mine.

119. Foucault, *The Order of Things*, p. 313.

120. Ibid., p. 315.

121. Ibid., p. 317.

122. Ibid., p. 319.

123. Ibid., p. 320, italics mine.

124. Ibid., p. 322.

125. Ibid., p. 324, italics mine.

126. Ibid., pp. 324–325.

127. Ibid., p. 328; cf. Coles, *Self/Power/Other*, p. 70.

128. Horkheimer and Adorno, *Dialectic of Enlightenment*, pp. 4–5.

129. Coles, *Self/Power/Other*, p. 70.

130. Ibid., pp. 70–71; Coles claims that this is the "*fundamental trajectory*" of modern thinking. Foucault, *Order of Things*, p. 328.

131. Coles, *Self/Power/Other*, p. 71. I owe the choice of the word "frenetic" to Coles.

132. See Foucault, *Order of Things*, p. 342. I am grateful to Romand Coles for this way of putting this matter. He reminds me that it is Nietzsche's point that the modern awareness of the "death of God" (who was executed by Kant!) makes the sovereignty of modern man an infrequently recognized impossibility.

133. MacIntyre, *After Virtue*, p. 68.

134. Ibid., p. 71.

135. Ibid.

136. Ibid., pp. 74–75; 84–87.

137. Michel Foucault, "Two Lectures," in *Power/Knowledge: Selected Interviews and Other Writings, 1972–1977*, ed. Colin Gordon and trans. Colin Gordon, Leo Marshall, John Mepham, Kate Soper (New York: Pantheon, 1980), p. 105.

138. Ibid., p. 106.

139. Ibid. Foucault notes here that individual right and corporate discipline are "heterogeneous. . . [and] cannot possibly be reduced to each other."

140. Michel Foucault, *The History of Sexuality*, vol. 1, *An Introduction*, trans. Robert Hurley (New York: Random House/Vintage, 1978/1990), pp. 94–95.

141. Foucault, "Body/Power" in *Power/Knowledge*, p. 59.

142. Foucault, "Two Lectures," p. 93. It seems that in a certain way the two points of reference of which Foucault speaks here correspond to the two poles of his "analytic of finitude" in *The Order of Things*: the "rules of right" resisting and limiting the exertion of power correspond to the "transcendental" aspect of the analytic, whereas the "effects of truth" (i.e., the knowledges) produced by power correspond to the "empirical" aspect.

143. See Foucault, "Truth and Power," in *Power Knowledge*, p. 131: "Each society has its regime of truth, its 'general politics' of truth: that is, the types of discourse which it accepts and makes function as true; the mechanisms and instances which enable one to distinguish true and false statements, the means by which each is sanctioned; the techniques and procedures accorded value in the acquisition of truth; the status of those who are charged with saying what counts as true."

144. Foucault, "Two Lectures," pp. 93–94.

145. Coles, *Self/Power/Other*, p. 57.

146. Ibid., p. 60.

147. Lupton, *Medicine as Culture*. p. 104.

148. Foucault, *The History of Sexuality*, pp. 99–100.

149. Foucault, "The Eyes of Power," in *Power/Knowledge*, p. 148.

150. See Michel Foucault, *Discipline and Punish* (New York: Vintage, 1979), pp. 200f.

151. Foucault, *Discipline and Punish*, pp. 205, 214.

152. Ibid., p. 218; see also p. 183, where Foucault speaks of internalized surveillance as "the perpetual penalty that traverses all points and supervises every instant in the disciplinary institutions compares, differentiates, hierarchizes, excludes. In short, it *normalizes*."

153. Foucault, "The Subject and Power," in *Michel Foucault: Beyond Structuralism and Hermeneutics*, ed. Herbert L. Dreyfus and Paul Rabinow (Chicago: University of Chicago Press, 1982), p. 208.

154. Foucault, *Discipline and Punish*, p. 184.

155. Peter McMylor, *Alasdair MacIntyre: Critic of Modernity* (London: Routledge, 1994), pp. 129–130.

156. Ibid., p. 130; cf. p. 139, where McMylor takes this assertion to be central to MacIntyre's entire project: "our current conceptions are partly due to our market-based capitalist culture."

157. Ibid., p. 138.

158. See Foucault, "The Subject and Power," p. 209. An account of power and political economy that compliments those offered by Foucault, MacIntyre, and McMylor is offered by Anthony Giddens in *The Nation-State and Violence* (Berkeley, Calif.: University of California Press, 1987).

159. See Foucault, "The Eye of Power," pp. 88, 151–152.

160. Foucault, *The History of Sexuality*, p. 141.

161. Ibid., p. 144, italics mine.

162. Ibid.

163. See Milbank, *Theology and Social Theory*, pp. 27–45.

164. Foucault, "Truth and Power," p. 129; cf. "Body/Power," p. 62, where Foucault says that medicine is the "common denominator" in the coinciding of power and the body.

165. See Foucault, "Two Lectures," p. 107.

166. Edwin R. Dubose, *The Illusion of Trust: Toward a Medical Theological Ethics in the Postmodern Age* (Dordrecht, Holland: Kluwer Academic Publishers, 1995), p. 49.

167. See Berry, "Health Is Membership," p. 88f.

168. Dubose, *The Illusion of Trust*, p. 53.

169. This connection seems to me to be a good deal easier to show than the first. Dan Beauchamp has written about the "market prison," in which modern medicine has been incarcerated, in *The Health of the Republic: Epidemics, Medicine, and Moralism as Challenges to Democracy* (Philadelphia: Temple University Press, 1988).

170. Berry, "Health Is Membership," p. 93. A complimentary point is made by Neil Postman in his excellent book *Technopoly: The Surrender of Culture to Technology*, (New York: Vintage, 1993), pp. 102–103: "The ideas promoted by this domination of technology can be summed up as follows: Nature is an implacable enemy that can be subdued only by technical means; the problems created by technological solutions (doctors call these 'side effects') can be solved only by the further application of technology (we all know the joke about the amazing new drug that cures nothing but has interesting side effects); medical practice must focus on disease, not on the patient (which is why it is possible to say that the operation or therapy was a success but the patient died); and information coming from the patient cannot be taken as seriously as information coming from a machine, from which it follows that a doctor's judgment, based on insight and experience, is less worthwhile than the calculations of his machinery.

171. Foucault, "The Subject and Power," p. 225, italics mine.
172. Dubose, *The Illusion of Trust*, p. 61.
173. Foucault, "Two Lectures," pp. 81–85.
174. Ibid., p. 83.
175. Ibid., p. 85.
176. Foucault, "Truth and Power," p. 133.
177. Kant, *Foundations of the Metaphysics of Morals*, p. 85.
178. Horkheimer and Adorno, *Dialectic of Enlightenment*, p. 7.

## Chapter 2

1. This is not to say that knowledge is completely unnecessary for ethical conduct. In the Aristotelian sense, knowledge is in fact a kind of action. My concern here is simply not to concede too much to the modern notion that ethics is first of all about esoteric knowledge, rather than well-formed character.

2. Hence Aristotle refers in the *Nicomachean Ethics* to the etymological relationship between the Greek words *ethikos* (ethic) and *ethos* (custom); See Aristotle *Nicomachean Ethics* II.i.1. All references to this text are from the edition translated by H. Rackham (Cambridge, Mass: Harvard University Press, 1994).

3. Ibid., I.iii.7; II.i.1–8; X.ix.3–10; cf. Alasdair MacIntyre's account of Aristotle's ethics in *After Virtue*, 2d ed. (Notre Dame, Ind.: University of Notre Dame Press, 1984).

4. Aristotle *Nicomachean Ethics* X.ix.3.

5. Ibid., X.ix.11.

6. Hence Aristotle often compares becoming moral to being apprenticed into a craft. In the *Nicomachean Ethics* he refers to morality as being analogous to playing the flute, sculpting, carpentry, and shoemaking (I.vii.10–11). Alasdair MacIntyre offers an extended treatment of this notion in *Three Rival Versions of Moral Enquiry* (Notre Dame, Ind.: University of Notre Dame Press, 1990), pp. 61–63, 127ff. This is an especially significant point where medicine is concerned; as I have heard Stanley Hauerwas say many times, medical education itself is one of the few fundamentally moral enterprises remaining in modernity precisely *to the extent that it follows the master-apprentice model*. One of the profound difficulties with this, however, is the gradual erosion of the conception of medicine as a craft; another, as I shall show momentarily, is the rise of the "expert" bioethicist.

7. See Chapter 1, pp. 39f.

8. Neil Postman, *Technopoly: The Surrender of Culture to Technology* (New York: Vintage, 1993), p. 58.

9. H. Jefferson Powell explains that ours has become "a society defined by the (liberal) distinction between public and private in which it is common to describe the courts, a quintessential public institution, as the 'final interpreters' of 'our

values'"; see *The Moral Tradition of American Constitutionalism* (Durham, N.C.: Duke University Press, 1993), pp. 2, 3.

10. Stuart Hampshire, "Fallacies in Moral Philosophy," in *Revisions: Changing Perspectives in Moral Philosophy*, ed. Stanley Hauerwas and Alasdair MacIntyre (Notre Dame, Ind.: University of Notre Dame Press, 1983), p. 51 (italics original).

11. Ibid.

12. Ibid., p. 52 (italics original). The distinction between agent and judge or critic needs to be qualified. For the moral agent is in a sense always making judgments about her own actions or possible actions, and judgment itself is a form of action.

13. Ibid., p. 53.

14. Ibid.

15. Ibid., p. 58.

16. Wendell Berry, "An Argument for Diversity" in *What Are People For?* (New York: North Point Press, 1990), p. 116.

17. Ibid., pp. 116–117.

18. Erwin Ackerknecht, *A Short History of Medicine*, rev. ed. (Baltimore, Md.: Johns Hopkins Press, 1982), pp. 55–58, 63.

19. Ibid., pp. 143, 217.

20. Albert R. Jonsen, "The Birth of Bioethics," special supplement to the *Hastings Center Report* 23, no. 6 (1993), p. S1. Jonsen is admittedly ambivalent about naming the dialysis committee's appointment as the moment that modern bioethics was born. He makes reference as well to the uncovering of the Nazi doctors' work at the Nuremberg trials in 1945, to the formation of "'brain death' committees" in response to Pius XII's 1958 encyclical, to the 1954 publication of Joseph Fletcher's *Morals and Medicine*, and to the 1970 publication of Paul Ramsey's *The Patient as Person*, which he says marks the beginnings of bioethics as an academic discipline.

21. Ibid.

22. Ibid., p. S2.

23. Ibid.

24. Ibid. Daniel Callahan remarks that the mature discipline now called bioethics has chosen a middle ground between sanction and condemnation: "Instead of either going along the Joseph Fletcher route of totally blessing everything that came along, or the Paul Ramsey route of seeming to reject everything, bioethics chose a kind of middle course"; see "Why America Accepted Bioethics," special supplement to the *Hastings Center Report* 23, no. 6 (1993), p. S5.

25. Ruth Shalit, "When We Were Philosopher Kings," *The New Republic*, April 28, 1997, p. 24. I am well aware that Shalit's broadside against applied clinical ethics is neither scholarly in the traditional sense nor altogether fair. I find it nonetheless an occasionally insightful critique of certain trends in contemporary medical ethics that is well worth engaging.

26. Ibid.

27. Ibid.

28. Various forms of this problem are of course one of the significant issues in clinical ethics; I try to show this in the sections below dealing with three examples of modern clinical ethics.

29. Shalit, "When We Were Philosopher Kings," p. 27.

30. Ibid.

31. This is not to deny that there might be a role for "ethicists" but to suggest that to the extent contemporary clinical ethicists are part of the health care "system" they are also likely to be part of the problem.

32. These are of course the kinds of issues "medical ethics" is thought most frequently to deal with: difficult, "life or death" decisions.

33. David Waisel and Robert Truog, "The Cardiopulmonary Resuscitation-Not-Indicated Order: Futility Revisited," *Annals of Internal Medicine* 122, no. 4 (1995), p. 304.

34. Ibid., italics mine.

35. Ibid.

36. Shalit, "When We Were Philosopher Kings," p. 26.

37. Harmon Smith and Larry Churchill, *Professional Ethics and Primary Care Medicine: Beyond Dilemmas and Decorum* (Durham, N.C.: Duke University Press, 1986), p. 34.

38. Ibid., p. 58.

39. Ibid., p. 19.

40. Ibid., p. 61. I depend extensively upon Smith and Churchill—particularly on their critique of principalism—in the next section.

41. Tom Beauchamp and James Childress, *Principles of Biomedical Ethics* (New York: Oxford University Press, 1994), p. 3.

42. Gerald McKenny, *To Relieve the Human Condition: Bioethics, Technology, and the Body* (New York: SUNY Press, 1997), p. 11. McKenny further characterizes this shift by saying: "Now that there is such a [philosophically grounded] bioethics, religious and medical traditions can be dismissed as relics of the past, to be replaced by the application of common moral principles or casuistical techniques to these unprecedented problems" (p. 11).

43. Beauchamp and Childress, p. 3.

44. Ibid., p. 6. The authors recognize that the origins of these theories precede the twentieth century. They cite the eighteenth-century philosophers Rousseau, Hutcheson, Butler, Kant, and Hegel, and write: "An elegant and simple common-morality theory that resembles ours is William Frankena's version of Hume's postulate that the two major 'principles of morals' are beneficence and justice" (pp. 102–103).

45. Ibid., p. 100. Here the authors come quite close to the later work of Rawls discussed in Chapter 1 above.

46. Ibid., p. 10.

47. Ibid., p. 37; cf. pp. 100–104; see also, p. 23.

48. Ibid., p. 105.
49. Ibid., p. 100.
50. Ibid., p. 126.
51. Ibid.
52. Ibid., pp. 128–129.
53. Ibid., p. 121.
54. Ibid., p. 132.
55. Ibid., p. 136.
56. Ibid.
57. Ibid., p. 137.
58. Ibid., p. 163.
59. Ibid., p. 141.
60. Ibid.
61. Ibid., p. 190.
62. Ibid., p. 189.
63. Ibid., p. 193.
64. Ibid.
65. Ibid., p. 194.
66. Ibid., p. 262.
67. Ibid., p. 227.
68. Ibid., p. 235.
69. Ibid., p. 236.
70. Ibid., p. 265. Here the authors quote Michael Slote: "One has an obligation to prevent serious evil or harm when one can do so without seriously interfering with one's life plans or style and without doing any wrongs of commission"; see Michael Slote, "The Morality of Wealth," in *World Hunger and Moral Obligation,* ed. W. Aiken and H. Lafollete (Englewood Cliffs, N.J.: Prentice-Hall, 1977), p. 127.
71. By saying this arrangement would seem to work well I do not mean to imply that I necessarily find it desirable from a moral perspective. To the contrary, as I will suggest in Chapter 4, perhaps the most morally dangerous thing about the vast majority of interactions between patients and caregivers in a world that brings together remarkable technical capability and an attitude that anything may be commodified is that they are conducted without a second thought. Conflict is but a small part of ethics.
72. Here I use the term "provider" in the broadest possible sense to refer to all the persons and institutions in a culture that are involved in the provision of health care, including, but not limited to, caregivers, insurance companies and HMO's, and the assortment of local, state, and federal government agencies and NGO's that are involved in the distribution of health care.
73. Beauchamp and Childress, *Principles of Biomedical Ethics,* p. 327.
74. Ibid.
75. Ibid., p. 330.

76. Ibid.

77. Ibid., p. 348.

78. Ibid., pp. 355, 387.

79. Ibid., p. 355.

80. Ibid., p. 364.

81. Ibid., p. 362.

82. Ibid., p. 357.

83. Ibid.; see, for example, pp. 380, 382, and 384.

84. Ibid., p. 502.

85. Edmund Pellegrino and David Thomasma, *A Philosophical Basis of Medical Practice* (New York: Oxford University Press, 1981), p. 14.

86. Ibid., p. 23.

87. Ibid., p. 25. The authors are at this point exactly right. Because medicine concerns itself with the complexities of human agency, it *must*, if it is to be genuinely meaningful, be able to speak about the ends for which it is carried out.

88. Ibid., pp. 47–48.

89. Ibid., pp. 53, 63–65.

90. Ibid., p. 69.

91. Ibid., pp. 73–74.

92. Ibid., pp. 101–102. Here the authors follow Georges Canguilhem in acknowledging that "medical knowledge and craft are value-laden. Hence a critical concept such as 'normal' clearly engages the physician and philosopher in a discussion of personal, social, scientific, and cultural values. Canguilhem concludes, after a survey of positivistic leanings in medicine, that 'those who themselves tried most vigorously to give "normal" only the value of a fact have simply valorized the fact of their need for a limited meaning.'"

93. Ibid., p. 105.

94. Ibid., p. 107, italics mine. This turns out—as I show presently—to be a crucial distinction. Whether they mean to or not, in saying that the living body is "ontologically prior" to the lived body, the authors have left room for a kind of practical hegemony of science that *could*, in the right circumstances, be reduced to a simple positivism. (See note 97 below).

95. Ibid., p. 117.

96. Ibid. The authors suggest that this might point to an ethics of medicine based in a "modified natural law theory" in which "statements . . . made regarding commonalities . . . must be relativized somehow by the specificity and uniqueness of living bodies." Here I think Pellegrino and Thomasma are very close to being right; unfortunately, however, they do not in my estimation show how the relativization of which they speak might be carried out. If in fact the body is not reducible to mechanical terms, why is the practice of medicine to be based on an ontology of *living* bodies and not on an ontology of the *lived* body.

97. Ibid., p. 122. The terms "agent" and "patient" are not unimportant in the authors' treatment of this matter. They explain that medicine must "end in a decision to act for, and in behalf of, a human who seeks to be healed." Yet they also note that "the term 'patient' does not necessarily imply a passive restoration in which the physician is the sole agent" (p. 123).

98. Ibid., p. 124. On the same page, the authors say something that is a good summation of their philosophy, in that it reveals what I take to be both the strength (their concern for the irreducible moral particularity of the patient) and the weakness (their presumption of human agency as properly individualized, and perhaps even universalizable, autonomy) of their thought: "Clearly, value considerations and moral issues—for both the patient and physician—can color the selection of the facts and reasons which justify placing one diagnosis over another, the justifications accepted for taking action, and the degree to which the physician persuades or the patient assents to the final decision. The end must, therefore, be understood in all its fullness, because it projects itself so forcefully on the entire sequence."

99. Ibid., p. 125.

100. Ibid., pp. 126–132.

101. Ibid., p. 132.

102. Ibid., p. 135.

103. Ibid., p. 155.

104. This is my aim in Chapters 3 and 4.

105. Ibid., p. 166.

106. Ibid., pp. 178–181.

107. Ibid., p. 177f.

108. Ibid., p. 180.

109. Ibid., p. 181, italics original.

110. Ibid.

111. Ibid., pp. 181, 183.

112. Ibid., p. 186.

113. Max Horkheimer and Theodor Adorno, *Dialectic of Enlightenment* (New York: Continuum, 1997), p. 7.

114. H. Tristram Engelhardt, *The Foundations of Bioethics*, 2d ed. (New York: Oxford University Press, 1996), p. vii.

115. Engelhardt does not name any of these persons, but one gets the impression in reading his work that Beauchamp and Childress would be listed among them, as his discussion of the difficulty of basing bioethics on principles indicates; see pp. 102–131.

116. Ibid., p. ix.

117. Ibid.

118. What I mean when I say that Engelhardt's understanding of neutrality is skeptical will become more apparent presently. Suffice it to say that for him "neu-

trality" may mean nothing more than minimal order. For examples of political theories espousing what is perhaps a more optimistic account of moral neutrality, see Bruce Ackerman, *Social Justice in the Liberal State* (New Haven: Yale University Press, 1980), pp. 10–12, 356–371. Ackerman is a classical representative of the position that the liberal state is morally neutral. For a more pragmatic view of liberal neutrality that is in my mind closer to Engelhardt, see the later work of John Rawls: for example, *Political Liberalism* (New York: Columbia University Press, 1993).

119. Engelhardt, p. x.

120. Ibid. Engelhardt says that "the moral life is lived within two dimensions: (1) that of a secular ethics, which strives to be content-less and which thus has the ability to span numerous divergent moral communities, and (2) the particular moral communities within which one can achieve a content-full understanding of the good life and of content-full moral obligations" (p. 78).

121. Ibid., pp. 8–13, 65–67.

122. Ibid., p. 78.

123. Ibid., pp. 14–15. Engelhardt remarks: "Diversity with substance offends. To have particular beliefs over against others is to invite judgment. A canonical content-full vision has teeth . . . Even if . . . religions are tolerant in the sense of not using coercive force to constrain those who persist in their errors, they are not tolerant in the sense of viewing these matters as mere issues of personal choice or preference. They allow in the sense of not coercing, but they do not accept" (p. 14).

124. Ibid., p. 72.

125. Ibid., p. 136.

126. Ibid., p. 137.

127. Ibid., p. 138.

128. Ibid., pp. 141, 239.

129. Ibid., pp. 154–157.

130. Here Engelhardt's definition of personhood seems very close to that of Joseph Fletcher, who argues (in "Four Indicators of Humanhood—The Enquiry Matters" in *On Moral Medicine*, ed. Stephen Lammers and Allen Verhey (Grand Rapids, Mich.: Eerdmans, 1987, pp. 276, 277) "that neocortical function is the key to humanness, the essential trait, the human *sine qua non*. The point is that without the synthesizing function of the cerebral cortex (without thought or mind), whether before it is present or with its end, the person is non-existent no matter how much the individual's brain stem and mid-brain may continue to provide feelings and regulate autonomic physical functions. To be truly Homo sapiens we must be sapient, however minimally." Of Engelhardt's account of personhood, Fletcher remarks that "it is difficult, studying his language, not to believe that he gives cerebral function the determinative place, as when he says that 'for a person to be embodied and present in the world he must be conscious in it' (p. 21)."

131. Ibid., pp. 245–252.

132. Ibid., p. 239.

133. This means, for example, that those "who produced a fetus, at least within general secular morality, have the first claim on effectively determining its use." (p. 255).

134. A significant number of liberal political theorists, finding the liberal claim of moral neutrality indefensible, are willing to concede this point. Consider, for example, the work of William Galston, who argues (in "Defending Liberalism," *American Political Science Review* 76 (1982), pp. 621–629) that arguments for liberalism claiming moral neutrality are "fundamentally misguided. No form of political life can be justified without some view of what is good for individuals. In practice, liberal theorists covertly employ theories of the good." See also Charles Larmore, "Political Liberalism," *Political Theory* 18, no. 3, (August 1990), p. 341, who says that "the neutral ground on which we reason ... must continue to have some moral content." And Fletcher himself does not dodge this point, remarking: "Whether or not we ever knew in the past what man is, in the sense of having a consensus about it, we do not know now" ("Four Indicators of Humanhood," p. 275).

135. Stanley Hauerwas, who pursues this line of thinking in his discussion of Engelhardt, says that the "supervisory strategies necessary to sustain Engelhardt's peace are simply coercion called freedom"; see "Not All Peace Is Peace," in *Reading Engelhardt*, ed. Brendan Minogue et al. (Dordrecht, Holland: Kluwer Academic Publishers, 1997), p. 40.

136. Engelhardt, *Foundations*, p. 419; cf. Hauerwas, "Not All Peace Is Peace," p. 40.

137. Engelhardt, *Foundations*, p. 79.

138. MacIntyre, *After Virtue*, p. 252.

139. Engelhardt, *Foundations*, p. xi.

140. Engelhardt says that those who want more "should join a religion and be careful to choose the right one" (p. xi). But this admonition still takes choice to be the central human attribute. Whether one in fact actually "chooses" a religion is questionable, as Hauerwas points out; see "Not All Peace Is Peace," pp. 33–36.

141. Engelhardt, *Foundations*, p. xi.

142. Ezekiel Emanuel, *The Ends of Human Life* (Cambridge, Mass.: Harvard University Press, 1991), p. 7.

143. Ibid., pp. 137–138.

144. Pellegrino and Thomasma, *A Philosophical Basis of Medical Practice*, pp. 171–172. They go on to say, on the same pages: "This is particularly true of modern science and technology, to which so many turn today because of their disaffection with religion and the humanities. As a result, we seem to lack the cultural wisdom to formulate moral policy without appealing to ends so vacuous as to be unobtainable, or so specific as to be acceptable only to a few."

145. Smith and Churchill, *Professional Ethics*, p. 47.

146. Ibid., p. 56.

147. Ibid., p. 61.

148. Ibid., p. 64.

149. Ibid.

150. I take this to be the particular weakness of Emanuel's otherwise excellent book, *The Ends of Human Life*. He is justifiably critical of the liberal character of most contemporary medical ethics and health care policy and is an excellent critic of liberalism's claims to moral neutrality. However, his advocacy of a "liberal communitarianism" based in a "pluralism of affirmation" (pp. 155–177) seems to be simply another version of liberalism, especially in his desire to make the state the final locus of authority.

151. Alasdair MacIntyre, *Whose Justice? Which Rationality?* (Notre Dame, Ind.: University of Notre Dame Press, 1988), p. 350 ff. MacIntyre notes that traditions *can*, however, be in conversation with and critique one another.

## Chapter 3

1. See Edmund Pellegrino and David Thomasma, *A Philosophical Basis of Medical Practice* (New York: Oxford University Press, 1981), pp. vii, 11. See also Leon Kass, *Toward a More Natural Science* (New York: Free Press, 1985), p. 159.

2. Flannery O'Connor, *The Complete Stories* (New York: Farrar, Strauss and Giroux, 1971), p. 275.

3. See Pellegrino and Thomasma, *A Philosophical Basis of Medical Practice*, p. 17, and Kass, *Toward a More Natural Science*, p. 165.

4. Rick J. Carlson, *The End of Medicine* (New York: John Wiley and Sons, 1975), p. 189. Kass, *Toward a More Natural Science*, points out that etymologically "health" is unrelated to disease, illness, and sickness in both the Greek and English languages (p. 170). Pellegrino and Thomasma, *A Philosophical Basis of Medical Practice*, note: "The normal cannot be reduced to a single form of physiological knowledge because it rests in part on man's action on his environment" (p. 105).

5. Carlson, *The End of Medicine*, pp. 189–190.

6. Wendell Berry, "Health Is Membership," in *Another Turn of the Crank* (Washington, D.C.: Counterpoint, 1995), p. 90. This conception of health is an implicitly theological one, which is to say that Berry does not arrive at it simply through abstract reasoning. He bases it on his participation in the Christian narrative, which holds that "divine love, incarnate and indwelling in the world, summons the world always toward wholeness, which ultimately is reconciliation and atonement with God" (p. 89). Only a purposeful world can be whole; only a body created by and reconciled to a loving God can be healthy in the fullest sense.

7. Kass, *Toward a More Natural Science*, p. 250.

8. This does not mean that the liberal ideal always collapses into hedonism. Self-interest, as many liberal thinkers have shown, can be quite "enlightened."

9. Thomas Aquinas, *The Treatise on Happiness*, translated by John Oesterle (Notre Dame, Ind.: University of Notre Dame Press, 1983), p. 3. The division of the

*Summa* into discrete treatises is perhaps somewhat arbitrary; Oesterle's edition is composed of the first twenty-one questions of the *Prima Secundae* (*I-IIae*) of the *Summa Theologia*. My references will refer to the divisions within the *Summa* itself, and I will include the pages of Oesterle's edition in parentheses.

10. Ibid., I-IIae 1.4-6 (pp. 8–12).

11. Ibid., I-IIae 2.5 (p. 21).

12. Ibid., I-IIae 1.7, I-IIae 3.2 (pp. 13, 28). The word used here for the greatest good (*eudaimonia* in Greek and *beatitude* in Latin), which I render as "flourishing," and which most translators render as "happiness," is not readily translatable into English.

13. Ibid., p. 39.

14. Ibid., p. 49.

15. Ibid., p. 52. My primary concern in what follows is to offer a theological account of the relationship of bodies to one another that does not deal specifically with friendship as a moral category. For an exceptional treatment of this topic, see Paul Wadell, *Friendship and the Moral Life* (Notre Dame, Ind.: University of Notre Dame Press, 1989).

16. Kass, *Toward a More Natural Science*, pp. 4–5.

17. This agnosticism also relates to certain historical developments in Europe at the beginnings of modernity, namely the wars of religion and the concern that the widespread willingness to kill in the name of being Protestant or Catholic would soon destroy civilization. This is the fundamental reason John Rawls gives in some of his later work for the rise of the modern liberal state; see, for instance, *Political Liberalism* (New York: Columbia University Press, 1993). I am grateful to Rom Coles for reminding me of the significance of the wars of religion in the rise of modernity.

18. In the history of philosophy prior to the Enlightenment there are a variety of accounts of the person as consisting in an autonomous individual will. Indeed, John Milbank, in *Theology and Social Theory* (Cambridge, Mass.: Basil Blackwell, 1990), suggests that Enlightenment accounts of autonomy were to some extent the reworking of older Greek philosophical views. He notes that "from the perspective of Christian virtue, there emerges to view a hidden thread of continuity between antique reason and modern, secular reason. The theme of continuity is the theme of 'original violence.' Antique thought and politics assumes some naturally given element of chaotic conflict which must be tamed by the stability and self-identity of reason. Modern thought and politics (most clearly articulated by Nietzsche) assumes that there is *only* this chaos, which cannot be tamed by an opposing transcendent principle, but can be immanently controlled by subjecting it to rules and giving irresistible power to those rules in the form of market economies and sovereign politics; antique thought—as Plato already saw, in *The Sophist*—is deconstructible into 'modern' thought: a cosmos including both chaos and reason implies an ultimate principle, the 'difference between the two, which is *more* than reason,

and enshrines a permanent conflict." These matters are from the beginning theological; John Zizioulas remarks that "*historically* as well as *existentially* the concept of person is indissolubly bound up with theology." *Being As Communion* (Crestwood, N.Y.: St. Vladimir's Seminary Press, 1993), p. 27.

19. Zizioulas, *Being As Communion*, p. 29.

20. Ibid., pp. 32–36.

21. Ibid., p. 39.

22. Ibid., p. 46.

23. Ibid., pp. 46–47.

24. Ibid., pp. 42–43.

25. Ibid.

26. Ibid., p. 49. Zizioulas goes on to note that the person who exists as what he calls a "biological hypostasis" is confronted by "two 'passions'." The first of these is the passion to exist, that is, to maintain one's biological existence; the second is the passion to be a free, autonomous individual (pp. 50–51).

27. Ibid., p. 43. I find this a compelling way of accounting for the "politics of modernity" introduced and discussed in Chapters 1 and 2.

28. Ibid., pp. 51, 53.

29. Ibid., p. 52.

30. Ibid., p. 53.

31. Ibid., p. 107.

32. All quotations from the Bible will be from the New Revised Standard Version (NRSV), unless otherwise noted.

33. Geoffrey Wainwright, *For Us and Our Salvation* (Grand Rapids, Mich.: Eerdmans, 1997), remarks: "God's revelation is always received, as Saint Thomas notes, 'after the manner of the receiver.' Humans are embodied creatures; and, while we are more than our senses, we receive through our senses" (p. 15).

34. Ibid., p. 18; cf. Dale Martin, *The Corinthian Body* (New Haven, Conn.: Yale University Press, 1995), pp. 3–15.

35. Thomas Aquinas, *Summa Contra Gentiles: Book Four: Salvation*, trans. Charles O'Neil (Notre Dame, Ind.: University of Notre Dame Press, 1975), p. 147.

36. See Stanley Hauerwas, *In Good Company: The Church As Polis* (Notre Dame, Ind.: University of Notre Dame Press, 1995); Hauerwas notes: "Our God is not some generalized spirit, but a fleshy God whose body is the Jews" (p. 37). Wainwright remarks that throughout the scripture God's self-disclosure is fundamentally material: "That the divine Word should have been made flesh is a sheer act of God's grace, but retrospectively we may find it at least congruous with the corporeal forms through which God spoke according to the Old Testament. If the higher Greek philosophy was suspicious of materiality, Hebrew faith by contrast confessed the material creation as made by God. As such, it could serve as the vehicle of God's self-communication, which was received by human beings in all their bodily existence. We may observe this by examining the way in which the scriptural writers use

terminology with the Hebrew root *dbr*. . . . Clearly, *dbr*, even the *dᵉbar-YHWH*, carries a certain material density. The 'Word of God' took solid flesh as Jesus of Nazareth" (*For Us and Our Salvation*, pp. 9–10).

37. 1 John 4:2b; 1:1b.

38. See Wainwright, *For Us and Our Salvation*, pp. 74–75; cf. Horton Davies, *Bread of Life and Cup of Joy: Newer Ecumenical Perspectives on the Eucharist* (Grand Rapids, Mich.: Eerdmans, 1993), p. 119.

39. This is a significant theme for Dale Martin in *The Corinthian Body*. He makes reference to the literary work of Michael Bakhtin in suggesting that because language is fundamentally social, its meanings always tend to be multiple; see, for example, p. 133.

40. Berry, "Health Is Membership," pp. 90–91, 94. To say that "we cannot distinguish these meanings absolutely" is not to say that "we absolutely cannot distinguish them." I am arguing simply that clear and complete distinctions cannot be made when talking about the theological body.

41. Edward Schillebeeckx, *Christ the Sacrament of the Encounter with God* (Kansas City, Mo.: Sheed and Ward, 1963), p. 47. On the same page, Schillebeeckx goes on to show how the man Jesus is linked with his community in salvation history: "Jesus the Messiah, through his death which the Father accepts, becomes in fact the head of the People of God, the Church assembled in his death. . . . Christ in his glorified body is himself the eschatological redemptive community of the Church. In his own self the glorified Christ is simultaneously both 'Head and members.'"

42. Ibid., p. 67.

43. Alasdair MacIntyre, *After Virtue*, 2d ed. (Notre Dame, Ind.: University of Notre Dame Press, 1984), pp. 205–225, explains the significance of this relationship. Human actions require for their intelligibility, he says, a certain narrative contextualization as, for instance, in "an annual cycle of . . . activity" (206); for "in successfully identifying and understanding what someone else is doing we always move towards placing a particular episode in the context of a set of narrative histories, histories both of the individuals concerned and of the settings in which they act and suffer" (211). Such narratives, he says, are always fundamentally teleological and hence establish one's identity, which I argue is a fundamentally ontological category. More importantly for the point I am trying to establish here, these narratives require for their sustenance a *certain network of social practices* (219).

44. See Geoffrey Wainwright, "From Word and/or Sacrament to 'Verbum Caro' = 'Mysterium Fidei'": Lessons Learned from the BEM Process," in *Studia Anselmiana* 123, pp. 141–175.

45. Geoffrey Wainwright, *Doxology: The Praise of God in Worship, Doctrine, and Life* (New York: Oxford University Press, 1980), pp. 31, 32.

46. See Catherine Pickstock, *After Writing: On the Liturgical Consummation of Philosophy* (Oxford, U.K.: Blackwell, 1998), p. 131. Pickstock, lamenting the loss

of a strong sense of the significance of the embodiedness of the liturgy, reminds us that in the Eucharist we see clearly the interconnection between ontology and social practice. In the eucharistic celebration, "the most abstruse theory coalesces with social practice and assists in its transformation, since the event of transubstantiation in the mediaeval epoch was the ever repeated miracle of the emergence of the 'social body' as such."

47. Zizioulas, *Being As Communion,* p. 53.

48. Karl Barth, *The Epistle to the Romans,* trans., from the 6th ed., Edwyn Hoskyns (New York: Oxford University Press, 1933), p. 193.

49. Ibid., p. 192.

50. Zizioulas, *Being As Communion,* p. 54.

51. Ibid., pp. 55–56.

52. Ibid., p. 40. Here I side more with what has come to be understood as an "Eastern" conception of God's triunity, as opposed to a "Western" conception (although I do have reservations about that distinction). Zizioulas explains that in the Western model, "the ontological 'principle' of God is not found in the person but in the substance, that is, in the 'being' itself of God" (p. 40).

53. Ibid., pp. 86–89, italics original.

54. Ibid., p. 56.

55. John Howard Yoder, *Body Politics* (Nashville, Tenn.: Discipleship Resources, 1992), p. 32, italics mine.

56. Zizioulas, *Being As Communion,* p. 58.

57. Ibid., p. 64.

58. Wainwright, "From Word and/or Sacrament," pp. 147, 150.

59. Harmon Smith, *Where Two or Three Are Gathered: Liturgy and the Moral Life* (Cleveland, Ohio: Pilgrim Press, 1995), p. 64.

60. Ibid., pp. 64–65.

61. *The United Methodist Book of Worship* (Nashville, Tenn.: The United Methodist Publishing House, 1992), p. 38.

62. Zizioulas explains that in the Eucharist there is "the expectation and hope of the ecclesial identity, by this paradoxical hypostasis which has its roots in the future and its branches in the present" (*Being As Communion,* p. 59). Alexander Schmemann, *The Eucharist,* trans. Paul Kachur (Crestwood, N.Y.: St. Vladimir's Seminary Press, 1988), suggests that "the kingdom of God is the content of the Christian faith—the goal, the meaning and the content of the Christian life" (p. 40).

63. Schmemann, *The Eucharist,* p. 11.

64. This does not mean, of course, that the agency of the community and the agency of God in constituting that community through Eucharist are *absolutely* indistinguishable. Clearly, the primacy of the narrative of salvation history of which the Eucharist is a re-enactment offers a critical tool by which the community's life may be evaluated. Thanks to Rom Coles for bringing this point to my attention.

65. Zizioulas, *Being As Communion,* p. 60.

66. Schmemann, *The Eucharist,* p. 23.

67. Zizioulas, *Being As Communion,* p. 63; he further explains: "The meaning of asceticism consists in the fact that the less one makes one's hypostasis rely on nature, on the substance, the more one is hypostatized as a person. In this way asceticism does not deny 'nature' but frees it from the ontological necessity of biological hypostasis; it enables it to *be* in an authentic manner" (pp. 62–63, n. 66); cf. Schmemann, *The Eucharist,* p. 33.

68. Zizioulas, *Being As Communion,* p. 149.

69. Ibid., p. 115.

70. Cyril of Jerusalem, *Lectures on the Christian Sacraments: The Procatechesis and the Five Mystagogical Catecheses,* F. L. Cross, editor (Crestwood, NY: St. Vladimir's Seminary Press, 1995), p. 72.

71. Schmemann, *The Eucharist,* p. 137.

72. Cyril, *Lectures,* p. 79.

73. Schmemann, *The Eucharist,* p. 147.

74. Ibid., p. 150.

75. Ibid., p. 151. Schmemann explains, on the same page: "Faith is the partaking of the *unity from above,* and in it of the 'beginning of another life, new and eternal.' And the Church is manifested in this world as the gift, the presence, the fulfillment of this *unity from above,* and thus of faith. The Church is not something 'other' in relation to faith, although linked with faith, but precisely the fulfillment of faith itself—that unity the reception of which, the entrance into which, the partaking of which, is faith."

76. Ibid., p. 144.

77. Hauerwas puts this perhaps as well as anyone when he says in the preface to *In Good Company* that "Christianity is connections" (p. xiii).

78. Zizioulas, *Being As Communion,* p. 46.

79. Ibid., p. 110.

80. Ibid., p. 47.

81. For a good historical overview and critical appraisal of the emergence of the notion of the immanent Trinity and of the distinction between the immanent Trinity and the economic Trinity, see Catherine LaCugna, *God for Us* (San Francisco: Harper Collins, 1991).

82. Zizioulas, *Being As Communion,* p. 111; see also pp. 112–113, 131–133.

83. The theological notion of the body of Christ of course has its origins in the New Testament. 1 Corinthians, particularly chapter 12, is the most significant passage and may be read as an abbreviated discourse on the politics and goods of the theological body. Richard Hays, *The Moral Vision of the New Testament* (San Francisco: HarperCollins, 1996), notes that although Paul's letters are undeniably occasional and that his emphasis on community is in part related to one of the particular tasks of those letters (which is to strengthen community), the arguments Paul makes are neither simply pragmatic nor radically contingent: "The weight placed

on community formation is not . . . merely a matter of practical necessity; Paul develops his account of the new community in Christ as a fundamental *theological* theme in his proclamation of the gospel" (p. 32). Hays has also said in another work that Paul's moral exhortations derive directly from the story of the life, death, and resurrection of Jesus of Nazareth, and that these exhortations are directed toward the common life of the community; see *The Faith of Jesus Christ: SBL Dissertation Series 56*, ed. William Baird (Chico, Calif.: Scholar's Press, 1983).

84. Significantly, Paul does not refer to Christ as the head of the body in 1 Corinthians 12; he does so, however, in Ephesians 1:22–23 (God "has made him the head over all things for the church, which is his body, the fullness of him who fills all in all") and also in Colossians 1:18 ("He is the head of the body, the church"). The only reference to Christ as head in 1 Corinthians is found in 11:2–6, where Paul suggests that the relationship between man and woman is analogous to that between God and Christ and Christ and man. This usage has led to a debate among contemporary New Testament scholars over whether the word Paul uses for head— *kephale*—is better understood to mean "ruler" or "source." That particular debate, interesting though it is, is not significant for the point I am making here. For Christ is both the ruler *and* the source of the church; he is the one who calls for discipleship and who by sending the Holy Spirit makes that discipleship possible. For an overview of that debate, see Gordon Fee, *The First Epistle to the Corinthians* (Grand Rapids, Mich.: Eerdmans, 1987), pp. 501–505; see also, Martin, *The Corinthian Body*, pp. 232, 296, n. 16.

85. Zizioulas, *Being As Communion*, p. 210. Again, it is important to note that this strong Christological turn does not represent a monistic abandonment of the Trinity. We can identify the Church so closely with Jesus, Zizioulas explains, "only if we let our *Christology be conditioned pneumatologically.* This can happen if we see the mystery of Christ as being *initiated* by the Father who actually sends the Son in order to fulfill and realize the eternal design of the Holy Trinity to draw man and creation in participation in God's very life. In this understanding of Christology, Christ cannot be isolated from the Holy Spirit in whom he was born of the Virgin; in whom he became able to minister on earth, in whom finally, and most significantly for our subject, he can now minister to this pre-eternal plan of God for creation *in* or rather *as* the Church" (pp. 210–211).

86. We are thus led back to Schmemann's argument that faith always involves a concrete reorientation toward the Other, that is, a transformation of relationships that is not simply existential; see n. 72 above.

87. Jurgen Moltmann, *The Way of Jesus Christ* (Minneapolis: Fortress, 1993), pp. 118–119.

88. John Howard Yoder, *The Politics of Jesus* (Grand Rapids, Mich.: Eerdmans, 1972), p. 39; for an extended discussion of the point, see pp. 32–40; cf. Moltmann, *The Way of Jesus Christ*, pp. 119–122.

89. Yoder, *Politics of Jesus*, p. 40.

90. William Kurz notes the significance of teachers as moral examples in all of the ancient Greco-Roman world; see his article, "Kenotic Imitation of Paul and of Christ in Philippians 2 and 3," in *Discipleship in the New Testament*, ed. Fernando Segovia (Philadelphia: Fortress, 1985), p. 106.

91. Yoder, *Politics of Jesus*, p. 116.

92. Ibid., p. 117.

93. Ibid., pp. 117–118.

94. Ibid., pp. 42–45.

95. Jurgen Moltmann, *The Crucified God* (Minneapolis: Fortress, 1993), p. 54.

96. Stanley Hauerwas, The *Peaceable Kingdom* (Notre Dame, Ind.: University of Notre Dame Press, 1983), p. 76.

97. Ibid., p. 74.

98. Stanley Hauerwas, *A Community of Character* (Notre Dame, Ind.: University of Notre Dame Press, 1981), p. 48.

99. Yoder, *Politics of Jesus*, p. 132.

100. Stanley Hauerwas, *Naming the Silences* (Grand Rapids, Mich.: Eerdmans, 1990), p. 85. Elsewhere in the same work Hauerwas suggests with regard to those who want to make a sharp distinction between kinds of suffering that "it is no simple matter to distinguish 'suffering that is part of our daily living' from suffering which comes as part of our discipleship" (p. 77). I take this to be an especially significant point, especially in a world so indifferent to Christianity; I am not persuaded that it is possible for Christians to readily *distinguish* discipleship from daily life.

101. Yoder actually comes close to this view when he says of the community of Jesus and his disciples that "the novelty of its character is not that it is social, but that it is marked by an alternative to accepted patterns of leadership" (*Politics of Jesus*, p. 46). I simply want to say that Jesus' example of servant leadership is not radically distinguishable from his willingness to suffer the cross.

102. For accounts of Philippians 2:6–11 as an early Christian liturgical hymn employed by Paul for hortative purposes, see: Ralph Martin, *Carmen Christi* (Cambridge: Cambridge University Press, 1967); Stephen Fowl, *The Story of Christ in the Ethics of Paul* (Sheffield: JSOT Press, 1990); Peter O'Brien, *Commentary on Philippians* (Grand Rapids, MI: Eerdmans, 1991), pp. 186–271. For this second point, see Kurz, "Imitation," p. 105.

103. For a detailed account of the significance of the cross in the Roman Empire, see Martin Hengel, *Crucifixion in the Ancient World and the Folly of the Message of the Cross* (Philadelphia: Fortress, 1977); see in particular pp. 33–34, 50–51, 87.

104. Ibid., p. 62.

105. Steven Kraftchick, "A Necessary Detour: Paul's Metaphorical Understanding of the Philippian Hymn," *Horizons in Biblical Theology* 15, (June 1993), p. 17–18.

106. An especially interesting account of the inexpressibility of pain is Elaine Scarry, *The Body in Pain* (New York: Oxford University Press, 1985). Scarry speaks

eloquently of the inexpressibility of pain and of the political consequences of that inexpressibility. She remarks: "Whatever pain achieves, it achieves through its unsharability, and it ensures this unsharability through its resistance to language" (p. 4). Part of the argument I am developing here and in Chapter 4 is that the body of Christ offers to its members a way of being-in-relation that makes possible, to some extent and in some ways, the sharing of suffering.

107. Hauerwas, *Naming the Silences*, p. 89.

108. John Zizioulas, "Communion and Otherness," *Sobornost: The Journal of the Fellowship of St. Alban and St. Sergius* 16, no. 1 (1994), p. 14.

109. Ibid., p. 8.

110. Ibid., p. 10.

111. Ibid.

112. Here I find myself both for and against Zizioulas, who suggests that "if this confusion between difference and division were simply a moral problem, ethics would suffice to solve it. But it is not" ("Communion and Otherness," p. 11). Zizioulas is by all means correct to suggest that the division characteristic of modernity is a theological problem, but his distinction between ethics and theology at this point is one that I reject. I am grateful to Hans Reinders for helping me clarify this point.

113. Ibid., p. 11.

114. Ibid., p. 12.

115. On this point, see Richard Hays, *Moral Vision of the New Testament*, p. 33; cf. Martin, *The Corinthian Body*, p. 39. Precisely what forms of social life characterize this being united in mind and purpose are discussed later in this chapter; for the present it will do to say simply that they do not necessarily entail a kind of difference-destroying, lock-step agreement.

116. Hays, *Moral Vision of the New Testament*, p. 33.

117. Martin, *The Corinthian Body*, pp. 38, 47–49. Martin argues persuasively that Paul's explicit renunciations of rhetoric in the early chapters of 1 Corinthians were a commonly used rhetorical strategy, that "rhetorical deprecations of rhetoric were quite common" (p. 48). "In fact," he notes, "in both his disparagement of rhetoric and his claim to be only a layman [with regard to being trained as a rhetorician], Paul stands in a great tradition of rhetorical disavowals of rhetorical activity" (p. 49).

118. Ibid., p. 39.

119. Ibid.

120. Ibid., p. 40.

121. Ibid., p. 43.

122. Ibid., p. 47.

123. Ibid., p. 50.

124. Ibid., p. 52. Martin notes in his preface and again on p. 58 that it has become common among scholars of the Corinthian correspondence to refer to the parties Paul is addressing as the "Strong" and the "Weak."

125. Ibid., pp. 52–55, 58–59.

126. Ibid., pp. 70–73.

127. See Fee, *The First Epistle to the Corinthians,* p. 535.

128. Martin, *The Corinthian Body,* p. 73.

129. Martin explains that these practices included specifying seating arrangements so as to honor certain people, giving them more and better food and wine (p. 74).

130. Ibid.

131. Ibid.

132. Fee makes an interesting suggestion here, saying: "What is most intriguing in the passage is what is left unsaid, or what is implied. Most likely Paul does not see the judgment as a kind of "one for one," that is, the person who has abused another is the one who gets sick. Rather, the whole community is affected by the actions of some, who are creating 'divisions' within the one body of Christ. Probably the rash of illnesses and deaths that have recently overtaken them is here being viewed as an expression of divine judgment on the whole community" (*The First Epistle to the Corinthians,* p. 565).

133. Ibid., pp. 583–588. Fee notes that Paul's language in these verses "is not in fact a Trinitarian construct as such; that is, Paul's interest is not in the unity of the *Persons* of the Godhead: the relations are not spoken to at all, nor does he say that the Father, Son, and Spirit are one. Nonetheless, such passages as this are the 'stuff' from which the later theological constructs are correctly derived" (p. 588).

134. Zizioulas, "Communion and Otherness," p. 12.

135. Ibid.

136. Ibid. Note that in Zizioulas' third point he again repeats the suggestion that morality is something radically distinct from ontology, a distinction I wish to resist, as I noted above.

137. Martin, *The Corinthian Body,* p. 57.

138. Martin explains: "Initially in verse 23, Paul seems to be saying that *we,* by our own choosing, accede greater honor to the less honorable members. But then, in the second half of the verse, his wording changes: 'and our ugly parts *have* greater beauty, while our beautiful parts have no need.' It is not our condescension that has attributed more beauty to the less comely; the supposedly ugly parts actually are more beautiful than the allegedly beautiful parts."

139. I make this claim with a certain reluctance, given what I regard as a dangerous tendency to make Jesus' life and death and the particular content of his teachings insignificant as a pattern for Christian discipleship. Such a tendency is represented, in my estimation, by John Milbank, who in his essay "The Name of Jesus," in *The Word Made Strange* (Cambridge, Mass.: Blackwell, 1997) suggests that although there remains a sense in which the "invocation of the name of Jesus" is a necessary part of the life of "the new universal community or Church," that name "cannot be given any particular content: for the founder of a new practice cannot

be described in terms of that practice, unless that practice is already in place, which is contradictory" (pp. 148, 152). Milbank's concern to critique "cultic" accounts of the atonement is appropriate, but the account of Jesus he develops in order to do so seems to me to disregard his Jewishness as well as his activity as a political subversive.

140. John Howard Yoder, *The Priestly Kingdom: Social Ethics As Gospel* (Notre Dame, Ind.: University of Notre Dame Press, 1984), p. 17.

141. Yoder, *The Priestly Kingdom,* refers here to Paul's discussion on the use of the gifts in corporate worship in 1 Corinthians 12–14. He briefly discusses as examples of essential voices in the process people he calls Agents of Memory (scribes), Agents of Direction (prophets), Agents of Linguistic Self-Consciousness (teachers), and Agents of Order and Due Process (pastors, elders, or even moderators); see pp. 29–34.

142. Ibid., pp. 26–27.

143. Thanks to Rom Coles for suggesting the use of this phrase to characterize the tradition. The phrase itself belongs to Alasdair MacIntyre; see *Three Rival Versions of Moral Enquiry: Encyclopaedia, Genealogy, and Tradition* (Notre Dame, Ind.: University of Notre Dame Press, 1990), pp. 230-231.

144. MacIntyre, *After Virtue,* p. 222. MacIntyre suggests in *Three Rival Versions of Moral Enquiry,* pp. 105–126, that a classical display of such a process is the Thomist synthesis of Augustinian Christianity with Aristotelian philosophy.

145. Yoder, *The Priestly Kingdom,* is thus quite critical of what he refers to as "punctualism," which is the "predilection within ethics to consider primarily those decisions that are made at one time and place. Others call it 'decisionism.' Such singular decisions serve best to illustrate the dilemmas of casuistry and the inadequacy of tired old rules. They correspond to our sense of where the hardest problems lie. They distort reality, however, by filtering out the longitudinal dimensions of preparing for a decision before the crunch and confirming it (or repenting) afterward. Of course every choice is owned at some time by someone's choosing. And there are times when an individual must make a decision without community process, and still more painful ones where the individual must disagree with a disobedient or misinformed community. But these are the exception. They test but do not replace the rule" (p. 35).

146. Yoder puts this in an interesting way when he says that for the "radical Protestant there will always be a canon within the canon: namely, that recorded experience of practical moral reasoning in genuine human form that bears the name of Jesus" (*The Priestly Kingdom,* p. 37).

147. Ibid., p. 36.

# Chapter 4

1. Aristotle *Nicomachean Ethics,* p. 75. All references to this text are from the edition translated by H. Rackham (Cambridge, Mass: Harvard University Press, 1994).

2. Owen Flanagan, *Identity, Character, and Morality*, ed. Owen Flanagan and Amelie Oksenberg Rorty (Cambridge, Mass.: Bradford/MIT Press, 1993), p. 2.

3. Ibid., p. 3.

4. Gilbert Ryle, *The Concept of Mind* (New York: Hutchinson's University Press, 1949).

5. Owen Flanagan, *Self Expressions* (New York: Oxford University Press, 1996), pp. 55–56; see p. 56.

6. Ibid., p. 6. Flanagan explains that these arguments typically appear in one of three forms. The first is a metaphysical argument that says that the "universe is just a complex causal network and what is 'me' is just a location." The second is a sociological argument that holds that the self is the convergence of a collection of roles "that seems to possess, but invariably lacks, any more than nominal unity." The third is a developmental argument that holds that "'I' am a series of self-stages" connected only by a common name.

7. Ibid., p. 7.

8. Ruth Anna Putnam, "The Moral Life of a Pragmatist," in *Identity, Character, and Morality*, p. 53.

9. Flanagan, *Self Expressions*, p. 65.

10. Alasdair MacIntyre, *After Virtue,* 2d ed. (Notre Dame, Ind.: University of Notre Dame Press, 1984), p. 216.

11. Ibid., p. 211.

12. Ibid., p. 222; cf. p. 149 above.

13. Flanagan, *Self Expressions*, pp. 69, 153. Flanagan here quotes the developmental theorist Erik Erikson.

14. Ibid., pp. 156–157. Flanagan makes these arguments over against the work of the philosopher Charles Taylor, who suggests, especially in his *Sources of the Self: The Making of the Modern Identity* (Cambridge, Mass.: Harvard University Press, 1989), that in order for one to be a moral agent one must be a "strong evaluator" who persistently reflects on his or her life. Flanagan—whose position I am following here—disagrees, citing as an example of strong moral agency the rather unreflective peasants who were frequently the heroes in the fictional works of Tolstoy. I would offer one qualification concerning my agreement with Flanagan, however: The sense of continuity of which he speaks is socially constituted.

15. Embodied habits are, in spite of Aquinas's systematic efforts, complex and difficult to characterize. Thanks to Stanley Hauerwas for reminding me of this.

16. Thomas Aquinas, *Treatise on the Virtues*, trans. John Oesterle (Notre Dame, Ind.: University of Notre Dame Press, 1984), p. 1. This treatise is Oesterle's translation of questions 44–67 in the *Prima Secundae* of Aquinas's *Summa Theologia*, identified hereafter as I-IIae 44–67 and so forth. Reference to the pagination of Oesterle's edition will be given in parentheses.

17. Aristotle *Nicomachean Ethics* p. 75.

18. Putnam, "The Moral Life of a Pragmatist," p. 69.

19. For an elaboration of this point, see Paul Wadell, *Friends of God: Virtues and Gifts in Aquinas* (New York: Peter Lang Publishing, 1991), p. 91; cf. Putnam, "The Moral Life of a Pragmatist," p. 69.

20. Aquinas, I-IIae 50.1, 4, 5 (pp. 11, 17, 19).

21. Ibid., I-IIae 51.2 (p. 26).

22. Ibid.

23. Ibid. Aquinas explains: "A habit is produced by act insofar as a passive power is moved by an active principle. But in order that some quality be caused in what is passive, the active principle must wholly dominate the passive. . . . Now obviously reason, which is an active principle, cannot wholly dominate an appetitive power in one act. For the appetitive power is inclined in different ways and to many things, whereas reason judges a single act that this should be willed for these reasons and in these circumstances. Consequently, the appetitive power is not at once wholly controlled so as to be inclined by nature to the same thing for the most part, which is proper to a habit of virtue. Hence a habit of virtue cannot be caused by one act, but only by many."

24. Ibid., I-IIae 55.1–2 (pp. 51, 52).

25. Ibid., I-IIae 55.4 (p. 54).

26. Ibid., p. 55. Thomas deals with the differentiation of the virtues into intellectual, moral, and theological in I-IIae 57–62 (pp. 67–123). I forgo a good deal of his analysis here because I am less concerned with enumerating the cardinal moral and intellectual virtues than I am with suggesting ways that virtue is developed in the Christian community.

27. Ibid., I-IIae 53.1 (p. 37).

28. Ibid., I-IIae 53.2 (p. 39).

29. In the next section I will show how what I have said in the previous chapter about the communal nature of practical moral reasoning might strengthen Aquinas's account of it as a virtue.

30. Ibid., I-IIae 57.4 (p. 73).

31. Ibid., I-IIae 57.2 (pp. 69–70); I-IIae 61.1–2 (pp. 108–110).

32. Ibid., I-IIae 57.4 (p. 74).

33. Ibid., I-IIae 57.5 (p. 76).

34. Ibid., I-IIae 61.5 (p. 116).

35. Ibid., I-IIae 57.3. Aquinas, in I-IIae 58.3, explains the notion of infused virtue. He says in response to the question of whether virtues other than the theological virtues are infused by God: "Effects must be proportionate to their causes and principles. Now all virtues, intellectual and moral, which are acquired by our actions, proceed from certain natural principles which pre-exist in us, as we have said. In place of these natural principles, God has bestowed on us theological virtues whereby we are ordered to a supernatural end, as we have also said. Hence it was necessary that other habits, *corresponding proportionally to the theological virtues,* be caused in us by God which are related to the theological virtues as the

moral and intellectual virtues are to the natural principles of virtues" (emphasis mine). In I-IIae 58.4, he explains that these virtues are *different* from acquired moral virtue in the sense that they are those virtues "which God works in us without us."

According to Aquinas, I-IIae 61.5, the theological virtues are not identical to the infused moral virtues; however, they are *proportional* to the infused moral virtues, meaning they are directed toward the attainment of the same end of friendship with God; see also I-IIae 57.1-2.

36. In the *Nicomachean Ethics* X.ix.11, Aristotle explains: "In order to be good a man must have been properly educated and trained, and must subsequently continue to follow virtuous habits of life, and to do nothing base whether voluntarily or involuntarily, this will be secured if men's lives are regulated by a certain intelligence, and by a right system, invested with adequate sanctions"; cf. MacIntyre, *After Virtue*, p. 156.

37. MacIntyre, *After Virtue*, p. 194.

38. Something like this is suggested by Aidan Nichols in his book, *Looking at the Liturgy* (San Francisco: Ignatius Press, 1996), an interesting historical, sociological, and anthropological assessment of the post-Vatican II liturgical reforms in Roman Catholicism. Nichols's work calls into question the general trend in Christian worship—and here I am thinking primarily of the contemporizing movements among some Protestants—away from ritual and formalism toward more casual, popular forms designed to address the "felt needs" of contemporary worshipers.

39. Nichols, *Looking at the Liturgy*, p. 84.

40. Vigen Guroian, *Ethics After Christendom: Toward an Ecclesial Christian Ethic* (Grand Rapids, Mich.: Eerdmans, 1994), p. 32.

41. Ibid., p. 33.

42. Aquinas, I–IIae 58.3 (emphasis mine).

43. I am a bit hesitant to put this exactly in this way; the one thing I want to avoid suggesting is that the liturgy itself is in any *mechanical* sense the efficient cause of the infusion of virtue. God, whose real presence in the sacraments has been promised to the gathered worship of the Church, is the ultimate cause of infused virtue.

44. Guroian, *Ethics After Christendom*, p. 39.

45. Catherine Bell, *Ritual Theory, Ritual Practice* (New York: Oxford University Press, 1992), p. 96.

46. Ibid., p. 98.

47. Ibid., p. 99.

48. James F. White, *Sacraments As God's Self Giving* (Nashville, Tenn.: Abingdon Press, 1983), pp. 21–22.

49. Ibid., p. 22; cf. p. 27, where White remarks: "Christianity does not try to out-spiritualize God by evading the physical order. Rather, it is precisely through actions that Christianity discovers God's expression of love to us."

50. See Wadell, *Friends of God*, pp. 96–103.

51. Aquinas, *Treatise on the Virtues*, I-IIae 65.3 (p. 144).

52. Paul Wadell, *Friendship and the Moral Life* (Notre Dame, Ind.: University of Notre Dame Press, 1989), p. 127.

53. Ibid., p. 151.

54. Ibid., p. 121.

55. Ibid., pp. 142, 150–151; see p. 151.

56. Harmon Smith, *Where Two or Three Are Gathered: Liturgy and the Moral Life* (Cleveland, Ohio: Pilgrim Press, 1995), p. 44.

57. Ibid., p. 37.

58. Geoffrey Wainwright, *For Our Salvation: Two Approaches to the Work of Christ* (Grand Rapids, Mich.: Eerdmans, 1997), p. 75.

59. Tom Beauchamp and James Childress, *Principles of Biomedical Ethics*, 4th ed. (New York: Oxford University Press, 1994), p. 462.

60. Edmund Pellegrino and David Thomasma, *The Virtues in Medical Practice* (New York: Oxford University Press, 1993), p. xii.

61. Ibid., p. xiii.

62. Ibid., p. 3.

63. Ibid., p. 32.

64. Benedict goes so far as to make this assertion explicitly in the first chapter of the *Rule*. There he remarks that the "best kind" of monks are the Cenobites, those who live a common life "in a monastery waging their war under a rule and an abbot"; see *The Rule of St. Benedict*, translated and introduced by Anthony Meisel and M. L. de Mastro (New York: Doubleday, 1975), p. 47.

65. Alasdair MacIntyre, "Patients As Agents," in *Philosophical Medical Ethics: Its Nature and Significance*, ed. S. F. Spicker and H. T. Engelhardt Jr. (Dordrecht, Holland: D. Reidel Publishing, 1977), p. 205.

66. Ibid., p. 209. MacIntyre's rationale for the abandonment of traditional models of physician authority comes of course from his broader assertions, common to much of his work, that contemporary American culture has become so morally fragmented that there is virtually no assurance that we might share an account of the good life sufficient to sustain meaningful moral conversation.

67. Ibid., p. 207.

68. Ibid., p. 211.

69. Ibid., p. 212.

70. This is perhaps one of MacIntyre's main points in "Patients As Agents," namely, that the contractual nature of medical practice in modernity renders the moral authority of the physician unintelligible.

71. Nel Noddings, *Caring: A Feminine Approach to Ethics and Moral Education* (Berkeley, Calif.: University of California Press, 1984), p. 19.

72. This is a difficult and delicate point that is not easily resolvable. I am not suggesting here that caregivers—especially those whose vocation is caring—should not

be well-compensated for their work. But to make that compensation an act on the same order as the care given, to make it a matter of pure economic exchange, suggests that the relationship is *constituted* by the transaction and not by the care. This is one of the reasons I am so generally concerned about fee-for-service health care.

73. John Milbank, "Socialism of the Gift, Socialism by Grace," *New Blackfriars* 77/910 (December, 1996), p. 535.

74. Ibid., p. 538, italics original.

75. In an essay entitled "Authority and the Profession of Medicine," in *Suffering Presence: Theological Reflections on Medicine, the Mentally Handicapped, and the Church* (Notre Dame, Ind.: University of Notre Dame Press, 1986), Stanley Hauerwas suggests that authority is "exactly that power which allows unified common action for the achievement of the common good" (p. 44). When members of the Body allow themselves to be appropriately dependent on their friends, they are exercising, together with their caregivers, the authority of the weaker members for the common good of the Body.

76. Rainer Maria Rilke, *The Book of Hours: Love Poems to God*, trans. Anita Barrows and Joanna Macy (New York: Riverhead Books, 1996), p. 131.

77. Stanley Hauerwas, "Happiness, the Life of Virtue, and Friendship: Theological Reflections on Aristotelian Themes," *The Asbury Theological Journal* 45, no. 1, p. 7.

78. Ibid., p. 16.

79. Ray Anderson, *Theology, Death, and Dying* (New York: Basil Blackwell, 1986), p. 17.

80. Ibid., p. 21.

81. An interesting critique of the medicalization of death from the perspective of a physician is Sherwin Nuland, *How We Die: Reflections on Life's Final Chapter* (New York: Alfred A. Knopf, 1994). Nuland notes: "Medical science has conferred on humanity the benison of separating those pathological processes that are reversible from those that are not, constantly adding to the means by which the balance shifts ever in favor of sustained life. But modern biomedicine has also contributed to the misguided fancy by which each of us denies the certain advent of our own individual mortality. The claims of too many laboratory-based doctors to the contrary, medicine will always remain, as the ancient Greeks first dubbed it, an Art. One of its most severe demands that its artistry makes of the physician is that he or she become familiar with the poorly delineated boundary zones between categories of treatment whose chances of success may be classified as certain, probable, possible, or unreasonable. Those uncharted spaces between the probable and everything beyond it are where the thoughtful physician must often wander, with only the accumulated judgment of a life's experiences to guide the wisdom that must be shared with those who are sick" (p. 10).

82. I refer here, of course, to the modern funeral industry, which I take to be to a significant extent the transmitter of these practices and attitudes.

83. Anderson, *Theology, Death, and Dying,* pp. 51–52.

84. Ibid., p. 56.

85. Ibid., pp. 82–83.

86. Ibid., p. 99.

87. Guroian, *Ethics After Christendom,* notes: "With the decline of traditional religion, the resources that help us die well seem to have dried up. There is renewed interest in old answers of suicide and euthanasia. Assisted suicide is now being debated by doctors and medical ethicists, state legislators, media pundits, and people in all walks of life. Our society is increasingly coming to view euthanasia as an appropriate solution to the problem of pain and suffering. Walker Percy referred to this trend as 'the thanatos syndrome.' The Greek from which the term *euthanasia* is derived means 'good death.' In our time, the term has come to cover both the choice of a painless death on the part of people suffering from debilitating or terminal illness and the deliberate putting to death of helpless or infirm persons. The Orthodox Christian tradition offers many important reasons why such deaths cannot be considered good" (p. 175).

88. Anderson, *Theology, Death, and Dying,* p. 147.

89. Edward Abbey, *Confessions of a Barbarian: Selections from the Journals of Edward Abbey, 1951–1989,* ed. David Peterson (Boston: Little, Brown and Company, 1994), p. 12.

90. Anderson, *Theology, Death, and Dying,* p. 149.

91. Ibid., p. 157.

92. I take this general biographical information from *Conversations with Flannery O'Connor,* ed. Rosemary Magee (Jackson: University Press of Mississippi, 1987), pp. xxv–xxvii.

93. Flannery O'Connor, *Mystery and Manners: Occasional Prose,* ed. Sally and Robert Fitzgerald (New York: Farrar, Strauss and Giroux, 1969), p. 44.

94. Flannery O'Connor, *The Habit of Being: Letters of Flannery O'Connor,* ed. Sally Fitzgerald (New York: Farrar, Strauss and Giroux, 1979), p. 114.

95. Ibid., p. 479. She remarked at one point in a strident criticism of liberal Protestantism: "I certainly don't think that the death required that 'ye be born again' is the death of reason. If what the Church teaches is not true, then the security and emotional release and sense of purpose it gives you are of no value and you are right to reject it" (p. 479).

96. Ibid., p. 126.

97. Ibid., p. 100; cf. p. 124. Importantly, this perspective did not mean that O'Connor rejected reason or science in any way. She simply understood scientific knowledge as having its place within the overall scheme of God's creation. As she remarked in her exchange with her friend, "I didn't mean to suggest that science is unreliable, but only that we can't judge God by the limits of our knowledge of natural things" (p. 102).

98. Ibid.

99. Ibid., p. 90.

100. Ibid., pp. 92–93.

101. Ibid., xvii.

102. Her understanding of and dependence on the Eucharist is wonderfully summed up in a story she told about a dinner party she once attended with a group of authors and publishers in New York: "Well, toward morning the conversation turned on the Eucharist, which I, being Catholic, was obviously supposed to defend. Mrs. Broadwater said when she was a child and received the Host, she thought of it as the Holy Ghost, He being the 'most portable' person of the Trinity; now she thought of it as a symbol and implied that it was a pretty good one. I then said, in a very shaky voice, 'Well, if it's a symbol, to hell with it.' That was all the defense I was capable of but I realize now that this is all I will ever be able to say about it, outside of a story, except that it is the center of existence for me; all the rest of life is expendable" (Ibid., p. 125).

103. Ibid., p. 163.

104. Ibid., p. 57.

105. For example, in a letter to Maryat Lee written just over a month before her death, she speaks at some length about the rather nasty side effects of the medication she was taking, saying: "So far as I can see, the medicine and the disease run neck & neck to kill you" (Ibid., p. 590).

106. Ibid., p. 591.

107. So observes her friend Sally Fitzgerald in a note on p. 560 of *The Habit of Being*.

108. Ibid., pp. 592–593.

109. Neil Postman, *Technopoly: The Surrender of Culture to Technology* (New York: Vintage Books, 1992), pp. 50–51.

110. John Koenig, *New Testament Hospitality: Partnership with Strangers As Promise and Mission* (Philadelphia: Fortress Press, 1985), p. 2.

111. Ibid., pp. 60–69.

112. Ibid., pp. 3–4, 15–19.

113. Ibid., pp. 5–7, 24.

114. Augustine perhaps understood time in this way as clearly as anyone. In Book XI of his *Confessions* he suggests that the only *real* time is the present, and that life lived only in anticipation of a future time is life lived at what might be called a less real level; see Augustine, *Confessions*, trans. R. S. Pine-Coffin (New York: Penguin, 1961). Thanks to Rom Coles for pointing this out to me.

115. Jean Vanier, *Community and Growth* (London: Darton, Longman, and Todd, 1979), p. 3.

116. Ibid., p. 80.

117. In this sense I find Koenig's connection of Christian hospitality to the house church tradition of the early Church especially appealing; see *New Testament Hospitality*, pp. 57–71.

118. Vanier, *Community and Growth,* p. 200.

119. Ibid.

120. Koenig, *New Testament Hospitality,* pp. 8–9.

121. Vanier, *Community and Growth,* pp. 139–140.

122. See O'Connor, *Habit of Being,* p. 394.

123. O'Connor, "Introduction to *A Memoir of Mary Ann,*" in *Mystery and Manners,* p. 214.

124. O'Connor, *Habit of Being,* p. 394.

125. O'Connor, *Mystery and Manners,* p. 215.

126. The book, entitled *A Memoir of Mary Ann,* was written by The Dominican Nuns of Our Lady of Perpetual Help Home of Atlanta, Georgia, and was published in 1961 by Farrar, Strauss, and Cudahy of New York, O'Connor's own publisher.

127. O'Connor, *Mystery and Manners,* p. 222.

128. Ibid., p. 217.

129. Ibid., pp. 218–219.

130. Ibid., p. 219.

131. Ibid.

132. Ibid., p. 223.

133. Ibid., p. 225–226.

134. Ibid., pp. 226–227.

135. Ibid., p. 227. This sentiment about tenderness is by no means unique to O'Connor. It appears also in Walker Percy's *The Thanatos Syndrome,* a novel that at times appears to draw directly from O'Connor's reflections on Mary Ann, and also in Walter Miller's *A Canticle for Liebowitz,* an almost prescient 1959 novel about nuclear holocaust and the dissolution of civilization at the hands of an extreme modernity.

136. Ibid., p. 228.

137. I am grateful to Harmon Smith for making me aware of the primary significance of this question for bioethics.

138. Hence we see two significant developments in modern biomedicine: Professional codes of ethics become increasingly procedural and void of material content, and difficult moral decisions are increasingly deferred to professional ethicists, who adjudicate them using utilitarian calculi. Thanks to Stanley Hauerwas for helping me understand the nature of the abandonment of moral authority in medical practice.

139. White, *Sacraments As God's Self Giving,* p. 79, notes that "it is impossible to separate healing from reconciliation entirely. Ultimately, both deal with the health of the body of Christ. The purpose of God's self giving seems to be the wholeness that is experienced spiritually, physically, and socially. This, of course, reflects the nature of creation itself, which, according to Genesis, is created good. 'God saw all that he had made, and it was very good' (1:31). Much is besmirched with sin, but the restoration of creation is directed toward its original goodness.

Healing is an expression of God's basic gift—life itself. The difference between the Creator and creature is our finitude. Thus the sacrament of healing does not always have the fruition that we might desire but that which is best in God's wisdom for us" (p. 79).

140. Karen Westerfield-Tucker, "Christian Rituals Surrounding Sickness," in *Life Cycles in Jewish and Christian Worship*, ed. Paul Bradshaw and Lawrence Hoffman (Notre Dame, Ind.: University of Notre Dame Press, 1997), p. 154.

141. Ibid.

142. Westerfield-Tucker notes that the prayer of consecration over the oil which "invoked the agency and power of Jesus himself (literally, the 'Christ' or 'anointed one') or the Holy Spirit, increasingly came to be regarded as imbuing the oil with a sacramental efficacy (though its identification as one of the seven sacraments in the West did not come officially until the thirteenth century)" (p. 159).

143. Ibid., p. 158.

144. Ibid., p. 156.

145. Ibid., pp. 157, 158, 160.

146. Pellegrino and Thomasma, *The Virtues in Medical Practice*, pp. 25, 79, 82–83.

147. Wendell Berry, "Health Is Membership," in *Another Turn of the Crank* (Washington: Counterpoint, 1995), p. 100.

148. Here everything I have said previously about the significance of charity as the form of the virtues is especially important.

149. Berry, "Health Is Membership," p. 101.

150. Ibid., p. 104. The question that is of course raised here is whether genuinely moral care can be given in some contemporary environments, and if not what the alternatives are.

151. This is something the Church seems to have known intuitively based on the close relationship between rituals of healing and rituals for the dying; see Westerfield-Tucker, "Christian Rituals Surrounding Sickness," p. 167.

152. Berry, "Health Is Membership," p. 105.

153. Ibid., p. 109.

## Afterword

1. John Howard Yoder, *The Politics of Jesus* (Grand Rapids, MI: Eerdmans, 1972), p. 238.

2. Denise Giardina, *Storming Heaven* (New York: Ivy Books, 1987), pp. 290–291.

# BIBLIOGRAPHY

Abbey, Edward. *Confessions of a Barbarian: Selections from the Journals of Edward Abbey, 1951–1989.* Edited by David Peterson. Boston: Little, Brown and Company, 1994.

Ackerknecht, Erwin H. *A Short History of Medicine.* Baltimore, Md.: Johns Hopkins University Press, 1982.

Anderson, Ray. *Theology, Death, and Dying.* New York: Basil Blackwell, 1986.

Aquinas, Thomas. *Summa Contra Gentiles: Book Four: Salvation.* Translated by Charles O'Neil. Notre Dame, Ind.: University of Notre Dame Press, 1975.

_____. *The Treatise on Happiness.* Translated by John Oesterle. Notre Dame, Ind.: University of Notre Dame Press, 1983.

_____. *The Treatise on the Virtues.* Translated by John Oesterle. Notre Dame, Ind.: University of Notre Dame Press, 1984.

Aristotle. *Nichomachean Ethics.* Translated by H. Rackham. Cambridge, Mass.: Harvard University Press, 1994.

Ashley, Benedict M. *Theologies of the Body: Humanist and Christian.* Braintree, Mass.: The Pope John Center, 1985.

Augustine. *Confessions.* Translated by R. S. Pine-Coffin. New York: Penguin, 1961.

Barth, Karl. *The Epistle to the Romans.* 6th ed. Translated by Edwyn Hoskins. New York: Oxford University Press, 1933.

Bates, Don. "Scholarly Ways of Knowing: An Introduction." In *Knowledge and the Scholarly Medical Traditions.* Edited by Don Bates. Cambridge: Cambridge University Press, 1995.

Beauchamp, Tom L., and James F. Childress. *Principles of Biomedical Ethics.* New York: Oxford University Press, 1994.

Bell, Catherine. *Ritual Theory, Ritual Practice.* New York: Oxford University Press, 1992.

Benedict of Nursia. *The Rule of St. Benedict.* Translated by Anthony Meisel and M. L. de Mastro. New York: Doubleday, 1975.

Berry, Wendell. *Another Turn of the Crank.* Washington: Counterpoint, 1995.

_____. *What Are People For?* New York: North Point Press, 1990.

Booth, Christopher C. "Clinical Research." In *Companion Encyclopedia to the History of Medicine.* Edited by Roy Porter and W. F. Bynum, 205–229. New York: Routledge, 1993.

Brieger, Gert. "The Historiography of Medicine." In *Companion Encyclopedia to the History of Medicine*. Edited by Roy Porter and W. F. Bynum, 24–44. New York: Routledge, 1993.

Browder, James P. "Elected Suffering: Toward a Theology for Medicine." Ph.D. dissertation, Duke University, 1991.

Bulger, Roger. *Technology, Bureaucracy, and Healing in America: A Postmodern Paradigm*. Iowa City: University of Iowa Press, 1988.

Callahan, Daniel. "Why America Accepted Bioethics." *The Hastings Center Report* 23, no. 6 (1993):S1–15.

Canguilhem, Georges. *The Normal and the Pathological*. Translated by Carolyn Fawcett in collaboration with Robert Cohen. New York: Zone Books, 1991.

Carlson, Rick J. *The End of Medicine*. New York: John Wiley and Sons, 1975.

Cassell, Eric J. *The Nature of Suffering and the Goals of Medicine*. New York: Oxford University Press, 1991.

Clark-Kennedy, A. E. *The Art of Medicine in Relation to the Progress of Thought: A Lecture in the History of Science Course in the University of Cambridge*. London: Cambridge University Press, 1945.

Coakley, Sarah. "Visions of the Self in Late Medieval Christianity: Some Cross-Disciplinary Reflections." In *The Special Nature of Women?* Edited by Anne Carr and Elizabeth Schussler Fiorenza. Special issue of *Concilium* 6. Philadelphia: Trinity Press International, 1991.

Coles, Romand. *Self/Power/Other: Political Theory and Dialogical Ethics*. Ithaca: Cornell University Press, 1992.

Coppleston, Frederick. *A History of Philosophy*. New York: Doubleday, 1974.

Cyril of Jerusalem. *Lectures on the Christian Sacraments: The Procatechesis and the Five Mystagogical Catecheses*. Edited by F. L. Cross. Crestwood, N.Y.: St. Vladimir's Seminary Press, 1995.

Dana, Charles L. *The Peaks of Medical History: An Outline of the Evolution of Medicine for the Use of Medical Students and Practicioners*. New York: Paul B. Hoeber, Inc., 1926

Davies, Horton. *Bread of Life and Cup of Joy: Newer Ecumenical Perspectives on the Eucharist*. Grand Rapids, Mich.: Eerdmans, 1993.

Descartes, René. *Discourse on Method and the Meditations*. Translated by F. E. Sutcliffe. New York: Penguin, 1968.

Dreyfus, Hubert, and Paul Rabinow. *Michel Foucault: Beyond Structuralism and Hermeneutics*. Chicago: University of Chicago Press, 1983.

Dubose, Edwin. *The Illusion of Trust: Toward a Medical Theological Ethics in a Postmodern Age*. Dordrecht, Holland: Kluwer Academic Press, 1995.

Emanuel, Ezekiel. *The Ends of Human Life: Medical Ethics in a Liberal Polity*. Cambridge, Mass.: Harvard University Press, 1991.

Engelhardt, H. Tristram, Jr. "Bioethics in Pluralist Societies." *Perspectives in Biology and Medicine* 26, no. 1 (1982): 64–78.

_____.*The Foundations of Bioethics*. 2d ed. New York: Oxford University Press, 1996.

Fee, Gordon. *The First Epistle to the Corinthians*. Grand Rapids, Mich.: Eerdmans, 1987.

Flanagan, Owen, and Amelie Oxenberg Rorty, ed. *Identity, Character, and Morality: Essays in Moral Psychology*. Cambridge, Mass.: MIT Press, 1993.

Flanagan, Owen. *The Science of the Mind*. Cambridge, Mass.: MIT Press, 1991.

_____. *Self Expressions*. New York: Oxford University Press, 1996.

_____. *Varieties of Moral Personality: Ethics and Psychological Realism*. Cambridge, Mass.: Harvard University Press, 1991.

Fletcher, Joseph. "Four Indicators of Humanhood—The Enquiry Matters." In *On Moral Medicine*. Edited by Stephen Lammers and Allen Verhey. Grand Rapids, Mich.: Eerdmans, 1987.

Foucault, Michel. *The Birth of the Clinic*. Translated by A. M. Sheridan Smith. New York: Vintage, 1975.

_____. *The Foucault Reader*. Edited by Paul Rabinow. New York: Pantheon, 1984.

_____. *The History of Sexuality: An Introduction*. Translated by Robert Hurley. New York: Random House, 1990.

_____. *Madness and Civilization*. New York: Vintage, 1988.

_____. *The Order of Things: An Archaeology of the Human Sciences*. New York: Vintage Books, 1973.

_____. *Power/Knowledge*. Translated and edited by Colin Gordon. New York: Pantheon, 1980.

Fowl, Stephen. *The Story of Christ in the Ethics of Paul*. Sheffield: JSOT Press, 1990.

Frank, Arthur. *At the Will of the Body: Reflections on Illness*. Boston: Houghton Mifflin, 1991.

Freund, Perter E. S., and Meredith B McGuire. *Health, Illness, and the Social Body: A Critical Sociology*. Englewood Cliffs, N.J.: Prentice-Hall, 1991.

Galdston, Iago, ed. *On the Utility of Medical History: Monograph I, The Institute on Social and Historical Medicine*. New York: International University Press, 1957.

_____. *Social and Historical Foundations of Modern Medicine*. New York: Brunner/Mazel, 1981.

Galdston, William. "Defending Liberalism." *The American Political Science Review* 76 (1982):621–629.

Giardina, Denise. *Storming Heaven*. New York: Ivy Books, 1987.

Giddens, Anthony. *The Nation-State and Violence*. Berkeley, Calif.: University of California Press, 1987.

Guroian, Vigen. *Ethics After Christendom: Toward an Ecclesial Christian Ethic*. Grand Rapids, Mich.: Eerdmans, 1994.

Gustafson, James. *The Contributions of Theology to Medical Ethics*. Milwaukee, Wis.: Marquette University Press, 1975.

Haggard, Howard W. *Mystery, Magic, and Medicine: The Rise of Medicine from Superstition to Science*. Garden City, N.Y.: Doubleday Doran and Co., 1933.

Hampshire, Stuart. "Fallacies in Moral Philosophy." In *Revisions: Changing Perspectives in Moral Philosophy*. Edited by Stanley Hauerwas and Alasdair MacIntyre. Notre Dame, Ind.: University of Notre Dame Press, 1983.

Hankinson, Robert J. "The Growth of Medical Empiricism." In *Knowledge and the Scholarly Medical Traditions*. Edited by Don Bates, 60–84. Cambridge: Cambridge University Press, 1995.

Hauerwas, Stanley. *Christian Existence Today*. Durham, N.C.: Labyrinth, 1988.

_____. "Happiness, the Life of Virtue, and Friendship: Theological Reflections on Aristotelian Themes." *The Asbury Theological Journal* 45, no. 1 (1990):49–63.

_____. *Naming the Silences: God, Medicine, and the Problem of Suffering*. Grand Rapids, Mich.: Eerdmans, 1990.

_____. "Not All Peace Is Peace." In *Reading Engelhardt*. Edited by Brendan Minogue et al. Dordrecht, Holland: Kluwere Academic Publishers, 1997.

_____. *The Peaceable Kingdom*. Notre Dame, Ind.: University of Notre Dame Press, 1983.

_____. *Suffering Presence*. Notre Dame, Ind.: University of Notre Dame Press, 1986

Hauerwas, Stanley, and Charles Pinches. *Christians Among the Virtues*. Notre Dame, Ind.: University of Notre Dame Press, 1996.

Hays, Richard. *The Faith of Jesus Christ*. SBL Dissertation Series 56. Edited by William Baird. Chico, Calif.: Scholar's Press, 1983.

_____. *The Moral Vision of the New Testament*. San Francisco: HarperCollins, 1996.

Hengel, Martin. *Crucifixion in the Ancient World and the Folly of the Message of the Cross*. Philadelphia: Fortress, 1977.

Horkheimer, Max, and Theodor Adorno. *Dialectic of Enlightenment*. Translated by John Cummin. New York: Continuum, 1997.

Ilich, Ivan. *Medical Nemesis*. New York: Pantheon, 1976.

Jonsen, Albert R. "The Birth of Bioethics." *The Hastings Center Report* 23, no. 6 (1993):S1–15.

Kahane, Ernst. "The Thought of Claude Bernard." Translated by Harry Chovnich and Paul M. Prebus. In *The American Institute for Marxist Studies: Occasional Papers* 3 (1966).

Kant, Immanuel. *Foundations of the Metaphysics of Morals*. Translated by Lewis Beck White. New York: Macmillan, 1989.

Kass, Leon. *Toward a More Natural Science*. New York: Free Press, 1985.

King, Lester S. *The Growth of Medical Thought*. Chicago: University of Chicago Press, 1963.

Kleinman, Arthur. *The Illness Narratives: Suffering, Healing and the Human Condition*. New York: Basic Books, 1988.

Koenig, John. *New Testament Hospitality: Partnership with Strangers as Promise and Mission.* Philadelphia: Fortress Press, 1985.

Kraftchick, Stephen. "A Necessary Detour: Paul's Metaphorical Understanding of the Philippian Hymn." *Horizons in Biblical Theology* 15 (1993):1–37.

Kurz, William. "Kenotic Imitation of Paul and of Christ in Philippians 2 and 3." In *Discipleship in the New Testament.* Edited by Fernando Segovia. Philadelphia: Fortress, 1985.

Lacugna, Catherine. *God for Us.* San Francisco: HarperCollins, 1991.

Larmore, Charles. "Political Liberalism." *Political Theory* 18, no. 3 (1990): 339–360.

Leder, Drew. *The Absent Body.* Chicago: University of Chicago Press, 1990.

Lederman, E. K. *Philosophy and Medicine.* London: Tavistock, 1970.

Lupton, Deborah. *Medicine as Culture: Illness, Disease, and the Body in Western Societies.* London: Sage, 1994.

Lysaught, Mary Therese. *Sharing Christ's Passion: A Critique of the Role of Suffering in the Discourse of Biomedical Ethics from the Perspective of the Theological Practice of Anointing of the Sick.* Ph.D. dissertation, Duke University, 1992.

MacIntyre, Alasdair. *After Virtue.* 2d ed. Notre Dame, Ind.: University of Notre Dame Press, 1984.

_____. "Medicine Aimed at the Care of Persons Rather Than What . . . ?" In *Philosophical Medical Ethics: Its Nature and Significance.* Edited by S. F. Spicker and H. T. Engelhardt Jr., 83–103. Dordrecht, Holland: D. Reidel Publishing Company, 1977.

_____. "Patients As Agents." In *Philosophical Medical Ethics: Its Nature and Significance.* Edited by S. F. Spicker and H. T. Engelhardt Jr., 197–212. Dordrecht, Holland: D. Reidel Publishing Company, 1977.

_____. "Theology, Ethics, and the Ethics of Medicine and Health Care: Comments on Papers by Novak, Mouw, Roach, Cahill, and Hart." *Journal of Medicine and Philosophy* 4 (1979):435–443.

_____. *Three Rival Versions of Moral Enquiry: Encyclopaedia, Genealogy, and Tradition.* Notre Dame, Ind.: University of Notre Dame Press, 1990.

_____. *Whose Justice? Which Rationality?* Notre Dame, Ind.: University of Notre Dame Press, 1988.

Martin, Dale. *The Corinthian Body.* New Haven, Conn.: Yale University Press, 1995.

Martin, Ralph. *Carmen Christi.* Cambridge: Cambridge University Press, 1967.

McKenny, Gerald. *To Relieve the Human Condition: Bioethics and the Technological Utopianism of Modern Medicine.* New York: SUNY Press, 1997.

McMylor, Peter. *Alasdair MacIntyre: Critic of Modernity.* London: Routledge, 1974.

Meilander, Gilbert. *Bioethics: A Primer for Christians.* Grand Rapids, Mich.: Eerdmans, 1996.

Midgley, Mary. *Science As Salvation: A Modern Myth and Its Meaning*. New York: Routledge, 1992.

Milbank, John. "Socialism of the Gift, Socialism by Grace," *New Blackfriars* 77/910 (December, 1996): 532–547.

_____. *Theology and Social Theory*. Cambridge, Mass.: Basil Blackwell, 1990.

_____. *The Word Made Strange: Theology, Language, Culture*. Cambridge, Mass.: Blackwell, 1997.

Moltmann, Jurgen. *The Crucified God*. Minneapolis, Minn.: Fortress Press, 1993.

_____. *The Way of Jesus Christ*. Minneapolis, Minn.: Fortress Press, 1993.

Morone, James A., and Gary S. Belkin, ed. *The Politics of Health Care Reform: Lessons from the Past: Prospects for the Future*. Durham, N.C.: Duke University Press, 1994.

Nichols, Aidan. *Looking at the Liturgy*. San Francisco: Ignatius Press, 1996.

Noddings, Nel. *Caring: A Feminine Approach to Ethics in Moral Education*. Berkeley, Calif.: University of California Press, 1984.

Nozick, Robert. *Anarchy, State, and Utopia*. New York: Harper Collins, 1974.

Nuland, Sherman. *Doctors: The Biography of Medicine*. New York: Vintage Books, 1988.

_____. *How We Die: Reflections on Life's Final Chapter*. New York: Alfred A. Knopf, 1994.

O'Brien, Peter. *Commentary on Philippians*. Grand Rapids, Mich.: Eerdmans, 1991.

O'Connor, Flannery. *The Complete Stories*. New York: Farrar, Strauss, and Giroux, 1975.

_____. *Conversations with Flannery O'Connor*. Edited by Rosemary Magee. Jackson: University of Mississippi Press, 1987.

_____. *The Habit of Being: Letters of Flannery O'Connor*. Edited by Sally Fitzgerald. New York: Farrar, Strauss, and Giroux, 1979.

_____. *Mystery and Manners: Occasional Prose*. Edited by Sally and Robert Fitzgerald. New York: Farrar, Strauss, and Giroux, 1969.

Pellegrino, Edmund D., and David C. Thomasma. *A Philosophical Basis of Medical Practice*. New York: Oxford University Press, 1981.

_____. *The Virtues in Medical Practice*. New York: Oxford University Press, 1993.

Pickstock, Catherine. *After Writing: On the Liturgical Consummation of Philosophy*. Cambridge, Mass.: Blackwell, 1998.

Polanyi, Michael. "Scientific Outlook: Its Sickness and Cure." *Science* 125 (March 1957).

_____. *The Tacit Dimension*. Gloucester, Mass.: Peter Smith, 1983.

Porter, Roy, and W. F. Bynum. "The Art and Science of Medicine." In *Companion Encyclopedia to the History of Medicine*. Edited by Roy Porter and W. F. Bynum, 3–14. New York: Routledge, 1993.

Postman, Neil. *Technopoly: The Surrender of Culture to Technology*. New York: Vintage Books, 1993.

Powell, H. Jefferson. *The Moral Tradition of American Constitutionalism*. Durham, N.C.: Duke University Press, 1993.

Rawls, John. "Justice As Fairness: Political Not Metaphysical." *Philosophy and Public Affairs* 14, no. 3 (1985):223–251.

_____. *Political Liberalism*. New York: Columbia University Press, 1993.

_____. *A Theory of Justice*. Cambridge: Belknap/Harvard University Press, 1971.

Reverby, Susan, and David Rosner, ed. *Health Care in America: Essays in Social History*. Philadelphia: Temple University Press, 1979.

Rilke, Rainer Maria. *The Book of Hours: Love Poems to God*. Translated by Anita Barrows and Joanna Macy. New York: Riverhead Books, 1996.

Risse, Gunter. "Medical Care." In *Companion Encyclopedia to the History of Medicine*. Edited by Roy Porter and W. F. Bynum, 45–77. New York: Routledge, 1993.

Rosenberg, Charles. "The Therapeutic Revolution: Medicine, Meaning, and Social Change in 19th-Century America." In *Sickness and Health in America: Readings in the History of Medicine and Public Health*. 2d ed. Edited by Judith Walzer Leavitt and Ronald L. Numbers, 39–52. Madison: University of Wisconsin Press, 1985.

Rossi, Paolo. *Francis Bacon: From Magic to Science*. Translated by Sacha Rabinowitch. Chicago: University of Chicago Press, 1968.

Ryle, Gilbert. *The Concept of Mind*. New York: Hutchinson's University Press, 1949.

Sandel, Michael. *Liberalism and the Limits of Justice*. Cambridge: Cambridge University Press, 1982.

Scarry, Elaine. *The Body in Pain*. New York: Oxford University Press, 1985.

Schillebeeckx, Edward. *Christ the Sacrament of the Encounter with God*. Kansas City, Mo.: Sheed and Ward, 1963.

Schmemann, Alexander. *The Eucharist*. Translated by Paul Kachur. Crestwood, N.Y.: St. Vladimir's Seminary Press, 1988.

Scott, Sue, and David Morgan. "Bodies in a Social Landscape." In *Body Matters: Essays on the Sociology of the Body*, 1–21. Edited by Sue Scott and David Morgan. London: Falmer Press, 1993.

Shalit, Ruth. "When We Were Philosopher Kings." *The New Republic*, April 28, 1997, 24–28.

Sigerist, Henry E. *The Great Doctors: A Biographical History of Medicine*. Garden City, N.Y.: Doubleday and Co., 1958.

Simon, W. M. "Claude Bernard." In *The Encyclopedia of Philosophy*. Edited by Paul Edwards. New York: Macmillan, 1967.

Smith, Harmon L. *Where Two or Three are Gathered: Liturgy and the Moral Life*. Cleveland, Ohio: Pilgrim Press, 1995.

Smith, Harmon L., and Larry R. Churchill. *Professional Ethics and Primary Care Medicine: Beyond Dilemmas and Decorum*. Durham, N.C.: Duke University Press, 1986.

Turner, Bryan S. *Regulating Bodies: Essays in Medical Sociology.* London: Routledge, 1992.

Vanier, John. *Community and Growth.* London: Darton, Longman, and Todd, 1979.

Verghese, Abraham. *My Own Country: A Doctor's Story.* New York: Vintage Books, 1994.

Wadell, Paul J. *Friendship and the Moral Life.* Notre Dame, Ind.: University of Notre Dame Press, 1989.

_____. *Friends of God: Virtues and Gifts in Aquinas.* New York: Peter Lang, 1991.

Wainwright, Geoffrey. *Doxology: The Praise of God in Worship, Doctrine, and Life.* New York: Oxford University Press, 1980.

_____. *For Us and Our Salvation.* Grand Rapids: Mich.: Eerdmans, 1997.

_____. "From Word and/or Sacrament to 'Verbum Caro' = 'Mysterium Fidei': Lessons Learned from the BEM Process," *Studia Anselmiana* 123:141–175.

Waisel, David, and Robert Truog. "The Cardiopulmonary Resuscitation-Not-Indicated Order: Futility Revisited." *Annals of Internal Medicine* 122, no. 4 (1995):304–307.

Walzer, Michael. *Spheres of Justice: A Defense of Pluralism and Equality.* New York: Basic Books, 1983.

Westerfield-Tucker, Karen. "Christian Rituals Surrounding Sickness." In *Life Cycles in Jewish and Christian Worship.* Edited by Paul Bradshaw and Lawrence Hoffman. Notre Dame, Ind.: University of Notre Dame Press, 1997.

White, James. *Sacraments As God's Self Giving.* Nashville, Tenn.: Abingdon Press, 1983.

Yoder, John Howard. *Body Politics.* Nashville, Tenn.: Discipleship Resources, 1992.

_____. *The Politics of Jesus.* Grand Rapids, Mich.: Eerdmans, 1972.

_____. *The Priestly Kingdom: Social Ethics As Gospel.* Notre Dame, Ind.: University of Notre Dame Press, 1984.

Zizioulas, John. *Being As Communion.* Crestwood, N.Y.: SVS Press, 1985.

_____. "Communion and Otherness," *Sobornost: The Journal of the Fellowship of St. Alban and St. Sergius* 16, no. 1 (1994):7–19.

# INDEX

Abbey, Edward, 137
*Absent Body, The* (Leder), 165(n48)
Ackerknecht, Erwin, 13
Ackerman, Bruce, 178(n118)
Adorno, T. W., 25, 32, 44, 71
Aesculapian authority, 57, 61
*After Virtue* (MacIntyre), 74–75, 118
Agency, 116, 123, 130, 131. *See also* Moral issues, moral agency
Alienation, 17, 19, 26, 45, 87, 104, 129, 130
Anatomy, 13, 165(n48)
Anaximander, 23
Anderson, Ray, 135, 136, 137–138
Antibiotics, 13
Apprenticeship, 48–49, 172(n6)
Aristotle, 26, 48–49, 50, 116, 121–122, 146, 168(n95), 172(n6), 193(n36)
Art, 48, 50, 51
Asceticism, 93, 185(n67)
Augustine (Saint), 95, 197(n114)
Autonomy, 9, 15, 29, 49, 55, 59, 60, 62, 63, 85, 87, 106, 181(n18)
  in conflict with caregiver authority, 56–57, 61, 64, 70, 71
  of physicians, 63–64
  relativization of, 86

Bacon, Sir Francis, 24–25, 26, 30, 49, 168(nn 90, 94, 95)
Baptism, 89–92, 102, 112, 114, 129, 137, 154
Barth, Karl, 91, 136
Beauchamp, Tom, 57, 58–67, 126
Being, 85–86, 91, 93

being-in-relationship, 93, 95, 96, 188(n106)
Bell, Catherine, 124
Benedictines. *See* Rule of St. Benedict
Beneficence. *See* Nonmaleficence/beneficence
Bentham, Jeremy, 37, 51
Bernard, Claude, 13, 165(n50)
Berry, Wendell, 16, 20–21, 25–26, 40, 41, 47, 51, 82, 89, 153, 154, 155–156, 180(n6)
Bioethics, 6, 173(n24)
  birth of, 47–77, 173(n20)
  virtue-based, 126–127
  *See also* Ethics; Moral issues
Biomedicine
  alternatives to status quo, 42–43
  assumptions of model, 165(n46)
  contemporary, 4, 6–10, 11, 13, 17, 28, 40, 44, 150, 151, 155, 195(n81), 198(n138). *See also* Modernity
Bland, James, 56
Blumenberg, Hans, 5
Bodies, 4, 5, 6, 8, 13, 35, 37, 85, 105–106, 116, 123–124, 132, 165(n48), 166(n63)
  descriptions of, 14, 164(n41), 165(n45)
  lived/living, 68, 71, 176(nn 94, 96)
  and machine metaphor, 20–21, 25–26, 29, 82, 84. *See also* Machine metaphor
  methodological assumptions concerning, 15
  normality of, 40–41. *See also* Normality

objectification of, 18–19
ontology of, 81, 82, 87–95, 97, 114
as passive, 6, 15, 16, 84
politics of the body, 98. *See also*
  Politics of the theological body
redemption of, 157
theological account of, 81
transformed, 90
*See also* Body of Christ;
  Resurrection
Body of Christ, 96–97, 102, 103, 104,
  107, 108, 110, 112, 115, 122,
  124, 129, 131, 132, 133, 137,
  138, 140, 141, 143, 152,
  185(n83), 188(n106), 189(n132).
  *See also* Community; Eucharist
Brieger, Gert, 164(n43)
Browder, James, 7, 11–12
Bureaucracy, 10, 33

Callahan, Daniel, 173(n24)
Canguilhem, Georges, 176(n92)
Capitalism, 33, 38–39, 40, 41, 42, 45,
  54, 133, 142, 155
Cardiopulmonary resuscitation (CPR),
  55
Care-giving, 41–42, 115, 126,
  128–130, 131, 150, 153, 155,
  156. *See also* Healing; Patient-
  caregiver relationship; Virtue(s),
  for caregivers
Carlson, Rick, 82
Cassell, Eric, 8
Catholicism, 139, 181(n17)
Character, 116, 117, 121, 126, 151,
  153, 172(n1)
Charity, 115, 121, 125, 129, 130, 150,
  154
  vs. efficiency, 155
  *See also* Love
Children, 147, 150
Childress, James, 57, 58–67, 126
Choices, 60, 74, 86, 100, 115–116,
  117, 120, 179(n140), 190(n145).
  *See also* Autonomy;
  Decisionmaking

Christianity, 6, 7, 23, 77, 79–81,
  83–84, 136, 151, 193(n49)
  vs. capitalism, 133
  *See also* Catholicism; Protestantism;
  Theology
Churchill, Larry, 57, 76
Clarke-Kennedy, A. E., 8–9
Class divisions, 105–106, 107, 110
Coakley, Sarah, 166(n51)
*Code of Ethics* (Percival), 52
Coles, Romand, 30, 32, 36, 37
Communion, 104, 107
Communion of Saints, 150
Communitarians, 77
Community, 76, 77, 82, 89, 92, 93, 96,
  97, 103, 104, 111, 112, 118, 121,
  122, 123, 127, 128, 130, 131,
  133, 135, 144, 152, 153–154,
  184(n64)
  compared with human body,
  105–106, 107
  in conflict with world, 111
  *See also* Body of Christ
Compassion, 151–152, 154
Competence issues, 60–61, 73
Comte, Auguste, 11–12
*Concept of Mind* (Ryle), 116
Concord, 105–106, 110
Conflicts of interest, 55
Consecrated oil, 152, 153, 199(n142)
Consent, 57, 60, 61
Constancy, 131, 134–138, 139, 141
Contingencies, 117, 141
Contracts, 131–132, 133, 194(n70)
Corinthians, 90, 93, 96–97, 103, 105,
  106, 107, 108, 109, 110, 124,
  132, 133, 143, 145, 152,
  185(n83), 186(n84), 188(n117)
CPR. *See* Cardiopulmonary
  resuscitation
Crucifixion/cross, 99–100, 101–102,
  103, 137, 153, 157
Cyril (bishop of Jerusalem), 93–94

Death/dying, 3, 4, 86, 87, 91, 108,
  113–114, 115, 134–138, 155,

158, 163(n23), 164(n40),
195(n81)
good death, 137
professionalization of, 135–136
*See also* Suicide
Decisionmaking, 6, 41, 47–48, 51, 53,
55, 60. *See also* Autonomy;
Choices
*De Humani Corporus Fabrica*
(Vesalius), 13
Delaporte, François, 165(n43)
Dependence, 131–134, 138, 139, 141,
144, 145, 195(n75)
Descartes, René, 15, 16, 31, 116,
166(n51). *See also* Dualism
Dialysis, 52–53
Differences, 104–105, 108, 109, 110,
188(n112)
Division of labor, 39, 142
Divisions, 104, 105–106, 107, 111,
188(n112), 189(n132)
DNR. *See* Unilateral do-not-resuscitate
order
*Doctors: The Biography of Medicine*
(Nuland), 13
*Dominium*, 23–24
Dostoevsky, Fyodor, 86
Dualism, 15–16, 17, 19, 88,
165(n48)
Dubler, Nancy, 54
Dubose, Edwin, 40–41, 43

Easter season, 126
Ecology, 22–26
Efficiency, 142–143, 145, 154, 155
Elderly people, 41–42
Emanuel, Ezekiel, 75–76, 180(n150)
Ends, 83, 117, 119, 121, 176(n87)
Engelhardt, Tristram, 58, 72–75, 76,
177(n118), 178(nn 120, 123,
130), 179(nn 135, 140)
Enlightenment era, 14, 25, 32, 44,
168(n94), 181(n18)
Ethics, 25, 28–29, 115, 123, 172(n1),
198(n138)
as applied science, 51

death and rebirth in modernity,
47–51
and faith, 97
*See also* Bioethics; Moral
issues
Eucharist, 89–90, 92–95, 107, 112,
114, 141, 152, 184(nn 46, 62,
64), 197(n102)
Euthanasia, 137, 196(n87). *See also*
Physician-assisted suicide
Examinations, 38
Experts, 34, 36, 38, 40–41, 44, 70,
136, 142, 151, 154, 155
in ethics, 50–51, 52–58

Faith, 95, 97, 99, 121, 152, 154,
185(n75)
Fee, Gordon, 189(nn 132, 133)
Finitude, 30, 31, 32–33, 76
Fitzgerald, Sally, 140–141
Flanagan, Owen, 116, 117–118,
191(nn 6, 14)
Fletcher, Joseph, 178(n130), 179
(n134)
Foucault, Michel, 29, 30–32, 33–35,
37–38, 39, 40, 43–44, 49,
165(n48), 170(nn 142, 143, 152)
*Foundations of Bioethics, The*
(Engelhardt), 58, 72–75
*Foundations of the Metaphysics of
Morals* (Kant), 15
Frank, Arthur, 19
Frankena, William, 59, 174(n44)
Freedom, 9, 12, 16, 29, 43, 49, 55, 85,
86, 87, 120. *See also* Autonomy
Freund, Peter, 15, 20, 165(n48)
Friendship, 84, 141
with God, 112, 115, 120, 121, 125,
126, 128

Galdston, Iago, 12, 22–23, 24,
164(n39), 168(n90)
Galston, William, 179(n134)
Giardina, Denise, 157
Gifts, 133, 199(n139)
Gilson, Etienne, 140

Gnosticism, 88
God, 6, 84, 88, 91, 93, 95–96, 100,
    102, 108, 112, 115, 120, 121,
    122, 123, 124, 137, 150, 151,
    182(n36), 184(n52),
    193(n49)
  Kingdom of God, 98, 184(n62)
  *See also under* Friendship
Good (the), 9–10, 49, 69, 71, 75, 83,
    84, 112, 115–116, 121, 149,
    179(n134)
  common, good, 96, 130, 152,
    195(n75)
  good life, 77, 81, 83, 102, 111, 118,
    120, 145, 194(n66)
"Good Country People" (O'Connor), 82
Grace, 124, 125
*Great Doctors, The* (Sigerist), 12
Greece (ancient), 22–23, 85, 107,
    181(n18)
Grief, 155
"Grotesque in Southern Fiction, The"
    (O'Connor), 139
Guroian, Vigen, 122, 123, 196(n87)
Gustafson, James, 161(n3)

Habits, 48, 119–120, 123, 140–141,
    192(n23)
Haggard, Howard W., 10
Hampshire, Stuart, 49, 50–51
Hankinson, Robert James, 22
Happiness, 84, 134
Hauerwas, Stanley, 1, 99, 100, 103,
    134, 135, 161(n3), 172(n6),
    179(nn 135, 140), 187(n100),
    195(n75)
Hawthorne, Nathaniel, 148
Hawthorne, Rose, 148–149
Healing, 150–156, 198(n139)
Health, 10, 20, 40, 41, 54, 68, 71, 84,
    110, 151, 152, 155, 180(n6)
  perspectives concerning, 81–83
Hippocratic Oath, 52
History of medicine, 10–14, 44
  classical Greece, 22–23
HMOs, 54

Horkheimer, Max, 25, 32, 44, 71
Hospitality, 142–144, 147
*How We Die* (Nuland), 164(n40),
    195(n81)
Human flourishing, 83–84
Humanism, 87
Hume, David, 174(n44)

Identity, 116, 117, 118, 122,
    183(n43)
Illich, Ivan, 6, 7–8, 14, 21, 166(n64)
Incarnation, 88–89, 96, 151
Individuals/individualism, 15, 25, 29,
    33, 36, 40, 49, 73, 82, 87, 89, 91,
    110, 111, 125, 190(n145). *See
    also* Autonomy
Interdependence, 23, 42, 97, 109, 133,
    142, 153, 154
Internalization, 37, 38
Irenaeus (Saint), 88
Isaiah (prophet), 98
Isolation, 102, 110, 131, 144

Jesus Christ, 88–89, 97, 111, 143–144,
    151, 183(n41), 186(nn 84, 85),
    187(n101), 189(n139)
  disciples' relation to, 98–99
  Nazarene discourse of, 98
  *See also* Body of Christ;
    Crucifixion/cross; Eucharist;
    Incarnation; Resurrection
Jews, 143
Jonsen, Albert, 52–53, 173(n20)
Justice, 59, 64–66, 174(n44)

Kant, Immanuel, 15, 26, 44, 49, 60
Kass, Leon, 84
Kissing, 93–94
Kleinman, Arthur, 18
Knowledge, 12, 14, 15, 19, 25, 27, 29,
    35, 53, 68, 84, 172(n1)
  as control, 21–22, 37, 49
  genealogies of, 43–44
  from moral discourse, 26
  and power, 24, 29–30, 32, 33, 34,
    36, 38, 41, 43, 49, 55

*See also* Experts; Positivism; Science; Truth
Koenig, John, 146
Kraftchick, Steven, 102

L'Arche communities, 144, 146
Law, 39, 86
Laying on of hands, 153
Leder, Drew, 165(n48)
Liberalism, 28, 29, 60, 65, 72, 77, 178(n118), 179(n134), 180(n150), 181(n17)
*Life* magazine, 52
Liturgy, 93(nn 38, 43), 122–126, 129, 140, 141, 152, 154
*Looking at the Liturgy* (Nichols), 193(n38)
Love, 86, 94, 96, 100, 125, 126, 137, 144, 154, 155, 193(n49). *See also* Charity
Lupton, Deborah, 11, 37

McGuire, Meredith, 15, 20, 165(n48)
Machine metaphor, 16, 17, 19. *See also under* Bodies
MacIntyre, Alasdair, 9, 14, 16, 26–27, 28, 33, 34, 74–75, 111, 118, 122, 130, 131, 161(n3), 165(n43), 168(nn 100, 101), 183(n43), 194(nn 66, 70)
McKenny, Gerald, 8, 29, 59, 174(n42)
McMylor, Peter, 38–39
Maritain, Jacques, 140
Markets, 65, 155
Martin, Dale, 105, 106, 107, 109–110, 188(n117), 189(n138)
May, Thomas, 53
Mental retardation, 41–42, 144
Metaphysics, 30–31
Middle Ages, 23
Milbank, John, 5, 23, 133, 163(n16), 167(n87), 181(n18), 189(n139)
Mill, John Stuart, 60
Modernity, 6–7, 8, 9, 26, 27, 28, 29–31, 32, 33, 34, 35, 40, 47–51,

54, 67, 81, 104, 127, 129, 130, 135, 142, 145
meaning of, 163(n16)
politics of modernity, 47, 56–57, 58, 62, 69, 72, 86
Moltmann, Jurgen, 97–98, 99
Monism, 85
Moral issues, 6, 8–9, 10, 25, 26, 28, 73, 105, 125, 127, 161(n3)
and biomedical model, 17
and care of elderly, 42
common morality, 59, 63, 64, 66, 72, 77
moral agency, 117, 118, 119, 191(n14)
moral criticism, 50–51
moral neutrality, 72, 151, 177(n118), 179(n134), 180(n150)
moral pluralism, 9, 70, 72, 131
moral vs. factual judgments, 49, 71, 168(nn 100, 101)
practical moral reasoning, 110–111, 111–112, 120
and public policy, 59
secular morality, 74, 75, 76
*See also* Bioethics; Ethics

Narratives, 117–118, 119, 122, 128, 146, 183(n43)
*Nature of Suffering, The* (Cassell), 8
Needs, 64, 65
New Testament, 146. *See also* Corinthians
Nichols, Aidan, 122, 193(n38)
*Nichomachean Ethics* (Aristotle), 116, 122, 172(n6), 193(n36)
Nominalism, 23, 24, 30, 163(n16), 168(n90)
Nonmaleficence/beneficence, 59, 61–64, 174(n44)
Normality, 36–37, 38, 39, 40–41, 42, 68, 176(n92), 180(n4)
*Novum Organum* (Bacon), 24
Nuland, Sherwin, 13–14, 164(n40), 195(n81)

Objectification, 30, 38. *See also under* Bodies
Objectivity, 22, 47, 51
O'Connor, Flannery, 82, 138–142, 147–150, 196(nn 95, 97), 197(nn 102, 105)
*Order of Things, The* (Foucault), 170(n142)
Otherness, 87, 95, 104, 105, 108–109, 125
*Our Old Home* (Hawthorne), 148

Pain behavior, 17–18
Panopticism, 37
Patience, 157
Patients, 130–142
    patient-caregiver relationship, 43, 56–57, 61, 67–68, 69, 70, 76, 130, 153, 175(n71)
"Patients as Agents" (MacIntyre), 131, 194(n70)
Paul (apostle), 96–97, 103, 105, 106–108, 109–110, 124, 132, 133, 143, 185(n83), 186(n84), 188(n117), 189(nn 133, 138)
    Christ hymn of, 100–101
    *See also* Corinthians
Pellegrino, Edmund, 57, 67–71, 76, 127, 176(n96), 180(n4)
Perception, 19
Percival, Thomas, 52
Persons, 73–74, 85–86, 87, 91, 178(n130), 181(n18), 182(n18)
*Philosophical Basis for Medical Practice, A* (Pellegrino and Thomasma), 57, 67–71
Physician-assisted suicide, 63, 136, 196(n87)
Pickstock, Catherine, 162(n7), 183(n46)
Pinches, Charles, 161(n3)
Polanyi, Michael, 16, 19, 27, 28, 168(n108)
Politics of modernity. *See under* Modernity
Politics of the theological body, 95–110

Positivism, 11–12, 13, 14, 21, 44, 71, 81–82. *See also* Science
*Possessed, The* (Dostoevsky), 86
Postman, Neil, 49, 142, 171(170)
Postmodernism, 116–117
Powell, H. Jefferson, 172(n9)
Power, 23–24, 35, 67, 70, 119, 170(n142)
    and medicine, 40
    and normality, 38, 39–40
    and surveillance, 37
    *See also under* Knowledge
Prayer, 152
Presence, 135, 138, 142–143, 144, 145, 146, 147
*Principles of Biomedical Ethics, The* (Beauchamp and Childress), 57, 58–67, 126
Private property, 136
Production/consumption, 40, 42
Profit, 54, 55
Progressivism, 11, 12
Protestantism, 99, 122, 181(n17), 190(n146), 196(n95)
Prudence, 120, 127, 129, 153. *See also* Moral issues, practical moral reasoning
Punctualism, 190(n145)
Putnam, Ruth Anna, 117, 119

Rationality, 6, 33, 61, 74, 115
Rawls, John, 9–10, 181(n17)
Reductionism, 17, 19, 26, 82
Renaissance, 23, 24
Respirators, 56
Resurrection, 137, 139–140, 157
Rhetoric, 69–70, 105, 106, 188(n117)
Rideout, Brianne, 56
Rights, 29, 33, 57, 62, 65, 73, 74
Rilke, Rainer Maria, 79, 134
Roman Empire, 101–102
Rossi, Paolo, 24–25, 168(nn 90, 94, 95)
Rule of St. Benedict, 128–129, 194(n64)
Ryle, Gilbert, 116

Sacraments, 124. *See also*
  Liturgy
Scarry, Elaine, 187(n106)
Schillebeeckx, Edward, 89, 183(n41)
Schmemann, Alexander, 92, 93, 94, 95,
  184(n62), 185(n75)
Science, 5, 7, 9, 12, 13–14, 21–22, 40,
  47, 49, 51, 67, 84, 162(n8)
  and abandonment of ecology,
    22–26
  and abandonment of teleology,
    26–28
  vs. ethics, 28–29
  *See also* Positivism
Secularism, 5, 23. *See also* Moral
  issues, secular morality
Self-interest, 104, 180(n8)
Selves, 116, 117, 118, 125, 191(n6)
Shalit, Ruth, 53–54, 56
Sidgwick, Henry, 59
Sigerist, Henry, 12
Slavery, 101–102
Slote, Michael, 175(n70)
Smith, Harmon, 57, 76, 92, 126
Social body, 20, 124
Social constructions, 164(nn 41, 43)
Specific etiology, doctrine of, 16
States, 29, 65, 73, 178(n118),
  181(n17)
  state terror, 100, 101
*Storming Heaven* (Giardina), 157–158
Storytelling. *See* Narratives
Subjectivity, 17, 28–29, 33, 36, 117,
  118, 133
Suffering, 8, 17, 62, 97–103, 109, 145,
  151, 187(n100)
  of children, 150
  inexpressibility of, 102, 188(n106)
Suicide, 63, 86, 136, 196(n87)
Surveillance, 37, 39, 170(n152)

Taylor, Charles, 168(n94), 191(n14)
Technology, 53, 171(n170)
*Technology: The Surrender of Culture
  to Technology* (Postman),
  171(n170)

Teleology, 26–28, 67, 84, 183(n43)
Tenderness, 150, 198(n135)
Theology, 5, 6, 11, 14, 23–24, 28, 81,
  83–84, 87–95, 104, 107, 115,
  149–150, 161(n3), 182(n18)
Thomas Aquinas, 83–84, 88, 115,
  119–121, 123, 125, 140, 146,
  192(nn 23, 35)
Thomasma, David, 57, 67–71, 76, 127,
  176(n96), 180(n4)
Time, 144, 145, 146, 154,
  197(n114)
Tolerance, 73, 74, 110, 178(n123)
Tradition, 111, 118, 122–123, 128,
  131, 165(n43)
Training, medical, 17, 18
Truog, Robert, 55
Truth, 14, 25, 31, 32, 35, 36, 37–38,
  40, 43, 44, 45, 51, 140, 170(nn
  142, 143). *See also* Knowledge
Turner, Bryan, 19, 166(n63)

Unilateral do-not-resuscitate order
  (DNR), 55, 56
United Methodist eucharistic liturgy,
  92
Unity, 105, 108, 112, 185(n75)

Values, 26, 29, 70–71, 110, 176(n92).
  *See also* Moral issues, moral vs.
  factual judgments
Vanier, Jean, 144, 145, 146
Vesalius, 13
Virtue(s), 119–122, 125, 126–130
  cardinal moral virtues, 129, 130
  for caregivers, 142–150
  infused, 121, 123, 192(n35),
    193(n38)
  for patients, 130–142
  virtue theory, 114–115, 118–119
*Virtues in Medical Practice, The*
  (Pellegrino and Thomasma),
  127

Wadell, Paul, 125
Wagener, Robert, 54

Wainwright, Geoffrey, 88, 90, 126,
    182(nn 33, 36)
Waisel, Daniel, 55
Walzer, Michael, 7, 162(n7)
Westerfield-Tucker, Karen, 151,
    199(n142)
White, James, 124, 193(n49),
    98(n139)
Will, 15, 23, 24, 103, 104, 181(n18)

Yoder, John Howard, 92, 98–99,
    99–100, 110–111, 112, 157,
    187(n101), 190(nn 145, 146)

Zizioulas, John, 85–86, 87, 90–91,
    92, 93, 96, 97, 103–104,
    104–105, 108–109, 182(nn 18,
    26), 184(nn 52, 62), 185(n67),
    186(n85), 188(n112)